Poverty in America

Recent Titles in the
CONTEMPORARY WORLD ISSUES
Series

Religious Belief and Science
Glenn H. Utter
Foster Care in America
Christina G. Villegas
Women in Media
Amy M. Damico
Income Inequality in America
Stacey M. Jones and Robert S. Rycroft
Rape and Sexual Assault
Alison E. Hatch
Campus Free Speech
Lori Cox Han and Jerry Price
Global Terrorism
Steven J. Childs
Food Insecurity
William D. Schanbacher and Whitney Fung Uy
Conspiracy Theories
Jeffrey B. Webb
Advertising in America
Danielle Sarver Coombs
Cyber Warfare
Paul J. Springer
Extremism in the Police
Carla Lewandowski and Jeff Bumgarner
The U.S. Criminal Justice System
Sarah Koon-Magnin and Ryan J. Williams
Women and Girls in STEM Fields
Heather Burns Page
Remote Learning and Distance Education
William H. Pruden III

Poverty in America

A Reference Handbook

Christina G. Villegas

BLOOMSBURY ACADEMIC
NEW YORK • LONDON • OXFORD • NEW DELHI • SYDNEY

BLOOMSBURY ACADEMIC
Bloomsbury Publishing Inc
1385 Broadway, New York, NY 10018, USA
50 Bedford Square, London, WC1B 3DP, UK
29 Earlsfort Terrace, Dublin 2, Ireland

BLOOMSBURY, BLOOMSBURY ACADEMIC and the Diana logo
are trademarks of Bloomsbury Publishing Plc

First published in the United States of America 2025

Cover image: Sergey Novikov/Adobe Stock

A catalog record for this book is available from the Library of Congress.

ISBN:	HB:	978-1-4408-7768-1
	ePDF:	979-8-2161-8303-7
	eBook:	978-1-4408-7769-8

Series: Contemporary World Issues

Typeset by Integra Software Services Pvt. Ltd.
Printed and bound in the United States of America

Contents

Preface

The United States has long been referred to as the land of opportunity based on the idea that each generation of Americans would be better off than the previous one and that individuals (regardless of their family, background, or creed) can improve their economic and social station if they work hard and play by the rules. While the country has experienced varying levels of poverty, opportunity, and prosperity over the course of its history, the twentieth century witnessed significant material progress and a steady growth in the number of Americans who were able to improve their standard of living and see their children surpass them in income, education level, social status, and overall quality of life.

In recent decades, however, the prospect of living out the American Dream has become less and less a reality for a large percentage of Americans. Homeownership, once a mainstay of the middle class and a primary steppingstone for upward mobility, is now out of reach for tens of millions of Americans thanks to rapidly increasing housing costs and a decline in real incomes. Class-based neighborhood segregation has become a permanent fixture of American life, and the soaring cost of living in American cities has led to a significant decline in the living standards of middle- and lower-income residents in some metropolitan areas. The benefits of economic growth over the past several decades have gone overwhelmingly to the wealthiest segment of the population and overall income and asset inequality are on the rise. Marriage, community involvement, and associational ties have declined, life expectancy has fallen, and impoverished individuals, families, and communities are more vulnerable to drug addiction and crime. Many observers of American society worry that old and young alike are increasingly living atomized lives disconnected from the social bonds of local communities, associations, families, and churches and the social capital and support they provide.

Indications that America is becoming an increasingly bifurcated society between the "haves" and the "have nots" present an opportunity for individuals and organizations from across the political spectrum to revisit and assess the various historical approaches to poverty in America, to understand its current contexts, controversies, and effects, and to explore solutions aimed at improving the lives of America's poor, fortifying its crumbling middle class, and reinvigorating the social capital and thriving communities necessary for social and economic mobility and the achievement of the American Dream.

Poverty in America: A Reference Handbook is a valuable resource for students and general readers seeking to understand the history, scope, and contexts of poverty in America and to identify the key issues and controversies at stake in the struggle to alleviate its causes and effects. The book additionally highlights the growing gap in wealth and opportunity in modern America, outlines ongoing and proposed efforts to restore a thriving middle class and improve prospects for upward mobility, and provides a listing of key actors and resources as a foundation for further research and engagement of the topic.

Poverty in America is organized into seven chapters. Chapter 1, "Background and History," introduces the scope and nature of poverty in America. It highlights key historical moments, with a specific focus on shifting ideological views and approaches toward poverty, and outlines some of the major laws, programs, and policies that have been adopted to alleviate its causes and effects.

Chapter 2, "Problems, Controversies, and Solutions," outlines common and persistent problems that arise in defining and addressing poverty in America, examines the contexts in which it is most prevalent, and explores some of the most prominent controversies related to identifying its roots and responding to its effects. Included in this discussion is an examination of the difficulty of measuring poverty and the factors contributing to problematic trends in mobility and the growing bifurcation of wealth in America. The chapter additionally explores specific efforts and proposals aimed at alleviating poverty, promoting widely shared growth and opportunity, strengthening families and communities, and restoring a thriving and upwardly mobile middle class.

Chapter 3, "Perspectives," includes five essays written by authors from a variety of viewpoints and professional backgrounds on a range of topics related to the issue of poverty and class mobility.

Chapter 4, "Profiles," lists and describes key government-sponsored entities, policy and research institutions, faith-based groups, and other private nonprofits dedicated to providing direct services to the poor, researching the various causes and contexts of poverty, and promoting solutions and policies to address the complex and multifaceted scourge of poverty in America.

Chapter 5, "Data and Documents," offers data and primary source documents, including essays, speeches, testimony, and legislation to provide readers with firsthand information on the scope and nature of poverty, various ideological and policy approaches to poverty, and suggestions for how to alleviate poverty's causes and effects.

Chapter 6, "Resources," provides an annotated list of selected books, articles, and reports on a variety of topics related to poverty in America. Several documentaries addressing related topics are listed and annotated as well.

Chapter 7, "Chronology," offers a timeline of defining moments and major events pertaining to poverty in America.

The book concludes with a glossary of key terms related to poverty in America and its various contexts, as well as a comprehensive index.

Acknowledgments

I would like to thank Kevin Hillstrom of ABC-CLIO, who assisted me in various stages of this project. Thanks also to Martha Elwell, who reviewed drafts of a few of the chapters. I am additionally thankful to Scot Zentner, chair of the political science department at California State University, San Bernardino (CSUSB), and Brian Janiskee, professor of political science at CSUSB for their professional support and mentorship, and to my other colleagues at CSUSB, who help make it a pleasurable place to work. Above all, I am grateful to my husband Manuel and our children Alexander, Anna, Izabella, and Sophia for their support and for the profound joy they bring to my life.

1

Background and History

Introduction

Founded on the principles of economic and political freedom, America has long been known as the land of opportunity based on the belief that even the most poverty-stricken citizens and their progeny are not condemned to a life of social isolation and destitution. In fact, up until a generation ago, a faith in the possibility for economic and social mobility prevailed. It was generally assumed that by the time children reached adulthood they would exceed their parents' standard of living at any given age.

More recently, prominent economists have cited aggregate data on wage growth, rising GDP, existence of economic opportunity, and increased access to consumer goods to assert that social mobility and growth in financial stability over the course of generations were still strong (Strain 2020). Others have pointed out, however, that for most Americans the American Dream refers to an overall state of well-being that requires a host of factors that extend beyond the accumulation of wealth (Cass 2019). According to a PEW Research Center (2017) study, the most important of these factors include freedom of choice in how to live, a good family life, and the ability to retire comfortably and make valuable contributions to the community. Despite signs of economic progress, in the aggregate, Americans currently face an array of economic and social challenges—such as the cost of living outpacing wages, rising housing and healthcare costs, burdensome student loans and other forms of debt, decline in the availability and quality of gainful full-time employment, growing income and wealth inequality, and deteriorating community life—that are making it

---

A migrant agricultural worker's family living in a pea picker's camp in California in 1936 during the Great Depression, an approximately decade-long period that saw unprecedented levels of unemployment, foreclosures, bankruptcies, and hunger in the United States. (Photo by Dorothea Lange. Courtesy of the Library of Congress)

more and more difficult for middle-to-lower-income Americans to build a good life based on those goals.

Furthermore, recent research demonstrates that the rate of upward mobility among younger generations born into poverty is on a downward trajectory (Chetty et al. 2017). The dwindling prospect of mobility for younger generations, combined with a host of economic and social challenges facing those at the lower and middle rungs of the income scale, has begun to affect Americans' general sense of economic well-being and their hope in the future. Lower- and middle-income Americans from across the political spectrum regularly express feelings of economic insecurity and pessimism. According to an October 2023 poll conducted by *The Wall Street Journal* and the National Opinion Research Center (NORC), only 36 percent of voters said the American Dream still holds true (Zitner 2023). This was substantially fewer than the 53 percent who reported that it still held true in 2012. According to another NBC News poll, only 19 percent of those surveyed felt confident that life for their children's generation would be better than for the current one—a record low since the group first started surveys in 1990 (Bowman 2023).

Regardless of one's beliefs concerning the status and achievability of the American Dream, it is evident that poverty remains a persistent economic, political, and social challenge in modern American life. To provide a foundation for further analyzing the nature, scope, causes, and contexts of poverty in America, this chapter reviews key historical moments. Specifically, this review focuses on the transformation of ideological approaches and attitudes toward economic opportunity and poverty and major actions, statutes, programs, and practices adopted to alleviate poverty's various causes and effects.

Property Rights and Free Markets in the Early American Republic

The birth of the United States dates to July 4, 1776, the day the Continental Congress endorsed the Declaration of Independence. Technically, the thirteen British American colonies had formally declared themselves free from allegiance to Great Britain two days earlier with the Lee Resolution; but the Declaration did something more important. It outlined a formal justification for the establishment of a new people and governing system rooted in what the

Declaration refers to as self-evident truths (truths that are discoverable through reason and a common-sense observation of humankind). The central and most fundamental of these is the claim of natural human equality. This proposition is based on the logic that although human beings are unique in characteristics and circumstances, none of these inequalities establishes select human beings as the rightful and natural rulers over others. Human beings are not divided by nature into castes of rulers and ruled. Individuals, therefore, have a right to govern themselves and a rightful claim to that which naturally belongs to them (their lives, bodies, minds, beliefs, talents, labor, etc.) and the right to use what belongs to them to acquire property and pursue happiness (Madison 1792). They also have a moral obligation to live in such a way that promotes the enjoyment of these rights by others. These inherent natural rights and obligations logically point to certain principles regarding the just establishment, operation, and continuation of systems of government. Government is necessary but ought to be rooted in the consent of the governed (through a system of political representation) and must be instituted to secure rights in a way that contributes to human flourishing.

The Right to Acquire and Possess Property

The view that government is instituted to promote the safety and happiness of society first and foremost by securing impartially those rights that individuals possess by nature had a profound impact on the policy approach to property rights and economics in early America. Despite bitter disagreement over such questions as how to pay the national debt, whether to charter a national bank, and the degree to which government ought to support manufacturing, there was widespread consensus that the right to acquire and possess property was intimately connected with the other rights of personhood and therefore indispensable for justice and human well-being. As one of America's leading founders James Madison (1829) observed, "It is sufficiently obvious … that the right of persons, and the rights of property, are the objects, for the protection of which government was instituted. These rights cannot well be separated. The personal right to acquire property, which is a natural right, gives to property when acquired, a right to protection, as a social right."

In practice, the belief that government is responsible for enabling individuals to exercise their right to acquire and possess property contributed to general acceptance of three broad economic policy principles in the early American republic: the legal right to own and use property in land and other goods, market freedom, and government support of sound money (West 2017). Based on these principles, the national and state governments, operating under the authority of the US Constitution, adopted laws defining property ownership and contracts along with legal safeguards against public and private injury and unreasonable seizure.

Other than minimal regulations aimed at protecting the public health, safety, and morals of society, very few restrictions were placed upon trade, professional pursuits, and the right of owners to dispose of and use their property as they saw fit. Furthermore, an animating factor leading to the creation and ratification of the US Constitution was the fact that the state legislatures under the Articles of Confederation had deliberately undermined the right to property through the cancellation of private debts, the adoption of inflationary policies, and the production of worthless paper money as legal tender—which effectively reduced or annulled the value of debts and investments.

Efforts to solve this problem and establish a stable and reliable measure of exchange included among other things a constitutional ban on state involvement with monetary policy, a constitutional requirement that the states could only require gold and silver coins as legal tender for the payment of debts, and an adoption of the precious metals standard, a system in which paper money is backed by actual gold or silver.

Opposition to Government-Imposed Privileges and Monopolies

These general economic principles in favor of property rights and market freedom inspired state laws forbidding practices, such as primogeniture (the requirement that inheritance be passed down to the oldest son) and entail (the requirement that owners keep their land intact for their descendants rather than being able to sell it off in whole or in part). Such practices had been used historically, throughout the British Empire and Europe generally, to interfere with the free use of individual faculties and to restrict the use and ownership of property based on birth, rank, and social class, ultimately contributing to arbitrary and permanent concentrations of wealth.

Legal opposition to government-imposed monopolies (apart from temporary patents and copyrights given to inventors and authors for their intellectual property) and government grants of exclusive economic privileges to particular persons was justified on the same grounds. Under colonial rule, the British government, motivated by a spirit of monopoly, accorded exclusive rights on trade to individual companies such as the East India Tea Company and placed onerous restrictions on the types of goods that could be produced and sold by American manufacturers. Such monopolies inhibited the development of American manufacturing and kept the young republic overly dependent on British goods. These state-imposed monopolies were criticized for arbitrarily favoring the well-connected and for depriving individuals of the free use of their faculties and the natural right to acquire and dispose of one's property. Revolutionary War Veteran and US Senator National Chipman (1793) observed, for example, "To give any individual, or class of men, a monopoly, an exclusive right of acquisition ... is an exclusion of the rights of others. It is a violation of the equal rights of man." In his widely read essay, "On Property," James Madison (1792) likewise condemned the spirit of legislation "where a manufacturer of linen cloth is forbidden to bury his own child in a linen shroud, in order to favor his neighbor who manufacturers woolen cloth; where the manufacturer and wearer of woolen cloth are again forbidden the economical use of buttons of that material, in favor of the manufacturer of buttons of other materials!" In this vein, several of the early state constitutions explicitly prohibited monopolies as being "contrary to the genius of a free state" and to the "spirit of free government" (West 2017).

Encouragement of Widespread Ownership

America's early leaders aspired to create a nation in which merit, honest productive work, and natural ability rather than birth, wealth, and legal credentials would provide the foundation for economic well-being and mobility. Alexander Hamilton, for example, contended that collective and individual prosperity would depend upon the protection of "the exertions of talents and industry, and securing to them their justly acquired fruits" (Hamilton 1795). Thus, equality of opportunity rather than equality of outcome was the primary political goal.

Although they acknowledged that equal protection of liberty and the individual right to employ varying degrees and types of talents and ability would lead to some level of economic inequality, America's early political leaders warned of the dangers of extreme discrepancies in wealth and property ownership. Instead, they typically embraced the idea that widespread property ownership and economic opportunity would contribute to the cultivation of self-reliance and civic responsibility, and the maintenance of political liberty, and would prevent the reemergence of a hereditary or class-based aristocracy. A 1794 Delaware law, for instance, specified: "it is the duty and policy of every republican government to preserve equality amongst its citizens by maintaining the balance of property as far as it is consistent with the rights of individuals" (Katz 1977). In this context, government programs to build commercial infrastructure, such as public roads and waterways, and policies easing the regulatory burdens of incorporation and facilitating widespread landownership were prevalent at both the federal and state levels (West 2017).

In 1785, a few years before the ratification of the US Constitution, the Congress of the Confederation passed the Land Ordinance of 1785. This act established a system in which settlers could purchase title to low-cost, subdividable lots of farmlands in the undeveloped western territories. This act set a precedent for nearly a century of federal policy encouraging widespread land ownership through the sale of public lands, culminating in the passage of the Homestead Act of 1862. Though most of the land made available was allocated to whites, the act was notable for providing plots of land to former slaves and other Black Americans as well. Additionally, a sizeable percentage of the proceeds from such public land sales was directed toward the maintenance of local schools, another important avenue for the promotion of economic opportunity and prosperity and the development of civic virtue among the citizenry.

Notable Exceptions

Despite the historically unprecedented expansion of property rights in early America, some glaring exceptions inhibited the full and impartial promotion of the founding principles in legal practice. Because of variations in state law, for instance, women did not immediately enjoy the same political and legal rights throughout the nation that men enjoyed. The dominant patriarchal view was that natural differences between the sexes made women more suited for domestic cares and that the legal system should promote public safety and happiness by strengthening the bonds of the nuclear family; this view led states to adopt policies that prohibited women from participating in certain forms of employment, limited property ownership to single women, and restricted the right to vote to males.

Nevertheless, the same Founding documents and principles that led to the broad expansion of property rights in early America eventually inspired the extension of those rights to women as well. The country's first women's rights advocates were able to contend that sexual difference is not a sufficient justification for not granting women the rights that flow from their equal status as rational human beings, such as the rights to legal property ownership, political representation, and freedom of occupation. Women's demand for expanded civil and political rights on this basis was first widely promulgated in the 1848 Seneca Falls's *Declaration of Sentiments*, which began by appealing to the same transcendent "Laws of Nature and Nature's God" that inspired the American Revolution. The signatories of the *Declaration* charged that laws and actions that construct barriers to higher education, property ownership, and profitable employment were unjust violations of women's equality and must be altered.

The most egregious violation and fatal exception to the protection of the natural right to property in early America was chattel slavery (a form of slavery in which human beings are bought and sold as property). Chattel slavery, which had been practiced throughout the world for millenniums and was introduced to America during its colonial period, represented a complete repudiation of personhood and property rights for a large portion of the population. Although slavery was not abolished with American independence for a variety of logistical and political reasons that were aggravated by both fear and economic self-interest, the principles at the heart of the American Revolution were directly relevant to the institution.

Based on the principles of just government espoused in the Declaration of Independence, slavery violates the equality of personhood by arbitrarily depriving human beings of their right to rule themselves, the right to the fruits of their labor, and their right to freely use their talents, faculties, and abilities to pursue happiness. In recognition of the incompatibility between slavery and America's founding principles, most of the original states outlawed slavery within their borders and federal legislation was adopted, when politically possible, to restrict the practice. One example is the Northwest Ordinance, which forbade the growth of slavery into US territories where it wasn't yet protected by law.

In fact, both free Blacks and slaves petitioned for liberation and the restoration of their inalienable right to their personhood and property by linking the cause of American freedom with the struggle of African Americans to the legal recognition of their inalienable right to liberty. In 1777, just a year after the signing of the Declaration, Prince Hall, a free Black living in Boston, presented a petition for freedom to the Massachusetts Legislature on behalf of a group of slaves. This petition declared, "[We] have in common with all other Men a natural right to that freedom, which the great Parent of the Universe hath bestowed equally on all Mankind & which they have never forfeited by any compact or agreement" (Hall 1777). Several years later, following other similar petitions, the Massachusetts Supreme Court ended slavery in the state, ruling that the institution violated the state constitution's declaration that "men are born free and Equal."

Ultimately, the Declaration's proclamation of human equality and inalienable rights laid the foundation for the complete abolition of slavery in the United States. It took more than half a century and a bloody Civil War (1861–5) that cost more than 600,000 lives, however, before Constitutional amendments were ratified to outlaw slavery and other forms of involuntary servitude nationally, to grant equal protection under the law, and to guarantee the right to vote regardless of race. While these amendments brought the Constitution into harmony with the principles of the Declaration of Independence, slavery and its undeniable repudiation of America's founding principles remain haunting and painful chapters in the nation's history.

Poverty and Poor Relief in Early America

Although early American leaders sought in many ways to democratize property ownership, they were adamantly opposed to significant government redistribution of property and resources. Thomas Jefferson (1816) opined, for instance:

> To take from one, because it is thought his own industry and that of his fathers has acquired too much, in order to spare to others, who, or whose fathers have not, exercised equal industry or skill, is to violate arbitrarily the first principle of association, the guarantee to everyone the exercise of his industry and the fruits acquired by it.

Despite the general opposition toward forced economic redistribution, however, support still existed in early America for local government involvement in poverty relief and a minimal government-funded safety net for those unable to work or provide for themselves.

In the essay "Poverty and Welfare in the American Founding," Thomas G. West (2015) counteracts two widely promulgated misconceptions: that early America did nothing to alleviate the plight of the poor and that poor relief was carried out entirely by private churches and charities. In fact, private and public provision of care for the poor in the United States has a history in the Christian and Jewish religious traditions in which caring for the indigent is mentioned in religious texts as a duty under law, in Lockean philosophy which taught that the law of nature requires the preservation of others when one's "own preservation come not in competition," and in the English Poor Law. This body of laws, first developed in sixteenth-century England, recognized the existence of involuntary unemployment and destitution, and established provisions governing relief for the poor.

During the seventeenth century, localities within the American colonies began to codify the English Poor Laws, allowing tax assessments for the provision of the poor and the appointment of town leaders to oversee the administration of such aid. Following the American Revolution, state governments adopted similarly patterned legislation establishing a public responsibility for the care of the destitute. When the US Constitution was ratified, it allocated specific, enumerated powers to the federal government such as the power to provide for the nation's security and the power to regulate commerce. The Tenth Amendment, however, specified that the exercise of all powers not granted to the federal government, nor forbidden to the states, would be reserved to the states or to the people. In the years following the Constitution's ratification, both the people and their representatives at the state level jealously guarded the prerogatives of their state and local governments, and poor relief continued to be handled almost entirely at the local level.

Besides the conviction that poor relief was a local responsibility, several features typified the poor laws of this time. The first was the assumption that the nuclear family and extended relatives ought to provide the primary line of defense. Husbands were legally expected to provide for their families and, in some localities, laws required parents and grandparents to care for their indigent children (Furner 2004). Neighbors, friends, and religious congregations also frequently assisted those struggling to meet their basic needs in moments of distress.

Poor citizens, without friends or family whom they could rely on for care, were generally divided into several categories for the purposes of public support: the impotent (the blind, elderly, disabled, etc.), widows, children, and the able-bodied. The impotent, or those unable to labor and to live on their own, were typically boarded in the houses of local families who received a public stipend for their care. Towns and parishes often provided clothing and medical care for such individuals (Trattner 1994). Supplementary aids in the form of money, goods, and services were given to widows and those who only needed partial assistance or temporary care, but who were able to continue to live on their own. Because towns and localities bore the primary financial responsibility for the care of the poor, transiency laws were introduced to keep strangers from moving from town to town to collect public funds. In some cases, constables would forcibly return individuals to their place of legal residence (Furner 2004).

Though early Americans exhibited a strong obligation to care for those in their communities who were unable to care for themselves, they also maintained a belief in the virtue of work and the vice of voluntary idleness. Orphaned, abandoned, and impoverished children were commonly placed in apprenticeships with a family under whose care they would have the opportunity to learn skills that would enable them to live independently once they came of age. Able-bodied unemployed men, commonly referred to as vagabonds, were either bound out as indentured servants or placed in almshouses or workhouses, where they were fed, clothed, and required to labor.

In the decades following the American Revolution, each town along with private citizens and religious groups continued to take on most of the financial burden for the indigent. Several forces of change, however, began to make it more difficult to maintain a local and insular poor relief system. Among these changes, large-scale immigration, rapid industrialization, an increase in travel and mobility, and widespread urbanization brought along with them both shifting populations and rising incidents of poverty. This, combined with a concern that the allocation of public assistance was destroying the incentive to work and contributing to permanent dependency and pauperism, led to calls for reform.

In 1824, the New York legislature enacted the County Poorhouse Act, which required that each county in the state establish one or more poorhouses for the care of all recipients of public assistance and created boards of County Superintendent of the Poor to manage these almshouses. The measure initiated two trends in nineteenth-century American welfare policy: a transfer of responsibility for public assistance from the town to the county and state level and a shift in emphasis toward "indoor relief" or the use of institutional care through poor houses (Trattner 1994). Meanwhile, nineteenth-century America also witnessed the growth of private ethnic and sectarian benevolent societies, hospitals, and educational institutions that aimed to provide material aid and instill character through education, religious instruction, and work.

Abolition, the Freedman's Bureau, Reconstruction, and Jim Crow

On December 6, 1865, in the aftermath of the Civil War, the necessary number of states ratified the Thirteenth Amendment to the US Constitution. This amendment declared: "Neither slavery nor involuntary servitude, except as a punishment for crime whereof the party shall have been duly convicted, shall exist within the United States, or any place subject to their jurisdiction." Widespread disagreement, however, existed over how to secure abolition and integrate back into the United States both the conquered Southern confederate states and the four million newly freed people. This was a particularly daunting task as the southern states sought to re-create a situation of *de facto* Black slave labor.

On March 3, 1865, just before the official conclusion of the Civil War, Congress passed "An Act to establish a Bureau for the Relief of Freedman and Refugees." The Bureau, which was to operate for the remainder of the war and for one year thereafter, was created to provide food, shelter, clothing, medical services, and land to freed slaves and destitute southerners who had been displaced during the war. The Bureau, which was housed in the Department of War, was additionally tasked with reuniting Black families, establishing schools for freed people, and supervising labor contracts between them and their employers. Northern missionaries and aid societies worked in conjunction with the Freedman's Bureau to establish more than 1,000 primary and secondary schools and colleges for former slaves (Butchart 2010). Several of these historically Black colleges are still in operation today.

Following the assassination of President Abraham Lincoln on April 14, 1865, Vice President Andrew Johnson ascended to the presidency. To the dismay of those concerned with guaranteeing political and economic rights to the newly freed slaves, President Johnson took a lax approach toward the Southern states and their readmission to the union. As a result of Johnson's leniency, numerous southern state legislatures enacted a series of Black Codes between 1865 and 1866. These codes imposed significant barriers to the protection of political rights and effectively re-enslaved freed persons by severely restricting their movement, the free use of their labor, and their right to acquire and possess property. Using the language of the Thirteenth Amendment that allowed for involuntary servitude in criminal cases, several southern legislatures passed vagrancy laws that allowed Blacks to be arrested for minor infractions and sentenced to unpaid penal labor. In a speech commemorating emancipation, Frederick Douglass, a former slave who had risen to a position of political and ideological influence, observed the kinship between slavery and the legal codes restricting freed people's opportunities for saving, accumulation, and geographical and economic mobility. In these Black Codes, Douglass contended "there is clearly seen the purpose to crush our spirits, to cripple our enterprise and doom us to a condition of destitution and degradation" (Myers 2008).

These Black Codes generated outrage among northern Republicans. Following the 1866 congressional election, Radical Republicans used their newly won power in Congress to override President Johnson's vetoes and enact the Freedman's Bureau Act of 1866, the Civil Rights Act of 1866, and the Reconstruction Act of 1867. The Freedman's Bureau Act extended the work of the agency for an additional two years and gave it more extensive authority to implement its provisions.

The Civil Rights Act of 1866 defined all persons born in the United States as citizens "without distinction to race or color, or previous condition of slavery or involuntary servitude"—thereby entitled to the rights of citizenship in every state and US territory. Among other provisions, the act declared that, as citizens, Blacks were entitled to the right "to make and enforce contracts," the right "to inherit, purchase, lease, sell, hold, and convey real and personal property," and the right to enjoy "full and equal benefits of all laws and proceedings for the security of person and property, as is enjoyed by white citizens" (U.S. Congress 1866). This act served to define in legislative terms the meaning of the freedom granted under the Thirteenth Amendment. It also ushered in a drastic transformation of the federal-state relationship by giving the federal government more influence over the enforcement of individual rights (Moses 2021).

The Reconstruction Act of 1867 divided former Confederate states into military districts governed by Union Army general officers. The act imposed strict criteria governing the development of new state constitutions and guidelines for protecting the political and property rights of Blacks in order for these states to regain the right to federal recognition and representation in Congress.

These acts were shortly followed by the ratification of the Fourteenth and Fifteenth Amendments in 1868 and 1870. The Fourteenth Amendment enshrined in the Constitution the citizenship of Blacks and prohibited state efforts to deny Blacks their right to equal protection and due process of law. The Fifteenth Amendment forbade both the federal government and the states from denying anyone the right to vote on account of race, color, or previous condition of servitude. During the first few years of Ulysses S. Grant's presidency, the federal government actively enforced these amendments in the southern states. For a short time, the political and economic condition of freed people improved, and Blacks successfully used their newly secured right of suffrage to elect hundreds of Black representatives to state and local offices and more than two dozen to the US Congress.

Unfortunately, the gains made for Blacks through the ratification and enforcement of the Thirteenth, Fourteenth, and Fifteenth Amendments during the reconstruction period were short lived. In 1873, economic panic seized the nation following the collapse of a firm heavily invested in government bonds to fund railroad construction. The collapse led to bankruptcy for nearly a quarter of the country's railroads and the failure of thousands of banking firms and businesses.

The economic depression that ensued—an era of wage cuts, high levels of unemployment, and labor strikes—distracted northerners from the problem of addressing southern racism, plunged the already economically shattered South into deeper poverty, and contributed to the Democratic Party's electoral victory in the House of Representatives for the first time since the Civil War. White supremacist groups like the Ku Klux Klan, which had been suppressed by federal troops during the height of reconstruction, resumed their terror campaign against Blacks—who became a convenient scapegoat amid economic devastation.

In the contested presidential election of 1876, Rutherford B. Hayes agreed to end federal enforcement in exchange for the Democrats' certification of his election in Congress. Beginning in the 1890s, southern states made it nearly impossible for Black men to vote by enacting literacy tests, poll taxes, and other restrictions. The disfranchisement of Blacks was soon followed by a wave of state and local segregation laws. These ordinances, referred to as Jim Crow Laws, mandated the separation of the races and condemned Black citizens to inferior treatment, services, and spaces. Southern white planters additionally colluded together to increase their profits by arbitrarily holding down Black wages (Roback 1984). In an effort to overcome the economic incentives that individual planters had to offer Blacks higher wages and to secure their labor-market cartel, groups of planters lobbied for the passage of labor laws aimed at restricting the migration of Black workers, restricting the activities of labor recruiters from out of state, and limiting increases in Black wages. Among the most egregious of these laws were vagrancy codes that made it a crime to be unemployed or out of the labor force, effectively preventing Blacks from leaving low-paying jobs to search for higher-paying ones.

Eventually, nearly three-quarters of a century later, the era of Jim Crow and the arbitrary legal class system it created ended when a national movement of people from a variety of religious, racial, and political backgrounds committed to ending political, economic, and social discrimination against Blacks successfully lobbied for the passage of civil rights legislation in the 1960s. Though judicial interpretation has caused dispute over the application of these laws and the degree to which they permit racial preferences in response to past discrimination, the actual language of the Civil Rights Acts of 1964 and 1968 reinforced the idea that law and economic opportunity ought to be colorblind by officially ending legally enforced segregation and outlawing arbitrary barriers to the right to vote and discrimination in employment, housing, and public accommodations based on race, color, religion, sex, or national origin.

The Gilded Age

From the last quarter of the nineteenth century into the early twentieth century, a period coined the Gilded Age by American writer Mark Twain, the United States experienced rapid economic expansion and became the largest industrial nation in the world. Prior to the Civil War, agriculture was the mainstay of the US economy and a large percentage of Americans worked for themselves. Beginning with the expansion of the railroads from coast to coast, the country experienced a rapid growth of industry, the factory system, mining, and finance. By the end of the century, most Americans engaged in industrial work for an employer, and the economy was dominated by several wealthy individuals. These captains of industry, as they were called, included familiar names like railroad mogul Cornelius Vanderbilt, John D. Rockefeller of Standard Oil, Andrew Carnegie of Carnegie Steel, and financier and investment banker J.P. Morgan.

The growth of corporations with their large mills and factories increased the demand for cheap labor and attracted a wave of southern European, eastern European, Asian, and Jewish immigrants fleeing poverty, religious persecution, and political oppression in search of freedom and economic opportunity. Between 1860 and 1900, approximately 14 million immigrants arrived in the United States, and another 9 million arrived between 1900 and 1910 (Trattner 1994). Most of these immigrants settled in New York City or went West to help build thousands of miles of railroads and canals and to work in mining and farming. This influx of immigrants, along with Blacks fleeing the Jim Crow South, and Native Americans migrating to the cities from poverty-stricken reservations and the rural countryside led to a rapid increase of residents from varying linguistic, religious, and cultural backgrounds in America's eastern and Midwestern cities.

The economic growth that came from industrialization had several positive outcomes. It eventually contributed to a rise in per capita incomes, greater access to consumer goods, better standards of living, and a higher life expectancy for large segments of the population (Iceland 16). Wealthy industry leaders and philanthropists bankrolled libraries, museums, orchestras, institutions of higher education, and settlement houses for the poor. The era, however, was also marked by abject poverty. As the concentrations of wealth among the nation's corporate leaders became more visible, crowded urban areas were plagued by dilapidated tenements, poverty, filth, disease, and rising crime. Low wages and simplified mass production assembly lines drew women and children into harsh and dangerous factory work as they sought to supplement family income. Urban children not employed in factories were frequently deprived of parental supervision, leading to a significant increase in juvenile delinquency (Trattner 1994).

In 1890, Danish immigrant and journalist Jacob Riis used flash photography to expose the squalid, unsanitary, and violent conditions of urban slums in his book *How the Other Half Lives: Studies among the Tenements of New York.* Riis's work drew widespread attention to the plight of the urban poor, ultimately motivating the passage of local laws regulating the quality of tenements and an extensive tenement study published by the Department of Labor in 1895. His work additionally inspired the housing and labor reforms later advocated by President Theodore Roosevelt (Diner 2010).

During that chaotic time of economic change and urban growth, city services became insufficient for effectively integrating and meeting the needs of the growing urban poor. Churches and charities were also overwhelmed by the demand. Political parties, which at the time were highly organized at the local level, emerged to fill the void. Local party machines led by party bosses began the work of winning and holding power through the distribution of government jobs and social services (Shannon 1969). These political bosses divided up large cities and many smaller cities and towns into districts, wards, and precincts in which ambitious partisans would work to organize neighborhoods, arrange ethnically balanced tickets, and deliver votes for their party. Under a system referred to as patronage, the winning party would then distribute government jobs and contracts in exchange for support. The party bosses also ran a kind of ramshackle welfare state in which party leaders would reward their constituents by helping them find employment, offering legal advice and interceding in court proceedings, providing financial assistance and other goods such as food or coal, and organizing free entertainment such as parades and beach excursions. The exposure of pervasive corruption among party bosses eventually resulted in the passage of laws restricting patronage and the power of urban political machines. Some historians nevertheless contend that local parties fulfilled an important public service during the era by integrating poor immigrants into the broader community and by providing them with essential social welfare services (Reid and Kurth 1992).

Eventually, glaring concentrations of wealth and poverty, harsh and dangerous working conditions, and the frequent instances of political corruption and cronyism that defined the era contributed to growing unrest among the nation's working class. The last couple of decades of the nineteenth century witnessed a rise of political populism, anti-immigrant animus and legislation, and violent labor strikes. That unrest gave rise to the formation and organization of private labor unions and spurred federal antitrust legislation. Early antitrust laws included the Interstate Commerce Act of 1887, which created the Interstate Commerce Commission tasked with preventing discriminatory rates in the railroad industry, and the Sherman Act of 1890, which outlawed the creation of monopolies or contracts between corporate leaders that were aimed at curtailing trade. Furthermore, although standards of living overall were improving, the worsening of urban poverty and the poor working conditions in the nation's factories and mills eventually contributed to increased public support for state action to mitigate the effects of industrial capitalism through laws regulating work hours and wages.

The Progressive Era

The twentieth century witnessed substantial institutional changes in the nation's approach to poverty and poor relief, including the eventual growth of the federal bureaucracy, entitlement programs, and the welfare state. The ideological roots of these changes were in large part initiated during the American Progressive Era, which overlapped in part with the Gilded Age, lasting from around 1880 until 1920. Progressive thought first gained a foothold in the United States during the latter half of the nineteenth century as intellectuals educated in Europe according to German idealism and the political and social thought of thinkers like G.W.F Hegel and his disciples filled many of the academic appointments at America's elite institutions of higher learning (Pestritto 2021).

Progressive intellectuals differed in some respects, but they shared certain essential commonalities. These included adherence to the tenets of historical contingency (the belief that there are no permanent truths and that values evolve and change over time) combined with an enthusiastic faith that historical and scientific progress would lead incrementally to an overall improvement in the condition of mankind. In contrast with the belief espoused by America's Founders that individuals are born with inherent natural rights by virtue of their equal humanity, Progressives posited that individuals possess nothing of value by nature but are solely products of their historical circumstance and the social and political arrangements and institutions under which they live. For instance, John Dewey, one of the most influential theorists of the era, declared, "Social arrangements, laws, institutions ... are means of *creating* individuals ... Individuality in a social and moral sense is something to be wrought out" (Dewey 1920).

Individuals, according to this view, are not free by nature, but become free as they cultivate their intellectual and spiritual capacities through the progress of history and the advancement of the cultural, social, economic, and political conditions and institutions under which they live. Thus, Dewey and other like-minded theorists distinguished between negative freedom and positive freedom (Miller 2007). Negative freedom refers to "freedom from subjection to the will and control of others" and the legal right to exercise one's talents, faculties, and abilities and make decisions for oneself in pursuit of everything from the lowest to the highest ends of life. Effective or positive freedom on the other hand, as stated by Progressive Economist Richard T. Ely, consists in the actual "development in the most complete manner possible of all faculties, physical, mental, moral, spiritual" (Miller 2012).

Shift in the Nation's Collective Understanding of and Approach toward Poverty

The notion that individuals are a product of their historical, social, economic, and political environment and that effective freedom is achieved through the development of human potential or capacity profoundly influenced attitudes and approaches toward poverty. The typical approach to poverty and poor relief in early America was based on encouraging local accountability, personal responsibility, frugality, and industriousness, and distinguishing between the deserving poor (those whose poverty was caused by forces outside of their control) and the undeserving poor (those prone to personal vices such as drunkenness, profligacy, and idleness).

By the end of the nineteenth century, social scientists, social workers, and private religious organizations increasingly blamed poverty on adverse economic and social conditions or "the system" (Iceland 2013). As the poor increasingly came to be viewed as people oppressed and degraded by external circumstances beyond their control, social reform and social and intellectual development became the chief goals of those who advocated for the poor.

The settlement house movement that emerged in the late nineteenth century with the founding of Jane Addams's Hull House in Chicago was deeply influenced by this new understanding of poverty. Between the 1880s and the 1920s, hundreds of settlement houses were established in urban centers by those who viewed themselves as social reformers rather than charity workers. Settlement houses were organizations designed to provide support services including education, healthcare, childcare, and employment resources to the poor and to immigrants. Eventually, the services were expanded to include activities such as men's clubs, courses in arts and crafts, libraries, art galleries, and gymnasiums. Leaders typically equated human progress with the development of middle-class values, and the houses were primarily staffed by educated middle- and upper-class women who sought to elevate the lives of the laboring classes by living and working among them (Trattner 1994).

A striking deviation from efforts to elevate the lives of the poor and laboring classes through social and legislative reform during the Progressive Era was the growth and entrenchment of Jim Crow, disfranchisement, and racial violence in the South. In fact, as historian C. Vann Woodward (2002) observes, many of the same progressive reformers who fought party machines, corporations, and the railroads and who secured "humanitarian legislation for miners, factory workers, child labor, and the consumer" rode "to power in the South on a disfranchising or white-supremacy movement."

Though this reality is frequently deemed a paradox, political theorist Tiffany J. Miller (2012) maintains that the sharp increase in the racial character of state law was the logical outgrowth of progressive idealism and the paternalistic character of the age. "In embracing the idealists' conception of positive freedom, and the process of historical development or 'social evolution' through which the ideal of freedom progressively unfolds," Miller writes, "The Progressives also accepted the idea that the different races of the human family are advancing at dramatically different rates." Consequently, they replaced the idea that "government is obliged to secure the equal rights of all" with the belief that legal and political rights ought to be granted to groups in accord with their moral and rational development. Furthermore, the belief that the more developed races and classes serve as the agents of progress and have a moral duty to promote the intellectual and moral cultivation of the less advanced informed both domestic policy reforms (such as wages and hours legislation, social insurance, and public housing) and a host of policies—including colonialism, disfranchisement, and segregation—designed, according to the language of Progressive economist Richard T. Ely, to subjugate the "backward," "inferior," and "degenerate" (Miller 2012).

This same rationale likely informed the treatment of Native Americans during the era and the adoption of federal policy forcing Native American children to leave their family homes and attend state-sponsored boarding schools. This misguided effort was justified on the grounds that it would promote the intellectual cultivation and cultural assimilation of these children into mainstream "white" society. The practice, however, inflicted terrible damage on tribal children, often permanently severing their connection with their family, tribe, and heritage.

Increased Focus on Children

In addition to a shift in the approach to poverty and poor relief generally, the Progressive Era saw widespread adoption of the view that childhood is a distinct, important, and vulnerable stage of life deserving greater protection—and that the state and federal governments should take a more involved role in promoting the health and welfare of children (Villegas 2022; Yarrow 2009). This growing concern with child welfare did not necessarily directly grow out of pity or compassion. Walter Trattner contends that "it resulted above all from the fact that most citizens viewed the child as the key to social control. If future generations were to possess the strength of mind, body, and character to become good, self-supporting citizens, able to assume the responsibilities and burdens of democratic rule, they had to be protected as children" (Trattner 1994).

Childhood poverty, reformers argued, hinders progress and contributes to all sorts of social ills including corruption, crime, greed, and incompetence by depriving children of the resources they need to develop their mental, intellectual, and spiritual capacities.

Social reformers became particularly concerned with the effects of growing up in an orphanage on child development. Consequently, they advocated for organizing orphan asylums as smaller dwelling units partitioned into bedrooms and began to experiment with alternatives such as promoting adoption, placing children with foster families, and giving "widow's pensions" to mothers to enable them to keep their children at home (Gates 1994). By the early 1900s, several states had passed laws to prevent child abuse and neglect and had authorized the creation of children's aid societies to represent children's legal interests. State social service agencies also began to place greater weight on children's individual needs when making placements and to inspect foster homes and supervise and compensate foster parents.

In 1909, President Theodore Roosevelt called together the First White House Conference on the Care of Dependent children in response to concerns about the institutional placement of children. The conferees recommended that measures be taken to prevent the removal of children from their homes except under extreme circumstances, and to place those children who did have to be removed with families instead of institutions. The conferees also pressed for the creation of a federal agency with the goal of overseeing state legislation and disseminating data on child welfare.

In response to such recommendations, President William Howard Taft signed the law establishing the Children's Bureau on April 9, 1912. The Bureau, originally housed in the Department of Labor and now part of the Department of Health and Human Services, was the first federal government department devoted to the welfare of children. It was given the responsibility to investigate and report on all matters pertaining to infant mortality, the birth rate, orphanages, juvenile courts, dangerous occupations, accidents and diseases of children, and employment.

Ideological Groundwork for Institutional Changes

The ideological climate of the Progressive Era not only effected a transformation in attitudes and approaches toward poverty and poor relief, including an increased focus on the welfare of children, but it also contributed to a shift in the American mind regarding the purpose, scope, and foundation of just government. It thereby laid the foundation for major institutional and political changes in the future.

Previously, American constitutionalism was grounded in the idea that individuals have rights that cannot be repealed or infringed by human law. Therefore, the Constitution was intended to limit the scope of democracy with a view to securing those things that are naturally our own, including as James Madison (1792) summarized, our personhood, opinions, religious beliefs, faculties, and possessions. As Madison posited, individuals' ability to pursue happiness is threatened both by "an excess of liberty" and by "an excess of power" of other citizens or government over us. Consequently, while a government is necessary to secure individuals' ability to pursue happiness by protecting them against injury from foreign actors or other citizens, a government also threatens individuals' pursuit of happiness when it becomes too intrusive or gives preferential treatment to certain classes of citizens at the expense of others. A constitutional government, according to this view, provides a framework for the individual pursuit of happiness both by effectively empowering governing authorities to protect the weak against injury and by subordinating them to a set of principles and procedures—such as representation, separation of powers, checks and balances, and federalism—that minimize abuses or overextension of that power.

While the Constitution defined and delineated power with a view to preserving individual liberties and electoral accountability, progressive thinkers posited that the threat of tyranny had been mitigated by an improvement in the condition of mankind through the advancement of the sciences. Thus, scientifically educated experts could be trusted to rule with a greater degree of unhampered discretion. They further embraced a much more expansive view of government and its purpose. In a survey of the political thought of the era, Charles Merriam (1903) summarized this change stating, "Whereas the revolutionary generation thought that the end of the political society is to protect life, liberty and the property of its citizens ... In the new view, the state ... may positively advance the general welfare by means and measures expressly dedicated to that end." Alternatively, as John Dewey put it, "The state has the responsibility for creating institutions under which individuals can effectively realize the potentialities that are theirs" (Dewey 2000). In the realm of the economy and the marketplace, this would require the state to proactively eliminate the social and economic forces producing poverty and degrading living and working conditions.

This new understanding of government's purpose demanded a much more active government at every level. The constitutional order which defined and limited authority and prohibited government interference with certain rights did not account for the redistribution of resources, legal privileges, and government intervention in social and economic conditions that would be necessary for individuals to effectively realize their potentialities. Nor did it facilitate the rule of credentialed experts whom Progressives believed would be best suited to direct society through rules and regulations appropriate for the times.

One of the most influential figures in laying the groundwork for actual institutional changes based on this critique of American constitutionalism was Woodrow Wilson (Pestritto 2005). In the decades leading up to his election to the presidency in 1912, Wilson was a prominent social scientist and theoretician, serving as a university professor and then president of Princeton University. In his book *Congressional Government*, Wilson (1900) contended, "The government of a country so vast and various must be strong, prompt, wieldy and efficient." Throughout his work, he critiqued the machinery of American constitutional government as outmoded and inefficient, arguing instead for a living constitution that could evolve to meet the social and economic challenges and complexities of the day. He further advocated minimizing the influence of political parties and locally elected officials (whom he argued tended toward corruption and parochialism) in favor of the discretionary rule of public-spirited, scientifically trained experts who could direct society through rules and regulations appropriate to the currents of the time (Pestritto 2005).

The ideas espoused by Wilson and other like-minded Progressives ultimately culminated in certain immediate legislative changes, such as passage of state labor and school attendance laws, the implementation of corporate trust busting and civil service reform, and the establishment of the first federal regulatory agencies—including the Interstate Commerce Commission, the Federal Reserve, and the Federal Trade Commission. In 1913, the Sixteenth Amendment was ratified establishing Congress's right to adopt a federal tax on personal income. Previously, federal revenue was generated almost entirely from tariffs and excise taxes on select commodities. The unhampered ability to tax incomes drastically increased the federal government's ability to produce revenue, paving the way for the further expansion of its powers into the economic life of the nation.

Nevertheless, the full implementation of the Progressive project was largely limited by the constitutional system, the attachment most Americans still retained to the idea of individual rights, and a general suspicion of an excessively strong or unrestrained national government. As political scientist Sidney Milkis explains, it was not until several decades later that FDR's skillful "reinterpretation of the American constitutional tradition" gave "legitimacy to progressive principles by embedding them in the language of constitutionalism and interpreting them as an expansion rather than a subversion of the natural rights tradition" (Milkis 2002).

The "Golden" Decade

The election of Republican Warren G. Harding to the presidency with over 60 percent of the popular vote in 1920 gave the appearance of an end to Progressivism for a time. Harding campaigned on the platform of a "return to normalcy." This included a rejection of continued involvement in world affairs following the World War and a laissez-faire or non-interventionist approach to economics and domestic governance. After a series of scandals within his administration and his own death in office, Harding was succeeded to the presidency by his vice president, the even more restrained and popular Calvin Coolidge, who is known by both admirers and detractors for his role in reducing the national debt, lowering tax rates, encouraging legislative moderation, and defending limits on federal authority. Nevertheless, the Progressive faith in managerial expertise, social science knowledge, and human progress continued to impact private and public life.

The 1920s are often remembered as the "golden decade" thanks to technological advances, increased production and economic growth, consistently low unemployment rates, an average rise in real wages, and the dramatic expansion of the middle class (Witcher and Horton 2013). The decade also marked a seismic transformation into a vibrant consumer society, as advances in technology and product development raised standards of living and revolutionized life through increased access to and affordability of goods and services like automobiles, electricity, radios, and household appliances.

The traditional American focus on productive work, land ownership, free labor, and political independence was eclipsed by a growing concern with economic growth, business autonomy, and the ability of the consumer to purchase a wider array of tangible commodities. The development of mass media and new techniques in advertising, such as radio ads and nationwide mailing of catalogs, fueled this growing consumerism. *Newsweek* editor Philip Jeffrey (2023) observes that it was during this period that a surge of advertising began to promise "greater happiness and power—therapeutic release from the psychic burdens of daily life and tighter control over one's health and appearances—through purchasing." Business leaders and bankers transformed into the new managerial class or agents of economic and social progress, and the term "free enterprise" came to be associated less with the capacity and agency of individual citizens and more with the ideas of business autonomy, free trade, and the capitalist economic system (Glickman 2019).

Individual purchasing power increased considerably during the 1920s, both through wage growth and product affordability and through the growing financialization of the economy and expanded access to credit. Prior to the twentieth century, state usury laws prohibiting high-rate lending greatly inhibited small-loan or consumptive borrowing (Calder 2001). In the early 1900s Progressive activists had prompted the emergence of personal finances by setting up "remedial loan" shops as an alternative to the illegal loan sharks and pawnbrokers frequented by industrial workers and by leading a successful campaign to overturn usury laws (Jeffery 2023). The movement ultimately failed to end black market loansharking, but it did make consumer loans and easy credit more socially acceptable.

This growing acceptance of debt was compounded by the creation of the Federal Reserve in 1913, which allowed banks to operate and expand credit with lower reserves of cash. During the 1920s, the Federal Reserve maintained low interest rates and pursued a policy of credit expansion. Banks began to actively sell business and consumer credit. Following the Progressives' enthusiasm for "scientific management," they adopted formulae for evaluating individual credit worthiness.

As sellers of consumer goods joined banks in allowing individuals to take out lines of credit or sign up for installment plans for access to commodities and conveniences that they could not afford to pay for all at once, consumer debt skyrocketed—more than doubling between 1920 and 1930 (ushistory.org). Stock trading also increased as middle-class people could purchase stocks on borrowed funds and as companies increasingly relied on selling stock to raise funds. As a result, Wall Street replaced the western homestead as the primary site for achieving the American Dream (Jeffery 2023).

The Onset of the Great Depression and the Hoover Administration

On October 29, 1929, a day that lives in infamy, a sharp decline in US stock values led to a market crash. While the crash is considered the official start of the crisis that led to the Great Depression, economists and historians hotly debate the various contributing factors and causes of the depression. These include structural weaknesses in American agriculture and industry, the frailty of the international economy at the time, the overly speculative and unstable foundations of the American financial sector, overproduction and supply, the Federal Reserve's misguided monetary policy, and unnecessary government intervention and regulation (Field and Kim 2020; Hamilton n.d.; Shlaes 2007).

Another common claim is that President Herbert Hoover's hands-off approach caused the country to slip into the Great Depression. This claim, however, ignores the reality that—though he lacked an assertive nature and initially characterized the market crash as a temporary downturn—Hoover advocated for and adopted a somewhat vigorous response to mitigate economic fallout. Even Rexford Tugwell, one of President Franklin D. Roosevelt's main economic advisors, confessed, "We didn't admit it at the time, but practically the whole New Deal was extrapolated from programs that Hoover started" (Burner 1979). In 1929 alone, Hoover devoted 13 percent of the federal budget to public works spending. Between 1929 and 1932, Hoover supported and signed several laws, including the Agricultural Marketing Act (1929), which established a farm board to control agricultural surpluses and increase prices; the Smoot-Hawley Tariff Act (1930), which drastically increased tariff rates on a host of imported products; and the Emergency Relief and Construction Act (1932), which allocated an additional two billion dollars to public works programs. Hoover additionally pushed for the creation of the Reconstruction Finance Corporation (RFC) in 1931 to make emergency loans to businesses in danger of default. The RFC eventually provided more than a billion dollars in subsidized or low-interest loans to bail out businesses, mostly banks or railroad corporations. To counteract the deficit spending resulting from these acts, Hoover signed the Revenue Act of 1932, which among other things drastically raised the top marginal income tax rate, increased the corporate income tax, and created the gas tax.

Despite or—as some economists argue—because of these interventions, the recession following the crash became a full-blown depression. The unemployment rate skyrocketed, industries continued operating far below capacity, and foreclosures, bankruptcies, and hunger reached unprecedented levels. By the end of his first and only presidential term, he began to appear heartless and out of touch with the suffering of the American people. Hoover's downfall ultimately resided, as Milkis and Nelson (2020) contend, in the fact that his "philosophy and personality rendered him sadly incapable of the brand of leadership he advocated."

As the depression deepened, Hoover flip-flopped between advocating for massive government intervention and adhering to philosophy of rugged individualism and laissez-faire. By supporting the Reconstruction Finance Bill and the demands for monetary assistance from banks, agricultural corporations, and railroads, Hoover implicitly legitimized the idea of federal assistance for certain sectors of the economy—yet he adamantly opposed direct federal payments for unemployment relief. This put Hoover in an indefensible position ideologically. As historian David M. Kennedy (1999) points out, "If Hoover could be made to support federal relief for the banks, why not federal relief for the unemployed?" The public antagonism toward Hoover only deepened when he ordered the military to forcibly remove financially desperate First World War veterans who had gathered in Washington DC's Anacostia Flats to demand early payments of government bonuses due to them for their service. By the end of his term, Hoover's name was permanently tarnished, becoming synonymous with the Great Depression.

Roosevelt's New Economic Order

In 1932, Hoover lost in a landslide election to Franklin D. Roosevelt. Roosevelt had given few policy specifics during his presidential campaign. Instead, amid national economic despair, he calmed voter's fears, infusing them with a sense of hope through his bold and energetic leadership style and comprehensive promise of a "new deal." FDR first used this term in his nomination acceptance speech at the 1932 Democratic Convention speech. It eventually became the comprehensive title of the series of legislative acts, executive orders, and presidential proclamations issued during his presidency that were aimed at resolving the economic problems underlying the Great Depression.

Very much in line with his Progressive forebears, Roosevelt envisioned an unencumbered state and discretionary rule by public-spirited experts to bring about a new economic constitutional order. The Progressive project, however, had been largely curtailed by the attachment that many Americans still held to the idea of natural rights, individual liberty, limited government, and local governance. Consequently, when FDR took office, the federal government still operated within a very limited range of authority. Nevertheless, FDR's rhetorical innovations and skillful ability to calm reactionary elements made him far more successful than previous Progressives in spurring substantial and lasting institutional change. Beginning during his campaign and throughout his presidency, he consistently framed the expansion of government and its purposes as a continuation and fulfillment, rather than a repudiation, of America's founding principles.

One of the clearest examples of Roosevelt's rhetorical strategy is his 1932 campaign speech on progressive governance delivered to the Commonwealth Club in San Francisco, California. In this speech, which has been referenced by some as "the New Deal manifesto," FDR shrouds his vision for the creation of a new economic order in the language of individualism, rights, and freedom (Milkis 2002). In fact, the main theme of the address is the need to extend the power of government into the economic life of the nation to preserve individualism. FDR ultimately contends that given new economic circumstances, the perpetuation of the traditional understanding of limited government would result in poverty and oppression and would thereby destroy individualism.

This claim, as Tiffany J. Miller (2007) points out, "depend[ed] on a subtle redefinition of individualism, essentially equating it with economic prosperity rather than the legal freedoms arising from the protection of natural rights." For FDR, Miller explains:

> The key to ensuring economic security and hence individualism ... was not to leave individuals largely free to discover, produce, and acquire more goods, as had the Founders. On the contrary, the key to securing individuals was to expand the power of government in whatever ways were necessary to effect *a more equitable distribution* of the "wealth and products" that had already been created.

Ensuring the fruition of the economic security, and thereby individualism in this new sense, through a more equitable redistribution of resources would require a new and more expansive understanding not only of the responsibilities of government, but also of the substance of individual rights. "As I see it," Roosevelt (1932) proclaimed, "the task of government in its relation to business is to assist the development of an economic declaration of rights, an economic constitutional order."

Reversing the original social contract notion that individuals form a government and empower it to secure their permanent inalienable rights of personhood, he declares, that "the people [consent] to power on consideration that they be accorded certain rights." "The task of statesmanship," he continues, "has always been the re-definition of these rights in terms of a changing and growing social order." FDR concludes the Commonwealth Address with such a redefinition and corresponding call for government action. "The right to life," he declares, means "a right to make a comfortable living," and the right to property "means a right to be assured, to the fullest extent attainable, in the safety of his savings."

FDR laid out a more extensive listing of rights in his 1944 State of the Union Address, also known as his "Second Bill of Rights" speech. After devoting the near entirety of the speech to policies needed to effectively wage and win the Second World War, Roosevelt turns to domestic policy, equating the promotion of "economic security" and a high standard of living among the citizenry to his presidential responsibility to secure the nation's liberty from foreign threat.

He begins this turn by contending that the protection of the rights to life and liberty in the old sense, such as "the right of free speech, free press, free worship, trial by jury, [and] freedom from unreasonable searches and seizures" were no longer adequately ensuring "equality in the pursuit of happiness." Equating freedom with the achievement of a basic level of financial affluence, Roosevelt asserts, "True individual freedom cannot exist without economic security and independence." Thus, the ultimate purpose of government is to guarantee individuals protection against the uncertainties of the marketplace. As Milkis (2002) notes, "Security was to be the new self-evident truth of political life." Because the old understanding of rights would be inadequate to guarantee such security, FDR pronounced, "We have accepted, so to speak, a second Bill of Rights under which a new basis of security and prosperity can be established for all regardless of station, race or creed."

Whereas the traditional American understanding of rights was associated with the limitation of the power of government, FDR's new listing of economic rights would require largely unhampered government involvement in public and private life. These new rights, according to FDR's Second Bill of Rights, include:

- The right to a useful and remunerative job;
- The right to earn enough to provide adequate food and clothing and recreation;
- The right of every farmer to raise and sell his products at a return which will give him and his family a decent living;
- The right of every businessman, large and small, to trade in an atmosphere of freedom from unfair competition and domination by monopolies at home or abroad;
- The right of every family to a decent home;
- The right to adequate medical care and the opportunity to achieve and enjoy good health;
- The right to adequate protection from the economic fears of old age and sickness and accident and unemployment; and
- The right to a good education.

Though FDR's Second Bill of Rights was never formally added to the US Constitution or fully executed in practice, it did inform many of the precedent-setting actions and policies pursued during his administration. During his first term, Roosevelt oversaw two periods of major legislative activity. The first, which occurred between 1933 and 1934, resulted in the passage of several bold measures, the two most prominent being the Agricultural Adjustment Act of 1933 (AAA) and the National Industrial Recovery Act of 1933 (NIRA). The AAA was passed with the goal of ensuring that farmers receive a high return on their crops. It established the Agricultural Adjustment Administration to administer rules and regulations governing subsidies, production, and supply restrictions on certain commodities.

The NIRA was even broader in scope. Overriding antitrust laws, Title I of the NIRA empowered and, in some cases, mandated companies to collaborate to write "codes of fair competition" that effectively fixed prices and wages and instituted production quotas (National Archives n.d.). It also gave employees the right to join labor unions and bargain with their employers collectively. Under the authority of the NIRA, FDR issued an executive order creating the National Recovery Administration (NRA), which he empowered to draft industrial codes governing hours of work, rates of pay, and prices. More than 500 codes of fair practice were adopted within the NIRA's first year.

From its inception, the NIRA was widely criticized. It promoted harmful monopolies, inhibited production, raised prices, and contained no enforcement mechanism for ensuring the trade union rights of employees. In 1935, the Supreme Court struck down Title I of the NIRA on the grounds that it exceeded the Congress's constitutional power to regulate interstate commerce and that it permitted an unconstitutional delegation of legislative authority to the executive branch. In 1935, Congress passed the National Labor Relations Act, also known as the Wagner Act, reinstituting the right of private sector employees to organize into trade unions, engage in collective bargaining, and participate in concerted action such as strikes. To ensure enforcement of these rights, the act created the National Labor Relations Board (NLRB) to arbitrate disputes, oversee union elections, and penalize unfair labor practices.

The second Title of the NIRA established a national public works program called the Public Works Administration (PWA). In an effort to revive the economy and reduce unemployment, the PWA funded billions of dollars on contracts with private firms to build dams, bridges, roads, buildings, and other major public projects, many of which are still in use today. The creation of the PWA was followed by additional public works legislation establishing the Civilian Conservation Corps, which provided opportunities for unemployed young men to work on reforestation and flood and fire control, and the National Youth Administration, which provided part-time jobs to high school and college students. The PWA also established the first federal housing project.

This project was followed up by the passage of the National Housing Act in 1934, which created the Federal Housing Administration (FHA) to ensure loans to middle-income families seeking to repair, upgrade, or build new homes.

A subsequent flurry of legislative activity, which became known as FDR's Second New Deal, took place between 1935 and 1937. The most ambitious of the laws passed during this period was the Economic Security Act of 1935 (also known as the Social Security Act). While a provision for universal healthcare was dropped from the act for political reasons, the Economic Security Act in its final form provided funding for state welfare programs to support mothers and children, the elderly, the crippled, and the blind; created a federal-state unemployment and disability insurance program; and established a compulsory old-age retirement system (now known as Social Security). In 1939, Amendments to the Social Security Act added benefit payments to a spouse and minor children of a retired worker and survivor benefits to the families of prematurely deceased workers.

Additional legislation passed during FDR's Second New Deal period imposed higher wealth taxes; established the first federal minimum wage; created the United States Housing Authority (USHA) to facilitate the construction of low-rent housing and rent supplements for low-income tenants; provided federal grants-in-aid to the states for emergency unemployment relief; and authorized the creation of the Works Progress Administration, an agency which directly supplied jobs to the long-term unemployed to carry out public works projects.

According to historian William E. Leuchtenberg (2009), FDR's New Deal Programs were less notable for their achievements than for the precedent they set in redefining the role of government in the lives of ordinary Americans. "The Social Security Act of 1935," Leuchtenberg notes, "reversed historic assumptions about the nature of social responsibility, and it established the proposition that the individual has clear-cut social rights."

Thus, although FDR faced resistance during his presidency from the courts and conservatives within his own party, he made significant strides in establishing and promoting the legitimacy of administrative centralization and expansive national power, thereby paving the way for an even greater transformation of the American political order in the years to come. Additionally, by the end of Roosevelt's time in office, the federal courts—once a leading barrier to the implementation of FDR's most ambitious initiatives—began to acquiesce in the expansion of federal administration power.

The Affluent Society and the Reemergence of Poverty as a Salient Political Issue

The New Deal period represented a radical expansion of the scope of federal administration, introduced the concept of entitlements into federal policy, and marked the birth of a national social welfare system. In many ways, however, the policies adopted during this era were reflective of the nation's early approach to poor relief. They emphasized the value of work, focused primarily on preventing destitution, and distinguished between the deserving and undeserving poor. The two most important components of Social Security, unemployment insurance and old age and survivors' insurance, for example, were implemented to protect those workers and their families from economic downturns and from destitution resulting from old age or death. Benefits were based on previous pay rates, and both programs were restricted to those who had been employed. Direct public assistance was largely limited to those unable to work, such as the elderly and severely disabled. Even the Aid to Dependent Children program (later renamed AFDC, Aid to Families with Dependent Children), created by the Social Security Act of 1935, was established with the goal of ensuring that indigent widows were not forced to place their children in orphanages (Jencks 1992). Though the program did not explicitly limit benefits to widows, several state legislatures adopted "suitable home" requirements and disqualified mothers who had children out of wedlock or who were cohabitating with a non-spouse.

Even as state governments relaxed welfare eligibility standards in the 1940s and Congress amended the Social Security Act to add new categories of public assistance in the 1950s, average benefits and reliance on them were minimal. Public assistance was not yet viewed as a right that could be demanded regardless of conduct or circumstances, and programs were narrowly focused on meeting individuals' immediate needs for food, shelter, and medical care. Poverty-stricken individuals and families still largely subsisted or worked their way out of poverty through the help of family members and social relations.

Summarizing the role of these informal social relations, Katz and Stern (2004) describe how poor families "turned to kin and friends for donations of food, clothes, small amounts of money, and temporary housing." They additionally "were sustained by credit from landlords and local grocers," "found help when sick in free dispensaries and hospitals," and "turned to the network of private charities and mutual aid societies" whose mission was not to lift people out of poverty, but to ensure their survival. Furthermore, dependency was still largely considered dishonorable—and until as late as the mid-1960s, only about half of those eligible for public assistance benefits enrolled in them (Olasky 1992).

In the decades following the Second World War, the country entered a period of unprecedented economic growth, and America rapidly developed into the world's most affluent society. Poverty rates dropped dramatically among all groups and society experienced increases in income and wealth (U.S. Census Bureau n.d.). This contributed to the prevailing view that prosperity, economic growth, and federal market manipulation had solved the poverty problem (Galbraith 1958). Academics, politicians, and the media gave very little attention to the issue of poverty, and it soon subsided as a national concern. The change in this state of affairs, however, was unexpected and rapid. As Charles Murray (2015) points out, "As of the beginning of 1962, no one was talking about poverty; by the end of 1963 it was the hottest domestic policy topic other than civil rights." Three factors significantly contributed to this change: growing public disaffection toward AFDC, the emerging civil rights movement, and socialist activist Michael Harrington's publication of *The Other America: Poverty in the United States* in 1962.

From 1935 until the early 1950s, most federal aid and state welfare funds went to assist the elderly. By the mid-1950s, however, recipients of AFDC far exceeded all other recipients of public aid, and despite economic growth, reliance on public aid continued to grow. Furthermore, whereas earlier recipients of AFDC were mostly widowed mothers of dependent white children, an increasing number were now single Black women with illegitimate children (Trattner 1994). By the late 1950s, states began implementing eligibility policies to reduce the number of AFDC recipients and to deter new applicants. While mainstream America was becoming more and more disgruntled with public welfare, the civil rights movement was increasingly drawing attention to the poor economic condition of Black citizens and the pervasive discrimination and injustice committed against them in a way that was impossible for conscientious whites across the political spectrum to ignore. In an influential assessment of American welfare policy, Charles Murray (2015) recounts how statistics on Black unemployment, wages, infant mortality, and education alongside television images of young children needing military escorts to attend school, mob attacks on the freedom riders, and college students sitting at drugstore counters for the right to be served a cup of coffee created a situation in which "white indignation at the morals of welfare recipients and white guilt over who was responsible for putting them in that state collided."

As the civil rights movement placed a spotlight on the economic suffering of many Black families, Michael Harrington's bestseller *The Other America* (1962) further contributed to the reinvigoration of poverty as a matter of public concern. *The Other America* challenged assumptions about American affluence by drawing attention to the hidden subculture of poverty and the egregious living conditions prevalent among America's Black, white, Chicano, and American Indian under class. Foreshadowing President Lyndon B. Johnson's call for a "war on poverty" that would end poverty, not just alleviate it, Harrington contended that America needed a "comprehensive assault on poverty."

Harrington's book had a profound impact on President John F. Kennedy and his Council of Economic Advisors, who began proposing antipoverty legislation shortly after its publication (Isserman 2009). In fact, by the time Kennedy took office in 1961, a growing consensus had emerged in the political center that welfare should be designed to help the poor escape poverty and prepare them for economic self-sufficiency and a quality life. Give the poor "a hand, not a handout" became the slogan for this appeal. Kennedy built on this consensus, focusing his programs largely on assisting those in need through job training and placement programs, case work, and other rehabilitative efforts. In the whole scheme of things, the measures adopted during Kennedy's administration were modest and not overly costly. On these grounds, Murray (2015) observes that "Kennedy's legacy to Lyndon Johnson was not a new system, but a new tone and new expectations." "By shifting the focus of welfare policy away from the dole and toward escape from the dole," Murray writes, "Kennedy brought the federal government into a role that it had barely considered in the past." That role was to move beyond emergency measures to relieve poverty and unemployment, and to take instead "a continuing responsibility for helping Americans to help themselves."

The War on Poverty and the Great Society

On November 22, 1963, John F. Kennedy was assassinated in Dallas, Texas, placing the presidency in the hands of Lyndon B. Johnson. Johnson wasted no time turning "the country's grief into a moral crusade" (Tulis 1987). Invoking the memory of the former president, he secured the passage of the Civil Rights Act of 1964, effectively dismantling Jim Crow through the prohibition of discrimination based on race, color, religion, sex, or national origin in employment, public accommodations, federally funded programs, and schools.

Johnson simultaneously made the elimination of poverty and the elevation of qualitative liberalism central to his presidency. In his first State of the Union Address, delivered just two months after taking office, Johnson contended that one-fifth of the American people lived in poverty (1964a). He, thus, declared an "unconditional war on poverty," calling on Congress to enact a comprehensive multiple-point legislative program. Recommending more federal support for education, training, and healthcare than any previous president in history, Johnson pledged not just to fight the symptoms of poverty but to "cure" and prevent it (Shlaes 2019).

While implementing a program to combat and prevent poverty had been one of JFK's priorities, Johnson made clear that his aspirations extended far beyond the mere elimination of poverty. For Johnson, ending poverty represented only a steppingstone toward the loftier goal of realizing what he termed the "Great Society." On May 22, 1964, in a commencement address at the University of Michigan, Johnson gave what became the signature speech of his presidency (1964b). At the outset of the address, which is excerpted in Chapter 5, Johnson stated that the first century and a half of American history involved the struggle to create "an order of plenty for all of our people." Having accomplished this goal, the challenge now lies, Johnson asserted, in using that material security and prosperity as a foundation to "enrich and elevate our national life, to advance the quality of our American civilization."

This grandiose vision of a society dedicated to ensuring that each of its members fully develop their mental and spiritual capacities and potential hinged on a decisive turn away from the idea of limited government. Speaking to this point, Johnson declared in a speech to Swarthmore College students given just a couple of weeks after his Great Society address, "The truth is, far from crushing the individual, government at its best liberates him from the enslaving forces of his environment" (1964c).

Johnson's bold ambitions ultimately contributed to the introduction of a legislative program of extraordinary breadth. Within nine months of taking office, Johnson signed the first comprehensive antipoverty proposal, the Economic Opportunity Act, into law. Faithful to the aim of striking at the root causes of poverty and providing "a hand, not a handout," Johnson elatedly remarked at the signing ceremony that "the days of the dole in this country are numbered" (1964d). Among other things, the act provided basic job skill training programs; funded part-time jobs for teenagers and college students; established Volunteers in Service to America (VISTA), the domestic version of the Peace Corps; created the Community Action Program to fund local agencies and community organizations to develop activities aimed at empowering the poor; authorized financial incentives such as job-creating loans to small businesses; and founded Head Start, an early education program for low-income children.

The strong economy made it easier to justify the establishment of programs that went well beyond the provision of basic needs. The signing of the Economic Opportunity Act was followed, less than two weeks later, with the passage of the Food Stamp Act and then a barrage of other major programs. Using the popular mandate created by his landslide electoral victory in 1964, Johnson was able to convince the incoming Democratic super majorities in the House and Senate to pass a host of legislative priorities. In 1965 alone, Congress passed eighty of Johnson's policy proposals. Milkis and Nelson (2020) note that no Congress since the New Deal era had done more to reorder the nation. New laws included the Social Security Amendments of 1965, which created Medicare and Medicaid, the Older Americans Act, the Elementary and Secondary Education Act, legislation to create the Department of Transportation and the Department of Housing and Urban Development, and the Immigration and Nationality Act of 1965, which relaxed entry requirements for various nationalities leading to an influx of immigration in the late twentieth century from Latin America and Asia.

Measuring and Studying Poverty

In the years directly following Johnson's declared war on poverty, two major trends emerged. The first was an emphasis on the need to formally measure how many people were in poverty and how those numbers changed from year to year. In 1965, the Office of Economic Opportunity adopted a working definition of poverty and an official measure, known as the poverty line, based on methodology proposed by Social Security Administration analyst Mollie Orshansky, which compares household income and size against a set of thresholds defined by the cost of minimum necessities such as food, clothing, and housing (United States Census Bureau 2014). A couple of years later, the Office of Management and

Budget codified that measure for statistical purposes and charged the Census Bureau with providing annual poverty estimates based on the measurement.

Various efforts have been made over the years to improve poverty measurement, including the introduction in 2011 of a new Supplemental Poverty Measure (SPM), which accounts for geographical variation and family resources (such as cash and noncash benefits) and expenses (such as taxes and medical costs) that are not included in the official poverty measure.

The second major trend was the widespread adoption of outcomes-based assessment combined with a belief in "structural poverty," the idea that economic, social, and political systems subject certain demographics to systemic poverty regardless of their life choices or whether they have equal legal opportunities. This view, which was already gaining momentum in the early 1960s, became even more widespread in the direct wake of Johnson's war on poverty.

Despite Johnson's promise that the "days of the dole in this country are numbered," none of his programs succeeded in getting people off public relief. Instead, the number of individuals and families relying on federal aid and the total expenditures continued to climb as eligibility for such programs was expanded and more people became aware of the aid available to them (Trattner 1994). This was particularly true of the AFDC program. Court rulings overturned a variety of state rules restricting access to the program, and local organizations funded by the EOP's Community Action Program worked to encourage eligible parties to sign up for benefits and to spread the view of welfare as a fundamental right among the poor. In 1960 the average number of families receiving monthly AFDC benefits was 803,000, by 1970 the number had jumped to 1.9 million (Béland and Waddan 2012).

Furthermore, while the language of the Civil Rights Act had prohibited discrimination for reasons of race, color, religion, sex, and national origin, within a few years of the law's passage it was clear that a legal policy of nondiscrimination was not guaranteeing equality between groups in outcome and effect. Activists successfully argued that overcoming economic and social discrepancies between whites and Blacks would require that civil rights laws be interpreted to mandate racial quotas and affirmative action policies in contracting, education, and employment. This contributed to a seismic ideological shift away from equality being understood as the protection of equal rights and opportunity toward an emphasis on equality as a result produced, if necessary, through preferential treatment and permanent income transfers.

Johnson himself endorsed this view in a speech at Howard University, when he declared, "We seek … not just equality as a right and a theory but equality as a fact and equality as a result" (1965).

In practice, the belief that poverty persists solely because of societal defects (rather than the personal failings or life choices of individuals) along with the general objective of achieving relative equality in effect contributed both to the assumption that all poverty-stricken individuals are deserving of aid and to the ongoing use of outcome-based poverty measurement for various demographics as the primary indicator of whether opportunity exists for such groups and whether further social and political intervention is necessary.

The Era of Welfare Reform

As unprecedented spending on the unpopular and politically polarizing Vietnam War and Great Society programs subjected the economy to inflationary strains, Johnson's popularity waned. In March 1968, Johnson announced that he would not seek reelection as the Democratic nominee. The Republican challenger, Richard Nixon, squeaked out a victory over eventual Democratic nominee Hubert H. Humphrey, who had been vice president in the Johnson administration. Nixon's campaign reflected growing public skepticism and disillusionment about Johnson's Great Society and social reform generally (Milkis and Nelson 2020).

Upon assuming office, however, Nixon presided over a rapid rise in domestic federal spending, much of which was due to his own initiatives that reflected the same basic purpose as Johnson's programs (Nathan 1996).

Nixon's major domestic policy initiative the "New Federalism," for example, upheld the welfare state in theory, merely challenging the presumption that social and urban problems should always be addressed at the national level. It gave greater flexibility and control over the administration of education, workforce training, and direct social services to state and local governments, while simultaneously expanding federal benefits. Despite the lip service he paid to conservative ideals, Nixon—working with Democratic majorities in Congress and through executive fiat—oversaw the implementation of the most expensive and extensive expansion of federal licensing and regulation in the name of safety, health, and environmentalism than any other president to date. Furthermore, his proposed Family Assistance Plan (FAP), which passed the

House, but failed to garner enough support for passage in the Senate, would have effectively guaranteed a minimum income for American families through a negative income tax scheme (Béland and Waddan 2012).

The several decades following the onset of the War on Poverty were marked by the steady growth of entitlement expenditures, despite growing public and political opposition to what critics derided as the "welfare state." By the time Jimmy Carter took office in 1977, the economic growth of the previous decades was marred by stagflation (economic stagnation and inflation), an oil embargo, high levels of unemployment, increased dependency on social welfare systems, and rising debt.

As economic conditions continued to deteriorate throughout the late 1970s, federal entitlements and public aid began to undergo an even greater level of public scrutiny. Several indicators, such as the passage of Proposition 13, the property tax-cutting initiative in California, suggested a mounting backlash against high taxes and government spending. The 1970s additionally witnessed a rapid rise in teen pregnancies, single-parent homes, and absent fathers. By 1980, a vast majority of single mothers receiving AFDC benefits were not widowed, but divorced, separated, or never married (Garfinkel and McLanahan 1986). Many began to question the degree to which means-tested welfare programs were contributing to family breakdown by incentivizing out-of-wedlock births and penalizing low-income parents who chose to get married. Consequently, in the two decades that followed, combatting dependency on public assistance replaced poverty as the more politically salient issue.

Beginning most notably with the publication of George Gilder's book *Wealth and Poverty* in 1981, growing numbers of conservative thinkers made the intellectual case that current welfare programs were harmful to those they were intended to help, exacerbating poverty by reducing incentives to work and encouraging other self-destructive behaviors. The most renowned of these public intellectuals was Charles Murray (2015). Murray used social science methods in his book *Losing Ground* to support the contention that the welfare state built in the 1960s inadvertently created a poverty trap by "mak[ing] it profitable for the poor to behave in the short term in ways that were destructive in the long term." Specifically, Murray contended that the incentive structures created by AFDC and other benefit programs contributed to rising rates of illegitimacy, dependency, and idleness. As a result, Murray maintained that these programs exacerbated income poverty as well as social and moral poverty. Ultimately, Murray's proposal to scrap "the entire federal welfare and income-support structure for working-aged persons" and to require able-bodied persons to rely on the job market, family members, friends, and public or private local fund services proved too radical for public sentiment. Nevertheless, his claims about the harmful individual and societal effects of federal welfare provided fodder for the conservative welfare reform movement in the 1980s and 1990s.

Tying Welfare to Work

A second wave of thought, headed up by political scientist and policy analyst Lawrence Mead (1992), supported the continuation of federal aid, but emphasized engagement in the workforce as essential to escaping poverty. Thus, in contrast to Murray's proposal to replace federal aid with short-term local programs, Mead advocated new strategies aimed at more effectively integrating welfare beneficiaries into the workplace. Specifically, he recommended work requirements backed by sanctions to incentivize the transition from welfare to work. Mead's perspective eventually provided the foundation for the successful passage of comprehensive welfare reform legislation in 1996.

Some changes to the AFDC program were initiated during the Reagan presidency. The most significant of these were implemented in 1981 with the passage of the Omnibus Budget Reconciliation Act (OBRA). OBRA authorized states to implement their own work requirements as conditions for aid, reduced the amount of income individuals and families could earn and the amount of assets they could own to remain eligible for AFDC benefits, and reversed a provision that allowed AFDC recipients who found employment to keep some of their earnings from work and remain eligible for benefits. Ironically, a consequence of this OBRA reform was that it reduced the likelihood that AFDC recipients, particularly mothers, would transition from welfare to work in the formal economy (Béland and Waddan 2012). Despite these revisions, and Reagan's continued critique of federal welfare programs, AFDC survived the Reagan administration largely intact.

Eventually, however, public support for welfare reform drew the attention of politicians across the political spectrum, as demonstrated by Bill Clinton's 1992 campaign promise to "end welfare as we have come to know it." In 1996, following several months of intense and even hostile negotiations, President Clinton and the Republican-controlled Congress (acting under the leadership of House Speaker Newt Gingrich) finally agreed on a compromise measure. The resulting Personal Responsibility and Work Opportunity Reconciliation Act

(PRWORA), signed into law on August 22, 1996, initiated major changes in US welfare policy. The law replaced AFDC as an open-ended entitlement with the Temporary Assistance for Needy Families (TANF) block grants to the states. Under TANF, states were given broad discretion to determine benefit eligibility and operate their own programs. The program also placed a five-year lifetime limit on receiving federally funded cash benefits and required that beneficiaries must find employment or enroll in job training within a certain period.

Ultimately, the passage of the PRWORA demonstrated that conservative critics of the federal welfare state had succeeded by turning the compassion argument against welfare. As Béland and Waddan (2012) point out, "This approach had turned out to be so effective politically that by the mid-1990s a Democratic president signed into law a set of rules that would have been denounced as an example of right-wing extremism a quarter century earlier."

In the decades that followed, though, conservatives had less success in reducing spending on entitlement programs like social security, Medicare, Medicaid, disability insurance, and the Supplemental Nutrition Assistance Program (SNAP) expanded over time. Furthermore, although the argument that public welfare entitlements had incentivized rising rates of nonmarital childbearing and child rearing had served as a primary motivator for reform, a commitment to marriage promotion remained a secondary feature of the PRWORA. While the act resulted in a reduction in welfare caseloads and an increase in employment rates among low-skilled mothers, it had little to no effect on out-of-wedlock births and family structure (Teitler et al. 2009).

The Rise of Neoliberalism

While political moderates from both parties debated the merits of welfare reform and how to best incentivize work as a contingent for federal aid, a neoliberal consensus was developing among American political and intellectual elites. The policies that ensued contributed to a substantial transformation of America's economy and the lives and communities of its lower-income and working-class citizens.

Neoliberalism most distinctly arose in the United States following the demise of the Soviet Union and the adoption of market-oriented reforms in communist China (Steger and Roy 2021). The threat of global communism having been neutralized, prominent political scientist Francis Fukuyama (1992) hailed a so-called "end of history" in which Western liberal democracy and market capitalism had ascended as the final and universal form of human government and economics. The neoliberal ideation that global democracy and the free flow of goods and services could finally be unleashed in a way that would alleviate human misery and permit "more people everywhere to turn their aspirations into achievements" and that America ought to be at the forefront of this movement influenced leaders and intellectuals of both parties to varying degrees (Friedman 2010). America now had a mission, in the words of George H.W. Bush (1991), to bring about "a new world order."

While few late-twentieth- and early-twenty-first-century politicians would self-identify as neoliberal, many of the policies they espoused fall under the broad definition of the term, which among other priorities espouses the ideals of globalization, economic deregulation, and uninhibited trade. In fact—though significant disagreements existed concerning the degree to which the state should interfere in the domestic economy through the administration and expansion of entitlements and the imposition of ever more robust environmental, health, and civil rights regulations—a bipartisan consensus among America's elected leaders and bureaucrats emerged that lasted throughout the administrations of Reagan, Clinton, both Bushes, and Obama in the areas of trade liberalization, global labor arbitrage, and the relaxation of antitrust policies.

Liberalizing Trade

The strongest area of bipartisan consensus was in the realm of liberalizing international trade and finance. The belief that furthering commercial and financial interdependence, particularly with Asia and the global south, would promote mutual economic growth, create conditions of peace, and hasten the spread of American ideals regarding freedom, democracy, and human rights motivated several major legislative actions and treaties. Among these were the North American Free Trade Agreement (NAFTA), the creation of the World Trade Organization (WTO), and more than a dozen bilateral trade deals that opened the American market to China. Advocates of such deals saturated the public discourse with idealized images of a consumerist free market world in which the uninhibited worldwide flow of goods, services, and labor would improve the human experience (Steger and Roy 2021).

By the early 2000s, however, it was clear that many of the promised benefits of the unrestricted flow of goods, services, and labor were failing to materialize, and that the country was beginning to incur significant costs. Previously US trade policy had sought to maintain an equilibrium between the country's imports and exports and to balance the interests of workers and investors. Trade liberalization, however, which contributed to a shift from trade surpluses to hundreds of billions of dollars in deficits appeared to favor corporate leaders and financiers at the expense of America's working class. At the same time, high-income earners gained the most from the 2001 and 2003 tax cuts championed by the George W. Bush White House (Horton 2017). Between 1990 and 2003 the total share of wealth held by the top 1 percent of income earners drastically increased, while the share held by the bottom 50 percent declined (Federal Reserve 2023).

Job losses in the high-paying textile and manufacturing industries, hitherto mainstays of the non-college-educated middle and working class, were pronounced. Between January 2000 and December 2014 manufacturing alone, which had remained relatively stable between 1970 and 2000, lost 5 million jobs (Scott 2015). American workers upon finding their jobs outsourced, their wages decreased, and their communities decimated were frequently admonished to find solace in their increased access to inexpensive foreign-made products and commodities—even as their savings declined and they took on greater levels of consumer debt to pay for such goods (Associated Press 2006).

The threat of outsourcing and corporate relocation made possible through the opening of global markets, along with the increased availability of cheap foreign workers for overseas factories and other operations, further reduced the bargaining power of American workers, both union and non-union. In response to Americans' demand for higher wages, politicians and corporate leaders further implemented global labor arbitrage in which they could force low-skilled Americans to compete with non-unionized foreign labor or ship jobs overseas. Citing a report from the US Commerce Department, Lind (2020) points out, "Between 1999 and 2009 US multinational corporations cut 864,000 workers in the US while adding 2.9 million workers abroad." Furthermore, freed from national labor and environmental laws, multinational corporations have facilitated the relocation of American industry and outsourcing of production to locations where economic desperation and a dearth of property rights and labor laws facilitate either outright slave labor or sweatshop-like working conditions. This increasing reliance on cheaper foreign labor has coincided with a rise of black-market indentured servitude and forced labor among poverty-stricken foreign nationals residing within the borders of the United States as well (Villegas 2020).

Politicians generally responded to American working-class angst, aggravated by continued trade deficits and global labor arbitrage, by proposing increases to the federal minimum wage and the expansion of the earned income tax credit or other forms of assistance, but such policies have done little to counteract the loss of gainful employment among the working class.

Financialization and the Growing Subprime Mortgage Market

Another of the more radical changes wrought by the neoliberal consensus has been the financialization of the US economy, which refers to the increase in size and importance of the country's financial sector relative to its overall economy and the practice of making money from money rather than from engineered products. Financialization largely took off in the early 1970s. During this time, President Nixon, concerned that the gold supply would be inadequate to cover the number of US dollars in circulation, announced that the United States would no longer exchange gold for US currency. That decision effectively ended the Bretton Woods Agreement negotiated between the United States and its Second World War allies in 1944 (Garten 2021). The agreement tied international currencies to the US dollar and made the dollar convertible into gold. This created predictable exchange rates and limited speculation (the selling or purchasing of an asset with the hopes that it will quickly decline or increase in value). The abandonment of the gold standard allowed the US government to print more money and led to a surge in liquidity (available cash) and profitability in the credit market.

The extension and profitability of the credit market was further encouraged by financial deregulation throughout the 1980s and 1990s pushed by Wall Street lobbyists and senior economic advisors serving in the Reagan and Clinton administrations—particularly of financial institutions or savings banks that specialize in real estate financing known as Savings and Loans (S&Ls). Beginning in 1982, regulators at the Federal Loan Home Bank Board attempted to bolster the struggling S&Ls industry by reducing the percentage of deposits that insured S&Ls had to keep on hand from 4 to 3 percent, thereby freeing up capital for further investments. Regulators simultaneously eliminated mandates that S&Ls have at least 400 shareholders (more than a quarter of whom had to be from the local community) and removed regulations forbidding any one individual from owning more than 10 percent of S&L stock and any one group from controlling more than 25 percent (FDIC 2023). New rules allowed for a single owner and allowed buyers to purchase S&L stock with real estate rather than cash. President Reagan expanded on this initial deregulation by signing the Garn-St. Germain Act the same year. This act eradicated requirements that S&Ls fund fixed rate home mortgage loans. Now S&Ls were permitted to write adjustable interest rate mortgages and could diversify their activities funding anything from commercial mortgages to consumer and commercial loans with a view to increasing profits. Two years later, Congress passed, and Reagan signed legislation permitting private banks to bundle mortgages into pools known as mortgage securities which could be sold off to investors for a profit.

In 1999, a decade and a half later, President Clinton signed the historic Financial Services Modernization Act. The law repealed important components of the Glass-Steagall Act of 1933, which had prohibited commercial banks from engaging in investment activities on Wall Street. Because the Financial Services Modernization Act allowed for the consolidation of investment and commercial banks via financial holding companies, contributing to the creation of companies that were "too big to fail," some have argued that this act was primarily responsible for the financial crisis that led to the Great Recession in 2007 through 2009 (Rickards 2012). This contention, however, overlooks the simultaneous and equally significant role of the rise in subprime lending (loans to buyers with poor or non-existent credit histories) and the packing of lower-risk assets with high-risk loans that could be sold as securities to investors around the world—much of which was an outgrowth of government financing and policy that facilitated and encouraged risky and predatory lending practices (Carney 2009; CBO 2010; Steger and Roy 2021).

The Great Recession, Covid-19, and the Growth of Neo-Feudalism

In 2007, the US real estate market collapsed as homeowners with subprime mortgages and other risky loans began to default. Foreclosures shot up in record numbers, triggering a global financial crisis and the worst US economic disaster since the Great Depression. Beginning in 2008, some of the largest, most respected financial institutions, insurance companies, and government-sponsored underwriters of mortgages were facing insolvency. Home values and the stock market plummeted, wiping out trillions of dollars of investment value between late 2007 and 2009 (Merle 2018). Many Americans lost their homes and saw their retirement accounts decimated. The flow of global credit came to a halt, forcing businesses to cut back on production and to lay off workers. Unemployment soared, peaking at 10 percent in October 2009 (Merle 2018). Presidents George W. Bush and Barack Obama approved hundreds of billions of dollars in corporate bailouts and stimulus spending.

While large, politically connected industries and financial institutions were saved, small community businesses and banks suffered widespread stagnation and closure. Working-class Americans watched as corporations that had received billions in taxpayer bailouts continued to move production and investment overseas (Niedermeyer 2012). Despite the passage of the 2010 Dodd-Frank Act, which gave regulators broad new authority to police the banking industry, many of the country's largest financial institutions grew even bigger than they were before the financial crisis, more than doubling their assets within a decade (Merle 2018). Public anger at the financial services industry contributed to the rise of both the conservative Tea Party movement, which demanded the failure of over-leveraged banks and corporations, and the progressive Occupy Wall Street movement, which demanded government takeover of those entities.

The Great Recession further exacerbated public feelings of betrayal and distrust toward the US government that had been growing for decades. While 77 percent of Americans said they trusted their government in 1964, by 2015 that number had plummeted to just 19 percent (Pew Research Center 2023).

Although the recession officially ended in June of 2009, its effects—including higher unemployment numbers, which did not even include the large number of individuals who dropped out of the workforce entirely—lingered for years (U.S. Bureau of Labor Statistics 2017). In addition, the recovery did not reach all Americans equally. Many workers were unable to find jobs that paid as well as the ones they held prior to the recession. According to an estimate from the Federal Reserve Bank of San Francisco, "That shift, combined with the time spent out of work and other drops in productivity … led to a loss of about $70,000 in lifetime income for every American" (Merle 2018). Moreover, while political actions aimed at recovery secured corporate wealth and the investments of high-income earners, they less successfully protected the assets of America's working class.

Sociologist Manfred B. Steger and professor of public administration Ravi K. Roy contend that even President Obama's signature healthcare initiative, the Patient Protection and Affordable Care Act, which was designed to make healthcare more affordable and accessible, placed additional tax burdens on already beleaguered middle-class and working families while acquiescing to the interests of powerful insurance companies and medical firms (Steger and Roy 2021). As of 2023, however, the Kaiser Family Foundation reported that more than 16 million Americans were enrolled in the ACA for health insurance coverage.

The neoliberal trend of a decline in the number of stable, well-paying jobs continued as companies began replacing career employees with short-term or zero-hour contract workers, offering little to no job security or retirement pensions, in what has become known as the "gig economy." By 2016, wealth gaps between upper-income families and lower- and middle-income families were at the highest levels recorded. According to a Pew Research Center study, "In 2016, the median wealth of lower-income families was 42 percent less than in 2007 and the median wealth of middle-income families was 33 percent lower. Indeed, the net worth of these families in 2016—$10,800 for lower-income families and $110,100 for middle-income families—was comparable to 1989 levels" (Kochhar and Cilluffo 2017).

Though the nation experienced significant growth in domestic production and a parallel increase in stock values, home equity, and the number of available payroll jobs between 2015 and 2019, the onset of the Covid-19 pandemic in early 2020 and the corresponding government shutdowns over the course of 2020 and 2021 served to aggravate the growing bifurcation of America between the professional and affluent members of society and the less educated and less prosperous. Stress factors associated with social isolation, job losses, and increasing caregiving burden for children were especially pronounced among the lower economic classes. While lockdowns favored big corporations, many of which were deemed "essential," small businesses struggled to survive. By the end of May 2021, there were nearly 40 percent fewer small businesses open nationwide than at the outset of 2020 (Roth 2021). Generously expanded unemployment benefits and federal and state stimulus checks temporarily prevented many from falling into destitution, but they also contributed to harmful employment gaps and labor shortages, as well as post-pandemic inflationary conditions across many sectors of the American economy. The lifetime reduction in earnings from learning loss in K-12 education and disconnection from the workforce remains to be seen.

Conclusion

In many respects, America is the wealthiest and most economically successful country in history. Founded on the idea that individuals' ancestry and social and economic class should not inhibit their ability to pursue a prosperous and fulfilling life, the nation developed from a primarily agrarian society into an industrial powerhouse, and eventually became the largest economy in the world. Today, even Americans who are classified as poor typically enjoy access to goods and services, such as indoor plumbing, heating and air conditioning, cellphones, internet, and a variety of foods that were unattainable to most people throughout history and even today throughout much of the world.

Over the past several decades, the nation has weathered periods of recession followed by periods of relatively stable economic growth. Political efforts to eliminate structural and societal causes of poverty and to elevate quality of life have dominated the past century, but the results of those efforts have been mixed. Chapter 2 will explore in greater detail recent trends and persistent problems relating to poverty in America as well as some of the specific efforts and proposals aimed at mitigating its effects and reinvigorating the promise of the American Dream.

Bibliography

Associated Press. 2006. "Saving in 2005 Worst since 1933." *New York Times*. January 31. https://www.nytimes.com/2006/01/31/business/saving-in-2005-worst-since-1933.html.

Béland, Daniel, and Alex Waddan. 2012. *The Politics of Policy Change: Welfare, Medicare, and Social Security Reform in the United States*. Washington, DC: Georgetown University Press.

Bowman, Bridget. 2023. "Mourning in America: Poll Finds Pessimistic Voters." *NBC News*. November 23. Accessed February 10, 2023. https://www.nbcnews.com/meet-the-press/meetthepressblog/mourning-america-poll-finds-pessimistic-voters-rcna126180.

Burner, David. 1979. *Herbert Hoover: A Public Life*. New York: Knopf.

Bush, George H.W. 1991. "State of the Union Address." January 29. Accessed February 15, 2024. https://millercenter.org/the-presidency/presidential-speeches/january-29-1991-state-union-address.

Butchart, Ronald E. 2010. *Schooling the Freed People: Teaching*, Learning, *and the Struggle for Black Freedom, 1861–1876*. Chapel Hill: University of North Carolina.

Calder, Lendol. 2001. *Financing the American Dream: A Cultural History of Consumer Credit*. Princeton: Princeton University Press.

Carney, John. 2009. "Here's How the Community Reinvestment Act Led to the Housing Bubble's Lax Lending." *Business Insider*. June 27. Accessed February 18, 2024. https://www.businessinsider.com/the-cra-debate-a-users-guide-2009-6.

Cass, Oren M. 2019. "Economic Mobility: Is the American Dream in Crisis?" in *Exploring Barriers to Economic Mobility and Making the American Dream Attainable for All Americans*. Hearing before the U.S. Senate Subcommittee on Economic Policy of the Committee on Banking, Housing, and Urban Affairs 116th Cong. 1st Sess (July 17, 2019). Accessed February 10, 2024. https://www.govinfo.gov/content/pkg/CHRG-116shrg39541/pdf/CHRG-116shrg39541.pdf.

Chetty, Raj, David Grusky, Maximilian Hell, Nathaniel Hendren, Robert Manduca, and Jimmy Narang. 2017. "The Fading American Dream: Trends in Absolute Income Mobility since 1940." *Science* 356 (6336): 398–406.

Chipman, Nathaniel. 1793. *Sketches of the Principles of Government*. Rutland, VT: J. Lyon.

Congressional Budget Office (CBO). 2010. "Fannie Mae, Freddie Mac, and the Federal Role in the Secondary Mortgage Market." December. Accessed February 18, 2024. https://www.cbo.gov/sites/default/files/111th-congress-2009-2010/reports/12-23-fanniefreddie.pdf.

Dewey, John. 1920. *Reconstruction in Philosophy*. New York: Henry Holt.

Dewey, John. 2000. *Liberalism and Social Action*. Amherst, NY: Promethean Books.

Diner, Hasia R. 2010. "Introduction" in Riis, Jacob. *How the Other Half Lives: Authoritative Text, Context, and Criticism*. ed. Hasia R. Diner. New York: W.W. Norton & Company.

FDIC. 2023. "The S&L Crisis: A Chrono-Bibliography." Accessed February 17, 2024. https://www.fdic.gov/resources/publications/s-and-l-crisis/index.html.

Federal Reserve. 2023. "Distribution of Household Wealth in the U.S. since 1989." Accessed February 17, 2024. https://www.federalreserve.gov/releases/z1/dataviz/dfa/distribute/chart/.

Field, Anne, and Paul Kim. 2020. "7 Causes of the Great Depression, and How the Road to Recovery Transformed the U.S. Economy." *Business Insider*. September 18. Accessed January 23, 2024. https://www.businessinsider.com/personal-finance/what-caused-the-great-depression.

Friedman, Thomas L. 2010. *The Lexus and the Olive Tree*. New York: Random House.

Fukuyama, Francis. 1992. *The End of History and the Last Man*. New York: Free Press.

Furner, Mary O. 2004. "Nineteenth Century" in Gwendolyn Mink and Alice O'Connor, eds. *Poverty in the United States: An Encyclopedia of History, Politics, and Policy*. Vol. 1 A-K. Santa Barbara, CA: ABC-CLIO.

Galbraith, John Kenneth. 1958. *The Affluent Society*. Boston, MA: Houghton Mifflin.

Garfinkel, Irvin, and Sarah S. McLanahan. 1986. *Single Mothers and Their Children: A New American Dilemma*. Washington, DC: Urban Institute Press.

Garten, Jeffrey E. 2021. "When the U.S. Gave up Gold." *The Wall Street Journal*. July 1. Accessed February 17, 2024. https://www.wsj.com/articles/when-the-u-s-gave-up-gold-11625148788.

Gates, David. 1994. "History of the Orphanage." *Newsweek*. December 11. Accessed January 10, 2024. https://www.newsweek.com/history-orphanage-185444.

Glickman, Lawrence B. 2019. *Free Enterprise: An American History*. New Haven: Princeton.

Goodwin, Joanne L. 2004. "Progressive Era and 1920s" in Gwendolyn Mink and Alice O'Connor, eds. *Poverty in the United States: An Encyclopedia of History, Politics, and Policy*. Vol. 1 A-K. Santa Barbara, CA: ABC-CLIO: 19–25.

Hall, Prince. 1777. "Petition to the Massachusetts Legislature." *National Constitution Center*. Accessed December 9, 2023. https://constitutioncenter.org/the-constitution/historic-document-library/detail/prince-hall-petition-to-the-massachusetts-legislature.

Hamilton, Alexander. 1795. "Defense of the Funding System." *Papers of Alexander Hamilton* 19: 32.

Hamilton, David E. n.d. "Herbert Hoover: Domestic Affairs." University of Virginia Miller Center. Accessed January 23, 2024. https://millercenter.org/president/hoover/domestic-affairs.

Harrington, Michael. 1962. *The Other America: Poverty in the United States*. New York: Macmillan Publishing Company.

Horton, Emily. 2017. "The Legacy of the 2001 and 2003 'Bush' Tax Cuts." *Center on Budget and Policy Priorities*. October 23. Accessed May 1, 2024. https://www.cbpp.org/research/the-legacy-of-the-2001-and-2003-bush-tax-cuts.

Iceland, John. 2013. *Poverty in America: A Handbook*. Berkeley: University of California Press.

Isserman, Maurice. 2009. "Michael Harrington: Warrior on Poverty." *New York Times*. June 19. Accessed February 2, 2024. https://www.nytimes.com/2009/06/21/books/review/Isserman-t.html.

Jefferson, Thomas. 1816. "Thomas Jefferson to Joseph Milligan." *The Founders Constitution*. April 6. Accessed December 12, 2023. https://press-pubs.uchicago.edu/founders/documents/v1ch15s64.html.

Jeffery, Philip. 2023. "Flapper Economics: Turning the American Citizen into 'the Consumer.'" *American Compass*. Accessed on January 16, 2024. https://americancompass.org/flapper-economics/.

Jencks, Christopher. 1992. *Rethinking Social Policy: Race, Poverty, and the Underclass*. Cambridge, MA: Harvard University Press.

Johnson, Lyndon B. 1964a. "Annual Remarks to Congress on the State of the Union." *The American Presidency Project.* January 8. Accessed February 3, 2024. https://www.presidency.ucsb.edu/documents/annual-message-the-congress-the-state-the-union-25.

Johnson, Lyndon B. 1964b. "Remarks at the University of Michigan." *The American Presidency Project.* May 22. Accessed February 3, 2024. https://www.presidency.ucsb.edu/documents/remarks-the-university-michigan.

Johnson, Lyndon B. 1964c. "Address at the Centennial Commencement of Swarthmore College." *The American Presidency Project.* June 8. Accessed February 3, 2024. https://www.presidency.ucsb.edu/documents/address-the-centennial-commencement-swarthmore-college.

Johnson, Lyndon B. 1964d. "Remarks upon Signing the Economic Opportunity Act." *The American Presidency Project.* August 20. Accessed February 3, 2024. https://www.presidency.ucsb.edu/documents/remarks-upon-signing-the-economic-opportunity-act.

Johnson, Lyndon B. 1965. "Commencement Address at Howard University." *The American Presidency Project.* June 4. Accessed February 3, 2024. https://www.presidency.ucsb.edu/documents/commencement-address-howard-university-fulfill-these-rights.

Katz, Michael B., and Mark J. Stern. 2004. "1940s to Present" in Gwendolyn Mink and Alice O'Connor, eds. *Poverty in the United States: An Encyclopedia of History, Politics, and Policy.* Vol. 1 A-K. Santa Barbara, CA: ABC-CLIO.

Katz, Stanley N. 1977. "Republicanism and the Law of Inheritance in the American Revolutionary Era." *Michigan Law Review* 76 (1) (November): 1–29.

Kennedy, David M. 1999. *Freedom from Fear: The American People in Depression and War, 1929–1945.* New York: Oxford University Press.

Kochhar, Rakesh, and Anthony Cilluffo. 2017. "How Wealth Inequality Has Changed in the U.S. since the Great Recession, by Race, Ethnicity and Income." *Pew Research Center.* Accessed February 5, 2024. https://www.pewresearch.org/short-reads/2017/11/01/how-wealth-inequality-has-changed-in-the-u-s-since-the-great-recession-by-race-ethnicity-and-income/.

Leuchtenberg, William E. 2009. *Franklin D. Roosevelt and the New Deal.* New York: Harper Perennial.

Lind, Michael. 2020. *The New Class War: Saving Democracy from the Managerial Elite.* New York: Portfolio Penguin.

Madison, James. 1792. "Property". March 27 in Philip B. Kurland and Ralph Lerner, eds. *The Founders' Constitution.* Chicago: University of Chicago Press, 1987. 1: 598–9.

Madison, James. 1829. "Speech in Virginia Convention, 2 December 1829." *Founders Online.* National Archives. Accessed November 27, 2023. https://founders.archives.gov/documents/Madison/99-02-02-1924.

Massey, Douglas S., Jonathan Rothwell, and Thurston Domina. 2009. "The Changing Base of Segregation in the United States." *Annals of the American Academy of Political and Social Science* 626: 74–90.

Mead, Lawrence. 1992. *The New Politics of Poverty: The Nonworking Poor in America.* New York: Basic Books.

Merle, Renae. 2018. "A Guide to the Financial Crisis—10 Years Later." *The Washington Post.* September 10. Accessed February 15, 2024. https://www.washingtonpost.com/business/economy/a-guide-to-the-financial-crisis–10-years-later/2018/09/10/114b76ba-af10-11e8-a20b-5f4f84429666_story.html.

Merriam, Charles E. 1903. *A History of American Political Theories.* New York: MacMillan Company.

Milkis, Sidney M. 2002. "Roosevelt and the New Politics of Presidential Leadership" in Sidney M. Milkis and Jerome M. Mileur, eds. *The New Deal and the Triumph of Liberalism.* Amherst: University of Massachusetts Press: 31–72.

Milkis, Sindney M., and Michael Nelson. 2020. *The American Presidency: Origins and Development, 1776–2018.* 8th ed. Los Angeles, CA: Sage/CQ Press.

Miller, Tiffany Jones. 2007. "Transforming Formal Freedom into Effective Freedom: Dewey, the New Deal, and the Great Society" in Ronald J. Pestritto and Thomas G. West, eds. *Modern American and the Legacy of the Founding.* Lanham, MD: Lexington: 169–206.

Miller, Tiffany Jones. 2012. "Freedom, History, and Race in Progressive Thought." *Social Philosophy and Policy* 29 (2): 220–54.

Moses, Stacy. 2021. "The Civil Rights Act of 1866: A First Attempt to Protect the Rights of African Americans." *Teaching American History.* April 8. Accessed January 8, 2023. https://teachingamericanhistory.org/blog/the-civil-rights-act-of-1866-a-first-attempt-to-protect-the-rights-of-african-americans/.

Murray, Charles. 2015. *Losing Ground: American Social Policy, 1950–1980.* New York: Basic Books.

Myers, Peter C. 2008. *Frederick Douglass: Race and the Rebirth of American Liberalism.* Lawrence, KS: University Press of Kansas.

Nathan, Richard P. 1996. "A Retrospective on Richard M. Nixon's Domestic Policies." *Presidential Studies Quarterly* 26 (1): 155–64.

National Archives. n.d. "National Industrial Recovery Act (1933)." Accessed January 30, 2024. https://www.archives.gov/milestone-documents/national-industrial-recovery-act#:~:text=On%20June%2016%2C%201933%2C%20this,a%20right%20to%20collective%20bargaining.

Neidermeyer, Edward. 2012. "Even after Bailout, GM and Chrysler Invest Billions Abroad." *Washington Examiner.* November 12. Accessed February, 18, 2024. https://www.washingtonexaminer.com/news/1007623/even-after-bailout-gm-and-chrysler-invest-billions-abroad/.

O'Connor, Alice. 2001. *Poverty Knowledge: Social Science, Social Policy, and the Poor in Twentieth-Century U.S. History.* Princeton, NJ: Princeton University Press.

Olasky, Marvin. 1992. *The Tragedy of American Compassion*. Washington, DC: Regnery Gateway.

Pestritto, Ronald J. 2005. *Woodrow Wilson: The Essential Political Writings*. Lanham, MD: Lexington.

Pestritto, Ronald J. 2021. *American Transformed: The Rise and Legacy of American Progressivism*. New York: Encounter Books.

Pew Research Center. 2017. "Few See 'Becoming Wealthy' as Essential to Their View of the American Dream." October 31. Accessed February 10, 2024. https://www.pewresearch.org/short-reads/2017/10/31/most-think-the-american-dream-is-within-reach-for-them/ft_17-10-31_americandream_definitions/.

Pew Research Center. 2023. "Public Trust in Government: 1958–2023." September 19. Accessed February 16, 2024. https://www.pewresearch.org/politics/2023/09/19/public-trust-in-government-1958-2023/.

Reid, Joseph D., and Michael M. Kurth. 1992. "The Rise and Fall of Urban Political Patronage Machines." *National Bureau of Economic Research*. Accessed January 2, 2024. https://www.nber.org/system/files/chapters/c6971/c6971.pdf.

Rickards, James. 2012. "Repeal of Glass-Steagall Caused the Financial Crisis." *U.S. News and World Report*. August 27. Accessed February 18, 2024. https://www.usnews.com/opinion/blogs/economic-intelligence/2012/08/27/repeal-of-glass-steagall-caused-the-financial-crisis.

Riis, Jacob. 1890. *How the Other Half Lives: Studies among the Tenements of New York*. New York: Charles Scribner's Sons.

Roback, Jennifer. 1984. "Southern Labor Law in the Jim Crow Era: Exploitive or Competitive?" *The University of Chicago Law Review* 51: 1161–92.

Roosevelt, Franklin D. 1932. "Campaign Address on Progressive Government at the Commonwealth Club in San Francisco, California." September 23. Accessed January 25, 2024. https://www.presidency.ucsb.edu/documents/campaign-address-progressive-government-the-commonwealth-club-san-francisco-california.

Roosevelt, Franklin D. 1944. "State of the Union Message to Congress." *The American Presidency Project*. January 11. Accessed January 25, 2024. https://www.presidency.ucsb.edu/documents/state-the-union-message-congress.

Roth, Carol. 2021. "Lockdowns Were a Gift to Big Business Designed to Kill Small Biz." *New York Post*. July 5. Accessed February 18, 2024. https://nypost.com/2021/07/05/lockdowns-were-a-gift-to-big-biz-designed-to-kill-small-biz/.

Scott, Robert E. 2015. "Manufacturing Job Loss: Trade, Not Productivity, Is the Culprit." *Economic Policy Institute*. August 11. Accessed February 17, 2024. https://files.epi.org/2015/ib402-manufacturing-job-loss.pdf.

Shannon, William V. 1969. "The Political Machine I: Rise and Fall the Age of the Bosses." *American Heritage* 20 (4). Accessed January 2, 2024. https://www.americanheritage.com/political-machine-i-rise-and-fall-age-bosses.

Shlaes, Amity. 2007. *The Forgotten Man: A New History of the Great Depression*. New York: Harper Collins.

Shlaes, Amity. 2019. *Great Society: A New History*. New York: Harper Perennial.

Steger, Manfred B., and Ravi K. Roy. 2021. *Neo-liberalism: A Very Short Introduction*. 2nd ed. New York: Oxford University Press.

Strain, Micael R. 2020. *The American Dream Is Not Dead (But Populism Could Kill It)*. West Conshohocken, PA: Templeton Press.

Teitler, Julien O., Nancy E. Reichman, Lenna Nepomnyaschy, and Irwin Garfinkel. 2009. "Effects of Welfare Participation on Marriage." *Journal of Marriage and Family* 71 (4): 878–91.

Trattner, Walter I. 1994. *From Poor Law to Welfare State: A History of Social Welfare in America*. 6th ed. New York: The Free Press.

Tulis, Jeffrey K. 1987. *The Rhetorical Presidency*. Princeton, NJ: Princeton University Press.

U.S. Bureau of Labor Statistics. 2017. "State Unemployment Rates, January 2007 to January 2017." *Economics Daily*. March 17. Accessed February 19, 2024. https://www.bls.gov/opub/ted/2017/state-unemployment-rates-january-2007-to-january-2017.htm.

U.S. Census Bureau. n.d. *Historical Income Tables*, Table F-1. Accessed February 2, 2024. https://www.census.gov/data/tables/time-series/demo/income-poverty/historical-income-inequality.html.

U.S. Census Bureau. 2014. "Poverty the History of a Measure." Accessed February 6, 2024. https://www.census.gov/library/visualizations/2014/demo/poverty_measure-history.html.

U.S. Congress. 1866. "Civil Rights Act of 1866: An Act to Protect All Persons in the United States in their Civil Rights, and Furnish the Means of their Vindication." Ushistory.org. *A Consumer Economy*. Accessed January 23, 2024. https://www.ushistory.org/us/46f.asp.

Villegas, Christina. 2020. *Contemporary World Issues: Modern Slavery*. Santa Barbara: ABC-CLIO.

Villegas, Christina. 2022. *Contemporary World Issues: Foster Care in America*. Santa Barbara: ABC-CLIO.

West, Thomas G. 2015. "Poverty and Welfare in the American Founding." *The Heritage Foundation*. May 19. Accessed December 11, 2023. https://www.heritage.org/poverty-and-inequality/report/poverty-and-welfare-the-american-founding.

West, Thomas G. 2017. *The Political Theory of the American Founding: Natural Rights, Public Policy, and the Moral Conditions of Freedom*. New York: Cambridge University Press.

Witcher, Marcus M., and Joseph Horton. 2013. "From Prosperity to Poverty: The Story of American Economic Decline during the 1920s." *Journal of Applied Business and Economics* 14 (4): 79–87.

Woodrow, Wilson. 1900. *Congressional Government.* 15th ed. Boston: Houghton Mifflin.

Woodward, C. Vann. 2002. *The Strange Career of Jim Crow.* New York: Oxford University Press.

Yarrow, Andrew L. 2009. "History of U.S. Children's Policy: 1900–Present." *First Focus.* April. Accessed January 10, 2024. https://firstfocus.org/wp-content/uploads/2014/06/Childrens-Policy-History.pdf.

Zitner, Aaron. 2023. "Voters See American Dream Slipping out of Reach, WSJ/NORC Poll Shows." *The Wall Street Journal.* November 24. Accessed February 10, 2024. https://www.wsj.com/us-news/american-dream-out-of-reach-poll-3b774892.

2

Problems, Controversies, and Solutions

Introduction

Modern America presents reasons for measured optimism when it comes to the issue of poverty. According to macroeconomic and microeconomic data on unemployment, economic growth, and household-level finances, the early 2020s were off to a promising start in terms of projected increases in aggregate growth and per capita Gross Domestic Product (GDP), which refers to the value of the country's economic output divided by its population (U.S. Bureau of Labor Statistics 2021). Yet this prosperity has not been widely shared, and economic vulnerability and social isolation characterize the lives of an increasing number of Americans. This chapter explores in greater detail several of the persistent problems and controversies involved in measuring and understanding the scope of poverty in America and evaluating trends in inequality, mobility, class-based segregation, alienation, and despair. It concludes with an overview of some of the various efforts and proposals aimed at mitigating poverty, promoting opportunity, and reinvigorating the promise of the American Dream.

Measuring Poverty

Understanding the scope of poverty and whether progress has been made in effectively combatting it first requires its definition and measurement, but such

---

Demolition of a high-rise building in the Cabrini-Green Homes public housing project in Chicago in 2011. Poverty, crime, and neglect in the area were well publicized, and the housing development became a symbol of the problems associated with public housing in the United States. Most of the project's buildings, including all of its high-rises, were demolished by 2011. (Richie Diesterheft via Flickr, Creative Commons License CC BY-SA 2.0 DEED)

assessment is often difficult due to conflicting views of what poverty entails and how it ought to be quantified. Typically, poverty is measured in both absolute and relative terms. Absolute poverty refers to the inability to access a minimal level of life-sustaining essentials (e.g., food, clean water, shelter, clothing, healthcare). Relative poverty, on the other hand, measures disparities of wealth or inequality between groups in a particular social context rather than material deprivation.

Each year, the US Census Bureau estimates the number of individuals living in poverty in the United States using two measures: the official poverty measure and the Supplemental Poverty Measure (SPM) (U.S. Census Bureau 2022). The official poverty measure was developed during the Johnson administration by economist Mollie Orshansky of the Social Security Administration (Fisher 1992). Orshansky based her poverty thresholds, or levels, on the Department of Agriculture's economy food plan, which included the minimal combination of foods that department dieticians determined was necessary for a nutritionally adequate diet. Based on the Department of Agriculture's Household Food Consumption Survey, Orshansky concluded that the average family of three or more people spends about one-third of their after-tax income on food. Thus, to determine a baseline poverty income line, she calculated the dollar cost of the economy food plan based on family size and multiplied that cost by a factor of three to include all other family expenses.

This formula provided a basis for determining various income thresholds and was eventually adopted in 1969 as the official poverty measure by the Bureau of the Budget (now the Office of Management and Budget). Today, the official poverty measure continues to be calculated by multiplying the cost of a minimum food diet adjusted for inflation by three. This measure is used to produce the poverty thresholds issued by the Census Bureau each year (which estimate the number of Americans living in poverty) and the poverty guidelines issued by the Department of Health and Human Services (which are used to determine financial eligibility for certain federal programs).

Most economists, researchers, and policymakers agree that the federal official poverty measure has significant flaws and does not accurately measure poverty. There is widespread disagreement, however, over whether the measure sets the bar too low or too high for determining the number of Americans living in poverty and their eligibility for government aid. Those who believe that the official poverty rate overestimates the number of individuals living in poverty contend that its fatal flaw "is that it doesn't count most government subsidies, such as Treasury checks beneficiaries receive from refundable tax credits, debit cards loaded with food-stamp allowances, and Medicaid payments as income to the recipients" (Gramm and Early 2023). When all these benefits are counted, such critics point out, the percentage of Americans living in poverty drops to only 2.5 percent compared to the percentage in the high teens that is usually publicized. Average consumption levels of goods and services support this contention. In 2017, researchers at the University of Chicago and Notre Dame compared the actual goods and services consumed by the 13 percent of the population that was considered poor in 1980 with consumption levels of those counted among the poor in 2017. They similarly found that only 2.8 percent of households in 2017 were consuming at or below the actual poverty consumption level in 1980 (Meyer and Sullivan 2017).

Conversely, others have maintained that the official poverty measure grossly underestimates the number of individuals living in poverty because it "it is no longer grounded in the real-world cost of living" (Valdez 2009). For starters, the measure ignores skyrocketing costs in housing, healthcare, and childcare and does not account for the huge geographical variation in living expenses across the United States. It also does not factor in significant financial liabilities including taxes, work-related costs, and out-of-pocket medical expenses, nor is it adjusted for changes in the standard of living over time. As Mastrangelo (2022) points out, there are many financial demands now vital to a household's basic infrastructure—such as internet access and cell phone service—that were not envisioned or accounted for back when the official poverty measure was developed in the 1960s.

In recognition of significant shortcomings in the official poverty measure, the Census Bureau began releasing data in 2011 based on the newly developed Supplemental Poverty Measure (SPM). Unlike the official measure, which only accounts for pre-tax cash income, the SPM includes both cash-based income and non-cash benefits from government programs, such as the Supplemental Nutrition Assistance Program (SNAP), tax credits, and housing subsidies. The SPM also considers geographical variation in the cost of living, whether a family is renting or paying a mortgage, and a host of additional necessary and typical expenses that families face based on the Consumer Expenditure Survey (such as tax liabilities, childcare and other work-related costs, medical expenses, child support paid to another household, transportation, utilities, internet, and telecommunication). The SPM reveals some interesting distinctions compared to the official measure, including higher poverty rates than are reported under the official measure for some demographics and the effect that individual benefit programs have on reducing poverty (Center for Poverty and Inequality Research 2017). For example, refundable tax credits alone reduced poverty by about 2.5 percent in 2016, with the largest reduction among children.

Examining poverty rates during and after the Covid-19 pandemic using the official poverty measure in comparison with rates using SPM further exposes the defectiveness of the official measure. Between 2019 and 2021 government payments for social benefits—including expanded unemployment insurance, the increased Child Tax Credit, and economic-impact/stimulus payments—rose by $1.5 trillion or 47 percent, yet the official poverty rate increased slightly during this time. As Gramm and Early (2023) point out, "These results were predictable because the official poverty measure fails to count 88 social benefits that low-income Americans receive from the government as part of their income, including almost all of the pandemic benefits." This also explains why the expiration of pandemic-driven financial assistance programs, combined with inflation and overall increased cost of living expenses, caused the US poverty rate using the SPM to see the largest one-year increase in history between 2021 and 2022 (Childers 2023). As soon as temporary benefits were phased out, families experienced a drastic drop in their calculated income. The child poverty rate more than doubled from a record low of 5.2 percent in 2021 to 12.4 percent in 2022.

The SPM additionally reveals a wider variation of poverty from state to state and within states. For instance, according to the SPM, poverty levels increased most drastically across the south in 2022, but California had the highest percentage of residents living in poverty—a majority of whom reside in farming, mining, and manufacturing communities or in high-cost cities like San Francisco and Los Angeles (Ney 2023).

While the SPM has been pushed as a necessary corrective to the official poverty measure, as of 2024, it is not used to determine eligibility for federal government assistance programs. Moreover, critics have argued that it likewise contains significant flaws that inhibit it from accurately identifying those experiencing the greatest economic deprivation and how economic deprivation has changed over time. Among the most significant critiques are that the SPM uses flawed survey data that understates earnings and government benefits thereby biasing income downward, that it fails to include the full value of health insurance, and that it caps government rental housing assistance below its full value (Burkhauser et al. 2021). The primary critique of the SPM, however, is that it defines poverty in relative terms, so that the poverty level increases as median income in society increases (Gramm and Early 2023).

In contrast with the official measure, which defines the poverty threshold as "the inability to satisfy minimum needs," the SPM defines the poverty threshold as the amount of income necessary to purchase 83 percent of what a median income family spends on the consumption of food, apparel, shelter, and utilities plus an additional 20 percent of that total for additional necessities. "Under this relative definition," Gramm and Early explain, "members of families that don't have enough income to pay for that percentage of median household consumption will always be counted as poor, no matter how well off they are." Adopting the SPM as the official measure would, therefore, mean that economic growth would have little impact on the poverty rate unless that growth was combined with additional income redistribution, even when families living under the "poverty line" enjoy a higher standard of living than middle-class families maintained several decades ago.

Over the past couple of decades several organizations have proposed alternatives to the federal government's official and supplemental poverty measures to assess neediness more accurately. One of the most preeminent is the self-sufficiency standard administered by the Center for Women's Welfare at the University of Washington. Developed in the 1990s by center director Dr. Diana Pierce, the standard defines the level of income necessary for working families to meet their needs at a minimally adequate level without public or private assistance. Basic minimum needs factored into the measurement include housing, childcare, food, transportation, healthcare, clothing, telephone, household items, taxes, and emergency savings. The standard additionally accounts for family composition, ages of children, and geographical differences in costs. Today, over forty states and the District of Columbia use the standard to inform state policymaking and allocation of benefits.

Inequality

Recently, the issues of income and wealth inequality and economic mobility have surpassed mere economic deprivation as primary matters of political concern. In 2013, President Obama declared that reversing the trends of "increased inequality and decreasing mobility" has become "the defining challenge of our time." Today, two primary debates surround the specific issue of inequality. The first involves a disagreement over the actual extent of income and wealth inequality; the second involves a clash over whether the existence of significant inequality is in fact a serious threat to societal well-being.

Concerning the first debate, Gramm et al. (2022) have contended that measures showing increasingly unequal levels of assets and income are exaggerated because they leave out massive government transfers to the lower two income quintiles (the poorest 40 percent of Americans) and the high levels of taxes paid by households among the most affluent quintiles. Critics assert that once these government transfers are accounted for, income inequality is much less significant than reports from government agencies, such as the Census Bureau, would suggest.

Regardless of the extent to which government redistribution mitigates inequality, it is evident that inequality of earned income and wealth has been on the rise in America (Siripurapu 2022). Since the 1980s, the share of income held by the most affluent quintile of the population has steadily increased, while the share held by families in the three middle quintiles and bottom quintile of the income distribution has decreased. This trend was intensified by the uneven recovery from the 2008 global financial crisis and the Covid-19 pandemic. According to the Congressional Budget Office's annual report on "The Distribution of Household Income," income inequality before transfers and taxes rose to all-time high in 2020, which was temporarily mitigated by emergency government transfers in response to the economic crises caused by Covid-19 and government-imposed shutdowns (CBO 2023).

The reality of growing earned income and asset disparities has contributed to a second area of contention regarding the question of whether significant inequality is necessarily a cause for concern. On the one hand, academics, journalists, and politicians like Senator Bernie Sanders equate inequality, poverty, and exploitation as components of a unified menacing phenomenon (Tomasky 2022; Wilkins 2022). In the wake of the pandemic, for example, Senator Sanders (2022) declared, "When we talk about oligarchy in America we are talking about

700 billionaires who became nearly $2 trillion richer during the pandemic and pay a lower tax rate than a nurse while the child poverty rate soared by 41 percent in January because the expanded Child Tax Credit ended." For such egalitarians, therefore, eliminating inequality is a moral issue requiring massive government redistributive interventions and regulation aimed at ensuring that everyone gets their "fair share."

Others, however, challenge the idea that wealth and inequality are directly connected with or are the cause of economic deprivation and exploitation. Instead, they emphasize that an unequal distribution of income does not mean that those at the lower end of the income scale are poor in an absolute sense (Worstall 2015). In fact, if the overall amount of wealth in a society is growing thanks to favorable economic conditions, inequality of income in terms of the overall share of growth might increase while standards of living and purchasing power are improving across all income levels. Philosophy professor Harry Frankfurt (2015) has argued that the political obsession with inequality is a distraction from the more important issue of making sure that everyone has sufficient resources to live a decent life.

Another point sometimes raised is that the income level of top earners has no bearing on the ability of those in the bottom income quintiles to move up the ladder of success and that the American Dream has never required equality as a result or dragging some down to pull others up. Azerrad and Hederman Jr. (2012), for example, contend that the American Dream is rooted in the idea that economic freedom (which requires the rule of law, property rights, limited government, regulatory efficiency, and open markets) combined with a culture of work allows most persons who apply themselves and live responsibility to thrive and prosper.

Declining Mobility and Growing Concentration of Wealth and Poverty

Mobility is the most widely used measure for determining the vibrancy of the American Dream of economic mobility—the capacity for individuals to move up and down the economic ladder in terms of income and wealth, both over a lifetime and across generations. Intergenerational mobility has two dimensions: relative and absolute. Relative mobility refers to a dynamic in which individuals move up or down the social hierarchy in comparison to the socioeconomic position of their parents. McElwee (2014) explains, "If your parents were in the bottom quintile and you move into the second quintile, you have experienced relative mobility." High levels of relative mobility, however, do not necessarily mean that standards of living have improved—they merely signify that there is movement between the various income brackets in a society.

Absolute mobility, on the other hand, is a measure of whether the overall standard of living in a society has increased. Absolute mobility occurs when the members of each class in a particular generation are better off and enjoy a higher standard of living, on average, than their counterparts in the previous generation. It is not based on quintile rankings; instead, it examines whether adults have higher cost of living and inflation-adjusted incomes and assets than their parents did at the same age. Thus, absolute mobility is dependent on economic growth, and high rates of absolute mobility indicate that the growth has been broadly shared among the income quintiles leading all boats to rise, not just a couple of yachts (McElwee 2014).

Trends in Mobility

The three decades directly following the Second World War saw substantial economic growth, the benefits of which were largely shared across the income distribution (Price and Edwards 2020). Consequently, incomes grew at roughly the same rate up and down the income ladder and the nation experienced high rates of relative and absolute mobility, signifying the existence of widespread opportunity and improved standards of living. From the 1940s to the 1980s, the prospect of a stable income, home ownership, and a comfortable retirement became increasingly possible for working- and middle-class families (Kotkin 2019). During this period, the American middle class flourished and grew to become the largest of any country in the world (Offenheiser 2022).

Beginning in the 1970s, however, the yearly rate of economic growth slowed, and the income gap simultaneously began to widen as the distribution of growth was increasingly concentrated among the top income quintiles (Stone et al. 2020). Rates of upward intergenerational mobility were likewise impacted. In a landmark study published in 2017, Harvard economist Raj Chetty and a team of researchers found that rates of absolute mobility (the degree to which members of each class in a particular generation are better off and enjoy a higher standard of living, on average, than their counterparts in a previous generation) had fallen from 90 percent for children born in 1940 to only 50 percent for children born in the 1980s.

Some scholars counter warnings of growing inequality and diminishing intergenerational mobility by arguing that there is still a considerable degree of income fluidity in America and that the country remains by and large an upwardly mobile society (Strain 2020). In response, others contend that the continued existence of upward mobility should not be used to obscure evidence that rates of upward mobility have declined significantly, and that the concentration of wealth is becoming a more permanent fixture of American society (King 2020). Indeed, data suggests that the decline in upward mobility in modern times is connected, in large part, to the change in the distribution of aggregate economic growth that has resulted in a greater degree of wealth concentration.

For example, in an effort to understand why upward mobility rates have fallen so sharply over the past half century, Chetty et al. (2017) examined two important macroeconomic trends that have affected the income of children born in the 1980s relative to those born in the 1940s: lower GDP growth rates and greater inequality in the distribution of growth. Specifically, Chetty and colleagues considered two counterfactual scenarios to assess the relative contribution of these factors. The first scenario examined what absolute mobility percentages would look like if growth rates were consistently as high over the years as those experienced by individuals born in 1940, but the distribution of that growth between income levels occurred at today's actual income distribution rates. The results demonstrated that higher GDP growth rates alone were insufficient to restore absolute mobility to the levels experienced by children in the 1940s and 1950s. Secondly, Chetty and colleagues considered a scenario using actual GDP growth rates but changed the distribution of total growth across income groups to the more equal distribution experienced by the 1940 birth cohort. Interestingly, changing the distribution of growth across income groups to the levels experienced by the 1940 birth cohort would reverse more than 70 percent of the decline in mobility despite lower percentages of yearly economic growth. Thus, their research showed that the decline in absolute mobility is more attributable to the unequal distribution of economic growth than it is to lower rates of growth in recent decades.

Concentrated Wealth and the Decline of the American Middle Class

One of the most concerning trends in recent decades is not just that the growth in income has tilted toward upper-income households, but that the middle class—once made up of a clear majority of Americans—is shrinking. According to the Pew Research Center, the share of American adults who live in middle-income households has decreased from 61 percent in 1971 to 51 percent in 2019 (Horowitz, Igielnik, and Kochhar 2020). While part of this change resulted from middle-class adults moving into upper-income tiers, the share of middle-class adults moving to a lower-income tier also increased—both trends reflect and contribute to the growing income inequality that began in the 1980s.

While growing income inequality has become a prominent matter of public concern, it is only part of the story. A more ominous trend is the expanding gaps in wealth (which includes assets held minus debt owed). When families are unable to accumulate savings and assets that exceed their debts, they are vulnerable to significant financial risk and upward mobility is far less likely. Moreover, the gap in overall wealth among upper-income families and middle- and lower-income families is growing more sharply and rapidly than the income gap. Researchers at Pew report, "Upper-income families were the only income tier able to build on their wealth from 2001 to 2016, adding 33 percent at the median" (Horowitz, Igielnik, and Kochhar 2020). Middle-income families, on the other hand, "saw their median net worth shrink by 20 percent and lower-income families experienced a loss of 45 percent."

Consequently, in 2016, upper-income families had 7.4 times as much wealth as middle-income families (compared to only 3.4 times as much in 1983) and 75 times as much wealth as lower-income families (compared to only 28 times as much in 1983). These numbers may be even worse than they appear because they include the current value of the family's home in the calculation of financial assets. While rapidly rising home values give the appearance of greater wealth, selling the home and using the money for something else is rarely an option for working- and middle-class families, especially when other homes have gone up in price as well (King 2021).

Growing gaps in wealth have particularly affected Millennials compared to previous generations, but there is also significant wealth stratification occurring within the generation itself. Whereas Millennials as an entire class have accumulated billions of dollars less in net worth than their counterparts among Baby Boomers and Gen X did at the same point in their lives, the wealthiest Millennials—many of whom grew up in wealthy families and went to selective colleges—are actually better off than people at the same age in previous generations (Lowrey 2021). The typical older Millennial without a college degree, however, has almost 20 percent less wealth and 5 percent less income than would be expected (Kent and Rickets 2021). The divide is even greater when it comes to race. Ironically, the generation that grew up most committed to racial equality is the one that is least likely to manifest it in terms of the accumulation of wealth.

Much of the growing bifurcation in wealth occurred in the years following the onset of the Great Recession in 2007. In comparison to previous American recessions, which were followed by periods of innovation and widely shared economic growth, the recovery from the Great Recession was different. For example, writing in 2018 economist and investment officer John Michaelson observed, "the economic legacy of the last decade is excessive corporate consolidation, a massive transfer of wealth to the top 1 percent from the middle class, the creation of even more asset bubbles, and rising social tensions." According to Pew, the richest 20 percent of the population were the only ones to experience gains in wealth during the recession and recovery, while the wealth of those in the four lower tiers decreased by at least 20 percent between 2007 and 2016 (Horowitz, Igielnik, and Kochhar 2020). The greatest decline was among those in the second quintile of wealth. By 2017, the decline was affecting public perception and attitudes, as nearly two-thirds of American adults surveyed by Pew expressed the belief that the current generation of children would be worse off financially than their parents (Stokes 2017).

The Covid-19 pandemic only amplified this troubling trend by creating an even deeper wedge in wealth and employment-based income between the upper classes and the rest of society. Counteracting temporary gains in employment, income, and wealth that occurred between 2017 and 2019, the labor-market turmoil caused by the pandemic and corresponding lockdowns were devastating to ordinary working- and middle-class individuals, families, and small business owners. Almost 40 percent of those making under $40,000 a year lost their jobs during the first couple of months of shutdowns (O'Donnell 2020). Many others suffered pay cuts. The losses occurred among all races but were particularly pronounced among working-class Latino households (Parker, Horowitz, and Brown 2020). The long-term economic effects of learning loss among low- and middle-income students from school closures, prolonged periods of remote learning, and rising rates of depression and anxiety are beginning to appear, but the full extent of these harms remains to be seen (Kuhfeld et al. 2022).

Within the first year of the viral outbreak in the United States, more than 200,000 businesses above the historical average of yearly closures failed and were permanently shuttered (Simon 2021). This does not even include the number of businesses that later collapsed under the weight of back rent, unpaid loans, and other expenses or the number of closures among sole proprietorships (businesses run by an individual without employees) during the main pandemic years of 2020 and 2021.

In contrast, the professional and upper-middle class—which includes those who were able to seamlessly shift to remote work—were typically either not negatively affected financially by the pandemic or actually experienced financial gains (Kochhar and Sechopoulos 2022). A sizeable percentage of publicly held corporations directly benefited from arbitrary legal distinctions between "essential" and "non-essential" businesses. Others were able to adjust to changing market demands and reaped the rewards of increased online sales. For such firms, 2020 was a good year despite the economic crises plaguing the nation (Hoffman and Maloney 2020). Corporate titans and billionaires came out exceedingly ahead. According to the Institute for Policies Studies (2024) calculations of *Forbes* "Real Time Billionaire Data," in the four years between when the United States entered the Covid-19 pandemic in March of 2020 and March of 2024, the number of billionaires in the United States grew from 614 to 737. Their combined wealth during this period increased from $2.947 trillion to $5.529 trillion—a nearly 88 percent increase. Billionaires—such as Tesla CEO Elon Musk, Amazon Founder Jeff Bezos, and the Walton family heirs to the Walmart fortune—witnessed particularly sizeable increases in their wealth. America's tech giants Apple, Google, Microsoft, and Facebook likewise experienced a massive expansion of their influence and profit margins contributing to complaints of monopolization and calls for trust busting (Ovide 2021).

Declining Rates of Homeownership

Related to the overall trends of declining mobility and growing wealth accumulation at the top of the economic ladder is the simultaneous dying dream of affordable homeownership among the working and middle class. Purchasing a home used to be one of the surest ways for members of lower-income brackets to build wealth and financial security in retirement, and over 90 percent of Americans still believe that homeownership is either an essential or at least important component of the American Dream (Pew 2017). Yet a host of factors over the past several decades—including low supply, inflated prices, and elevated mortgage interest rates—have made such ownership largely inaccessible for all but the upper classes.

Historically, the average home has cost about 2.6 times the median income—a ratio that is often cited as the ideal threshold for affordability (Chang 2023). In the years leading up to the financial crash of 2007 and the ensuing housing market collapse, housing costs were rapidly and arbitrarily inflated thanks to reckless lending practices and government policies aimed at making home ownership more obtainable and attractive. Among these policies were the provision of easier access to taxpayer guaranteed credit and the mortgage-interest tax deduction. At the same time restrictive land use policies and zoning laws constrained the supply of new home construction putting additional upward pressure on the price of housing in certain areas.

In a vicious cycle, practices encouraging higher levels of ownership in a period of limited supply drove prices way up, making it difficult for lower-income families to enter the housing market. That in turn contributed to the further loosening of credit and lending standards to allow more buyers to qualify for larger mortgages. Millions of buyers purchased homes they ultimately could not afford using risky borrowing schemes like interest-only mortgages, adjustable interest-rate loans, and loans that required little to no down payment. By 2005, the price of an average single-family home was nearly five times the median income (Chang 2023). As historian Vincent Cannato (2010) concludes, "The result was a dangerous bubble that inevitably burst."

The collapse of the housing market led to plummeting home values. Millions of homeowners found themselves underwater on their mortgages, owing more than their homes were worth. Consequently, they were unable to sell what they could no longer afford to keep. Whereas the only option for many homeowners was foreclosure and bankruptcy, the financial titans who had issued and profited from risky loans were bailed out by taxpayers. In turn, many of them were able to benefit from the market crash by using their resources to buy undervalued homes and properties as investments. This began a new ownership phenomenon in which institutional investors buy single-family homes with the purpose of turning them into long-term rentals (Pascus 2023).

Institutional investment in residential real estate grew rapidly following the recovery from the Great Recession, adding to the competition for an already limited supply. In 2010, only about 10 percent of single-family homes were purchased by investors (Chang 2023). During the last quarter of 2023, investors purchased 26.1 percent of the country's most affordable homes and more than 18 percent of all homes (Katz 2024). US housing has also rapidly turned into a commodity traded by foreign individuals and investors, most of whom are from China (Lindsay 2023). Furthermore, unlike first-time home buyers, foreign and domestic investors often come in with all cash offers and no contingencies. This trend has further increased competition over an already inadequate inventory of homes, crowding out individual home buyers and pricing locals out of their own neighborhoods.

Despite a plummeting of home prices resulting from the market crash, housing prices during and after the recovery once again began to nudge upward. During the Covid-19 pandemic, mortgage interest rates hit a record low, supercharging home sales which correspondingly contributed to skyrocketing real estate prices, particularly in the Sun Belt and Mountain West regions. By 2022, the average single-family home was priced at a record 5.3 times more than the median household's income—more than double the threshold for affordability (Chang 2023). Between 2023 and 2024, a slight drop in housing prices was counteracted by increased borrowing costs as the Federal Reserve aggressively hiked interest rates to battle inflation trends elsewhere in the economy (Curry 2023). Meanwhile, home prices were arbitrarily driven up yet again due to continued low supply thanks to underbuilding and sellers sitting out of the market because they do not want to give up the lower interest mortgage rates they secured in the past (Mohammed 2023).

The soaring costs of insuring homes and higher property taxes tied to the assessed value of the home have additionally locked many potential home buyers out of the market. Moreover, housing inflation combined with debt burdens in other areas—most notably student loans taken out to pay for the corresponding inflated price of higher education—has delayed homeownership among younger generations (NAR 2021). Those who do buy a home often depend on help from their parents. Older generations fortunate enough to own homes have benefited greatly from the increased equity that has come from inflated home values. In turn, they can use that equity to help their children make a down payment. Younger generations without that help are often shut out from the market, which has pushed down their overall rate of early homeownership (Lowrey 2021).

Both the growing burden of student loans and the necessity of assistance from homeowning parents are in large part responsible for the sizeable racial gap in home ownership. Blacks, on average, hold the highest levels of student debt and are less likely to benefit from the assistance of intergenerational wealth. Although minority homeownership rates have ticked upward slightly in recent years, the racial gap in homeownership between Blacks and whites grew a percentage point between 2014 and 2024 (Bahney 2024).

While rising housing costs have made homeownership inaccessible for many, they have also been devastating for renters. Between 2008 and 2022, average rents increased progressively and substantially (Whitney 2024). Today a record number of renters are "cost burdened," meaning they spend more than 30 percent of their income on rent. Affordability worsened for renters at every income level, but deteriorated most rapidly for middle-income earners who are less likely to qualify for public support than lower-income households. With rents reaching unsustainable highs, many Americans are left with little in their budget to pay for other items such as food, utilities, and healthcare that have experienced rising costs as well. Saving for a down payment has become less and less feasible, making ownership and the accumulation of wealth through home value appreciation even more unreachable for households that don't have existing family wealth to fall back on.

Geographical Socioeconomic Inequality and Segregation

Another ominous trend that has been growing for decades across the country is the sharp geographical concentration of economic progress and the corresponding phenomena of class-based segregation. Throughout American history, regional economic disparities have been commonplace, but for most of the twentieth century poorer states and regions were progressively improving and catching up economically and high local employment rates were transitory. Incomes typically converged as migration flowed to high-income areas and capital and investment were attracted by the lower wages in poorer areas (Austin, Glaeser, and Summers 2018). Until 1975, poorer states were experiencing the highest levels of growth and were rapidly catching up to more wealthy ones (American Compass 2022a). Beginning in the late twentieth century, however, regional income convergence slowed, and eventually reversed, and non-employment became a more permanent fixture of life in certain areas.

National job-creation and unemployment statistics often conceal the fact that good jobs are being created in fewer and fewer places (King 2020). For instance, 50 percent of job growth in 2010 following the Great Recession took place in only 2 percent of US counties (EIG 2016). According to the Economic Innovation Group's "Distressed Community Index," between 2000 and 2017, little job growth occurred outside of the 20 percent of the nation's most prosperous zip codes. Between the years 2017 and 2021, the nation's most prosperous zip codes experienced a 15 percent increase in employment and an 11.8 percent increase in new business establishments, whereas the nation's most economically distressed communities contained 8.7 percent fewer jobs and 4.2 percent fewer businesses than they had at the start of the period. This was compounded by the shift away from manufacturing jobs to a financialized and service-based economy, which has meant that the jobs that are created tend to be at the very high end or at the very low end of the income scale (Collins 2023).

In addition to the macro-level regional disparities in economic growth and job creation, individual neighborhoods are becoming increasingly segregated along class lines at the micro level as well. Class-based segregation has replaced the rigid race-based segregation of the past, and economic divisions across space have become equally, if not more, pronounced than the nation's increasingly polarized political divisions (Masey, Rothwell, and Domina 2009). Citing data from the US Census Bureau, Robert Putnam (2015) points out that compared to the 1970s, fewer families today live in mixed or moderate-income neighborhoods and more families live in either uniformly affluent or uniformly poor neighborhoods. In fact, neighborhood segregation has affected each major racial group. Today, affluent and impoverished minority groups are less likely to live next to or interact daily with each other than they were in previous generations.

The increase in segregation by income and wealth has been accompanied by a corresponding increase in class isolation (Massey, Rothwell, and Domina 2009). As neighborhoods become more segregated, fewer and fewer young people—whether rich or poor—interact in their daily lives with people outside of their socioeconomic circle. This effect has extended to a decline in cross-class marriage, further reducing the bridge between classes. Children from wealthy and upper-middle-class families on the other hand are more likely to attend expensive universities, marry from within their same class, and take jobs and reside in cosmopolitan bubbles segregating themselves from the rest of society. Consequently, some areas are experiencing brain and wealth drain as young people with money and high IQs flee. Conversely, in prosperous urban and suburban areas that have become a destination for the wealthy and those with advanced degrees, gentrification is quickly displacing the long-established working and middle class.

Manhattan, New York, provides a glaring example. In 1980, Manhattan's residents were more reflective of the nation in terms of income and employment.

Today, the borough has a higher level of income and wealth inequality than that of South Africa before Apartheid ended in 1994 (Kotkin 2014). It is home to nearly all the city's billionaires. Though service and working-class jobs make up more than half of the area's jobs, they amount to less than a third of the area's residents (Florida 2017).

Likewise, in Chicago, the city's once-thriving middle class has almost disappeared (Lutton 2019). In 1970, fully half of the city was middle income, but today only 16 percent of the city's 797 census tracts are considered middle income. Furthermore, these tracts are confined to the outer corners of the city and to slivers between areas of wealth and poverty. The city has also become a national leader in joblessness among young people, particularly young Black people. Citing a report published by the Great Cities Institute, Alexia Elejalde-Ruiz (2017) observes that in addition to high youth unemployment, the city has one of the largest race disparities in terms of early 20-somethings who are both out of school and out of work. In 2015, among the city's population of 20- to 24-year-olds, 40 percent of Blacks and 7 percent of whites fell into this category compared to the national average disconnection rate for this age group of 25 percent for Blacks and 13 percent for whites, respectively.

A great deal of research suggests that both the unequal geographical distribution of opportunity and class-based segregation have played a role in the overall decline in intergenerational mobility in certain areas of the country. As University of Maryland economist Melissa Kearney (2017) discovered, "Places themselves have causal impacts on kids' outcomes." Likewise, in 2014, Harvard economist Raj Chetty and colleagues found that both relative and absolute intergenerational mobility varies substantially across geographical areas within the United States and that even adjacent neighborhoods can have dramatically different levels of mobility. In fact, some areas have relative mobility equivalent to the highest mobility countries in the world, while others have lower levels of mobility than the aggregate levels of any other developed country. For example, the probability that a child starting from a family in the bottom quintile of the national income distribution will reach the top quintile is only 4.4 percent in Charlotte, North Carolina, but is 10.8 percent in Salt Lake City, Utah, and 12.9 percent in San Jose, California. Chetty and colleagues, thus, determined that rather than characterizing the entire country as "the land of opportunity, the US is better described as a collection of societies some of which are 'lands of opportunity,' while others offer little chance of escaping poverty."

Decline in Social Capital

After exploring the factors correlated with upward mobility, Chetty and colleagues (2014) discovered that high-mobility areas have less residential segregation, less income inequality, better primary schools, greater social capital, and fewer single-parent homes. They conclude, therefore, that though economics certainly plays a role, opportunity and upward mobility are overwhelmingly shaped by a child's social environment. The most prevalent social factors include education, family stability, and high levels of social capital indices—which refers to the strength of social networks and community involvement in an area. In this sense the distinction between America's upper and upper-middle (or professional) classes compared to its working- and poverty-stricken classes is seen not just in bank balances, asset sheets, and salaries, but also in family structure, educational attainment, and civic and community life. In contrast to the typical child born into a working-class or poor home and neighborhood, the typical upper or upper-middle-class child is raised in a stable home by well-educated, married parents, lives in a great neighborhood, and attends the area's best schools, giving that child a nearly insurmountable advantage right from the start (Reeves 2018a).

As neighborhoods have become more and more segregated by income level and bridges between classes have further deteriorated—fewer and fewer young people—whether rich or poor—are interacting in their daily lives with people outside of their socioeconomic circle. Effectively, this means that members of the lower classes are simultaneously missing out on opportunities created by what social scientists term social capital. Social capital refers to the non-financial resources available to individuals through relationships to people and institutions. These informal resources include ties to family, friends, neighbors, mentors, and acquaintances; involvement in civic associations, religious institutions, athletic teams, volunteer activities; and access to job referral networks, educated professionals, good schools, and so on.

High levels of social capital have long proved a strong predictor of well-being for both individuals and communities no matter their economic class. Those who live in upper, middle, and working-class neighborhoods in which familial, civic, and religious institutions are strong are far less likely to suffer from social alienation and physical and economic decline (Carney 2019). Unfortunately, children born into poverty are more likely to grow up in communities with few public services, serious problems with crime and drug abuse, and few civic or religious institutional supports. In such cases, children are left without access to important steppingstones and resources crucial for educational success, gainful employment, upward mobility, and social well-being. The recent catastrophic increases in substance abuse, suicide, and homelessness among young and middle-aged Americans living in distressed communities are indicative of just how severe this problem has become.

Weakening Family Structures

In a nation in which families are the most important institution for raising children, the status of family structure and stability greatly affects both immediate opportunities and the likelihood of future financial well-being and upward mobility. Families are not only a source of financial and non-financial resources and support—including financing of educational and extra-curricular activities, time and energy, and emotional engagement—they also play a social role in instilling valuable habits, dispositions, and connections that can equip their children for a greater likelihood of future success. Using a social science data-driven approach to studying family life, University of Maryland economist Melissa S. Kearney (2023) concludes that "two parents tend to be able to provide their children with more resource advantages than one parent alone." Furthermore, she notes, "that a two-parent family is increasingly becoming yet another privilege associated with more highly resourced groups in society."

According to researchers at the Institute for Family Studies, prior to the 1970s there were no large class divides in American family life (Wilcox and Wang 2017). Most Americans, regardless of class status, got married and stayed married and most children were raised in two-parent homes. This trend began to change in the 1960s, first as poorer and less-educated Americans became less likely to get and stay married. By the 1980s, members of the working class were also becoming less and less likely to marry and stay married. Today, the United States has the world's highest rate of children living in single-parent households (Kramer 2019). Although declining marriage rates and the likelihood that children are raised in a single-parent home have become more prevalent across class lines, they are far more pronounced in the bottom two income quintiles. There are now striking differences in both marital status and single parenthood of Americans by both income and educational achievement levels.

Citing figures from the Census Bureau's American Community Survey, Wilcox and Wang (2017) show that low-income and less-educated Americans are more likely to be living outside of any kind of partnership, but this is particularly true when it comes to marriage. Only 26 percent of poor adults and 39 percent of working-class adults (age 18 to 55) are married compared to 56 percent of middle- and upper-class adults. Rates of single parenthood likewise diverge. Based on a tabulation of Current Population Survey data, Reeves (2018b) found that the single parenthood rate among those aged twenty-five to thirty-five in the top 20 percent of income earners is now 9 percent, up from 3 percent in 1980, but this is much lower than for other classes. The proportion of single-parent households in the bottom two quintiles, for example, is now 40 percent.

Working-class and poor adults are also far more likely to divorce even if they do marry. Among working-class and poor men and women who have married, more than 40 percent have been divorced, compared to less than one-third of middle- and upper-class men and women who have married (Wilcox and Wang 2017). This divide suggests that working-class and poor Americans not only have fewer resources, but also have more fragile families. They also have smaller extended families on average due to declining birth rates—fewer cousins, uncles, aunts, and other relations upon whom they might turn in times of financial or emotional need than in generations past.

Children's family structure additionally varies across racial and ethnic groups (Kearny 2023). In 2019, 77 percent of white children and 88 percent of Asian children lived with married parents compared to 62 percent of Hispanic children and 38 percent of Black children. While the racial gap in family structure existed before the late twentieth century, it has drastically widened since the 1960s (Kearney 2023). Furthermore, regardless of race, the rise in the share of children living with one parent (81 percent of which are mothers) reflects declines in marriage, not changes in childbearing patterns. According to Kearney (2023), the share of births to unmarried mothers has climbed steadily over the past forty years, despite a reduction in teen pregnancy and childbearing overall. Poor women, however, start bearing children younger on average and have significantly more children than do affluent women (Wilcox and Wang 2017).

Some attribute the growing class divide in marriage and family patterns solely to economic facts. They primarily focus on how the hardships created by financial insecurity among working-class and poor families have contributed to greater marriage instability (Greenstone and Looney 2012; Reeves and

Pulliam 2020). Others, such as economist Isabel Sawhill (2014), have contended, however, that "purely economic theory falls short as an explanation of the dramatic transformation of family life in recent decades." There was no discernible increase in divorce or single parenthood at the height of the Great Depression, for instance, despite widespread economic distress. Thus, as Wilcox and Wang (2017) observe, "A different policy, cultural, and civic context in that era meant that economic distress did not automatically lead to greater family instability."

By contrast, since the 1960s, a series of economic, social, and cultural changes have interacted to create a major transformation in the lives and structures of poor and working-class families. On the economic front the move to a postindustrial economy, the rise in automation, growing trade deficits, and the increased necessity of a post-secondary degree to obtain a well-paying job have made it more difficult for poor and working-class men to find stable, gainful employment, making them less attractive as husbands and more vulnerable to divorce.

Based on interviews with 162 single mothers about their lives and views on marriage and children, sociologists Kathrin Edin and Maria Kafalas (2005) conclude that many women don't marry the father of their children because they do not believe that he will be a reliable source of economic security or stability. Recent data on marriage rates does demonstrate a striking connection in the economic outcomes and marriage rates for men. Between 1980 and 2020, college-educated men, whose employment has remained high and whose earnings have increased, experienced little decline in marriage rates (Kearney 2023). Conversely, non-college-educated men—the same group that has primarily experienced stagnant earnings and falling employment rates—experienced a significant decline in marriage rates. Wilcox and Wang (2017) contend, however, that the seemingly causal relationship between the decline in men's employment and earnings does not tell the whole story. The decline of marriage and the corresponding rise in single parenthood first began, they contend, in response to cultural changes arising from the sexual revolution and the rise of expressive individualism in the 1960s and 1970s, which preceded the shifts in the economy that undercut men's wages and job security.

Wilcox and Wang (2017) discuss several possible reasons as to why these cultural changes have disparately affected poor and working-class Americans, even as more educated women who have taken full advantage of modern opportunities for women in the labor force continue to marry at higher rates. The first is that, in the absence of cultural supports for marriage, working-class and poor Americans have less of a social and economic stake in marriage than do their counterparts in the middle and upper class. Working-class and poor couples are less likely to share assets, such as a home, and thus have fewer financial incentives to marry or to avoid divorce. Secondly, poor and working-class Americans often lack the cultural and educational resources to successfully navigate the social, moral, and legal deregulation of sex, childbearing, parenthood, marriage, and divorce that have occurred since the sexual revolution, thereby leaving them more subject to short-term, fragile relationships.

In a study of diverging patterns of sexual behavior, childbearing, and family life by race and class, legal scholar Amy Wax (2011), for instance, traces disparities to distinct modes of assessing personal well-being when it comes to matters such as partner choice, reproductive behavior, and sexual fidelity. The more well-educated and privileged members of society, she contends, have been better equipped than those among the poor and working classes with the knowledge and resources to approach personal choices regarding sexual and relationship matters with a disciplined and long-term perspective.

Other scholars have similarly maintained that today's culture of freedom regarding childbearing and marriage has been more difficult for members of the lower classes to navigate but have argued that this is because the various stresses facing poor and working-class adults leave them with a diminished sense of control over their own lives (Sassler and Miller 2017). Thirdly, Wilcox and Wang contend that middle- and upper-class Americans have rejected several of the most permissive dimensions of the sexual revolution for themselves and their children, while poor and working-class Americans have adopted a more permissive, destigmatized approach toward infidelity, cohabitation, divorce, and out-of-wedlock childbearing than they held in the past. Finally, in addition to these economic and cultural factors, many have argued that the transformation of family law, along with the expansion of means-tested welfare programs since the 1960s, has both penalized and disincentivized marriage (Wilcox, Price, and Richidi 2016).

Available data suggests that a distinct social, psychological, and economic advantage exists for children who grow up with married parents (McLanahan and Sawhill 2015). While many children raised by single parents or in unstable family environments go on to live successful, happy, and healthy lives, in the aggregate, however, an abundance of social science evidence shows that growing up in an unstable or fatherless home undermines social mobility and perpetuates inequality across generations. The odds of graduating high school, completing a college and advanced degree, having higher earnings in adulthood, maintaining stable marital relationships in adulthood, and avoiding involvement with the justice system are substantially higher for children who grow up with married biological parents (Kearney 2023).

Using data comparing the income quintile that more than 5,000 Americans were born into compared to the income quintile they reached later in life, Reeves (2014) found that 50 percent of poor children raised by a never-married mother remained in the bottom quintile compared to only 17 percent of poor children raised by a married mother and father. Speculating as to why marriage itself produces better outcomes for children, over and above cohabitation, Reeves and Pulliam (2020) conclude that "On average, married-couple families experience the most stability, and for children, a stable family environment provides a solid foundation, while instability is linked to negative child outcomes including problematic behavior, poorer social development, lower educational attainment, poorer cognitive development, and a wealth penalty in adulthood." These negative outcomes are particularly pronounced for young men who grow up without their biological father (Wilcox, Wange, and ElHage 2022).

Interestingly, research has shown that marriage rates can impact the financial and social well-being of entire communities. In a landmark study on the relationship between geography, opportunity, and intergenerational mobility economist Raj Chetty and a team of researchers found that mobility is significantly lower among children of all races, even those living with their biological married parents, in areas with weaker family structures, as measured by the percentage of single parents in a neighborhood (Chetty et al. 2014). Conversely, children of single parents raised in areas with a high percentage of intact families had higher rates of mobility.

Educational Attainment

As Brookings Institution Senior Fellow Richard V. Reeves (2018a) recollects, "Americans have historically lauded education as the great equalizer, allowing individuals to determine their own path in life regardless of background." Today, however, he laments, "Education has become the main mechanism for the reproduction of upper middle-class status across generations."

Failures in Primary and Secondary Education

Once the envy of the world, America's primary and secondary education systems have fallen behind much of the developed world in preparing students, particularly in the lower classes, for success in the modern globalized economy (Desilver 2017). First, although the on-time high school completion rate has reached a record high in recent years, at least 13 percent of students nationally fail to graduate in four years (National Center for Education Statistics 2023). That number is much higher for low-income, disadvantaged, and minority youth—and, in many urban areas, as few as 50 percent of students complete their degree (Guryan and Ludwig 2014). Furthermore, in contrast with many advanced democracies like the UK, France, and Germany that measure completion of secondary education based on the passage of skill assessment exams, high school graduation in the United States is based on hours of attendance and credits completed. Thus, some districts can use questionable methods to increase graduation rates, such as relaxing grading requirements and allowing students to participate in abbreviated credit recovery programs for courses they have failed (Dynarski 2018). Consequently, those who do graduate often lack proficiency in basic skills.

Despite steadily increased spending on K-12 Education and various revisions of and efforts under the Elementary and Secondary Education Act to raise chronically low achievement rates among disadvantaged children, data from the National Assessment of Educational Progress reveals that less than 40 percent of graduating seniors are proficient in reading and less than 25 percent are proficient in math (NAEP 2024). These proficiency rates vary greatly by geography and state and appear even more tragic when broken down by race. Among Asian graduating seniors, 50 percent are proficient in math, compared to only 30 percent of whites, 11 percent of Hispanics, 9 percent of American Indians, and 8 percent of Blacks. In terms of reading, 50 percent of Asian graduating seniors are proficient, compared to 47 percent of whites, 25 percent of Hispanics, 23 percent of American Indians, and 17 percent of Blacks. Such abysmal low-achievement outcomes that predominantly affect lower-income students reveal that America's schools are failing to impart basic literacy and numeracy skills to a large percentage of the population, greatly reducing their chances of achieving a rewarding career and financial security.

The prolonged school closures in several states, following the Covid-19 pandemic, further aggravated this problem. As reported in the *New York*

Times, "Today, there is broad acknowledgement among many public health and education experts that extended school closures did not significantly stop the spread of Covid, while the academic harms for children have been large and long-lasting" (Paris 2024). Students who spent more time in remote or hybrid instruction in the 2020–1 school year had larger drops in test scores than students who spent most of the year fully in person. The combination of poverty and remote learning was particularly harmful, as the steepest learning losses from the move to remote and hybrid learning occurred in the nation's poorer districts.

Even after the return to in-person learning, there are signs that school closures, and the pandemic more broadly, had lasting effects on the culture of education. Schools across the country have seen sharp and sustained increases in absenteeism across demographic groups—but, as with learning loss, the problem has been more pronounced among the poor. Around 32 percent of students in the nation's poorest districts were chronically absent during the 2022–3 school year, up from 19 percent prior to the pandemic (Mervosh and Paris 2024). Absenteeism is negatively affecting the achievement of all students, including those who show up, because teachers are forced to slow down and adjust their approach to keep all students on track. The long-term damage from these trends of learning loss and absenteeism in terms of lost earnings and employment opportunities may not be known for years.

In addition to failing to ensure the achievement of basic academic skills, a large percentage of high schools have eliminated programs and courses focused on developing career-oriented or vocational skills. This process began in the 1960s and 1970s as the emphasis on secondary education aggressively shifted toward a focus on college enrollment (American Compass 2022b). In contrast to Europe's most economically competitive nations, in which nearly half of high school students are enrolled in vocational education programs, only 2 percent of US high school students attend schools that concentrate on vocational training (Wyman 2015). As a result, a large majority of US students are leaving high school tremendously ill-prepared for the workforce.

Higher Education and the Perpetuation of Inequality

The current state of postsecondary education in America additionally seems to be contributing to the growing depth and permanency of class divisions. A generation ago, career success was less dependent on secondary and postsecondary education. Workers with postsecondary education held only a small percentage of jobs. Youth, particularly males, who did not complete high school were able to find jobs in agriculture, manufacturing, the military, and so on that frequently led to a lucrative career. Over the past several decades, changes in the labor market have progressively diminished such opportunities for young people with limited education. In 2023, nearly 70 percent of jobs required postsecondary education or training, and a 2023 report published by Georgetown University's Center on Education and the Workforce predicted that by 2031, 72 percent of all jobs in the United States will require postsecondary education or training (Carnevale et al. 2023).

Consequently, today there are far fewer opportunities for those with a high school diploma or less to find a job that serves as a steppingstone to a well-paying profession. The completion of high school and at least some level of postsecondary education or training has become more and more crucial for stable employment and for higher earnings and job advancement. Even when those who have dropped out of high school or who only possess a high school degree are able to secure employment, they are more liable to be employed in short-term jobs long after they have left school, compared to college or career training program graduates who have a much easier time finding stable, long-term employment. While completing high school is no longer sufficient for ensuring reasonable prospects in the job market, failure to complete high school all but guarantees a life of poverty. High school dropouts are more than three times as likely to be unemployed as those who graduate from college (Bureau of Labor Statistics 2024).

Over the past couple of decades, many young people heeded the advice that they should go to college, and the nation made incredible strides toward increasing the percentages of high school graduates enrolled in various forms of postsecondary education. This progress was particularly notable when it came to youth from low-income and disadvantaged backgrounds. For instance, Holzer and Baum (2017) point out that in 1984 only 36 percent of high school graduates from the lowest family income quartile immediately enrolled in a two- or four-year college. By 2014, however, "67 percent of all recent high school graduates—and 52 percent of those from the lowest income group—went straight to college."

Nevertheless, a sizeable percentage of Americans still do not attend college, and college enrollment in recent years has been on a steady decline since its peak—yet another trend that accelerated following the Covid-19 pandemic. The enrollment rate for recent US high school graduates, ages 16 to 24, dropped to

62 percent in 2022 from 66.2 percent in 2019 (the year before the pandemic began) and from a high point of about 70 percent in 2009 (Torry 2023). Furthermore, it is important to note that enrollment alone does not ensure success. Other factors, including the institution attended, the choice of a major, and whether a student graduates, matter a great deal, and these factors all reflect highly segregated social and economic patterns (Carnevale 2012; Reeves 2018a).

Those who support universal access to college education generally point to data demonstrating significant earning premiums and greater job security associated with the attainment of a college degree. They contend that the financial gains resulting from the acquisition of a college degree far outweigh the large sums of money used to finance that degree. However, the data associating higher levels of income and employment opportunity with a college degree is based on an examination of the average earnings of the entire college graduate population, many of whom graduated 30 or more years ago (Vedder, Denhar, and Robe 2013). Critics of data purporting to be supportive of universal access to college also claim the data fails to distinguish between earning potential based on the prestige of the degree program and university and does not account for how individuals' preexisting cognitive skills, or their choice of a major, may contribute to better employment and earning rates.

Although many graduates over time have reaped substantial economic benefits from higher education, a large percentage of recent college graduates do not receive a good financial return on their temporal and monetary investment. Unfortunately, this is even more the case for many youths born at the bottom of the socioeconomic ladder, who end up disproportionately at institutions (or in majors) ill-equipped to help them succeed (Fischer 2016). Robert Putnam (2015), for example, points out that the class gap in admission to the most selective institutions with the best prospects for employment success has widened in recent years. Summarizing data from several recent studies, Putnam explains:

> The fraction of kids from the bottom quartile of the income distribution who ended up at a selective college or university rose from 4 percent in 1972 to 5 percent three decades later, but for kids from the top quartile, the equivalent figures were 26 percent and 36 percent. By 2004, in the nation's 'most competitive' colleges and universities … kids from the top quartile of the socioeconomic scale outnumbered kids from the bottom quartile by about 14 to one.

Today, despite the growth in access to higher education more generally, the representation of low-income students at high-mobility colleges (those that offer much higher completion rates and greater access to well-paying jobs or prestigious graduate and professional schools) has fallen (Opportunity Insights 2024). This is due to a host of factors, which include an admission process that favors legacy and well-connected students, and factors such as weak academic backgrounds and other constraints that are more prevalent among low-income students (Reeves 2018a).

Students from low-income and disadvantaged backgrounds who graduate from less selective institutions still, overall, have undeniably better prospects than nongraduates. Nevertheless, many of these graduates concentrate in fields with low levels of compensation and are leaving college unprepared for the workforce having few marketable skills (Hansen 2021). In 2012, *The Chronicle of Higher Education* and America's Public Media *Marketplace* conducted a nationwide survey of over 700 employers, asking employers a series of questions pertaining to their perception of how well colleges and universities were preparing their graduates for the workplace (Fischer 2013). Although most of the employers surveyed require applicants to possess a college degree—viewing it as an indicator that an individual can work toward achieving a goal—half of those surveyed reported trouble finding qualified graduates.

A third of those surveyed lamented that a large percentage of bachelor's degree holders lack basic workplace proficiencies, such as adaptability; written and oral communication skills; and the ability to problem solve, make decisions, analyze data, and construct cogent arguments. Consequently, most employers surveyed reported that, when given the opportunity, they prefer to hire applicants with a record of workplace competency in addition to possessing a degree. Furthermore, although college major was mentioned as the most important academic credential in evaluating a recent graduate for employment, a large percentage of employers testified that they give more weight to the applicant's previous work experience, including internships and employment, than to their academic credentials, including their GPA. Thus, those who graduate from college with a low-demand major and little to no work experience are automatically at a major disadvantage when seeking postgraduate employment.

The fact that those from well-connected, upper-class and professional homes have much higher access to prestigious internships and other work-related experiences further compounds inequality (Reeves 2018a). Moreover, as more ordinary people have earned college degrees, upper-middle-class families have simply upped the ante with an ever-increasing pursuit of postgraduate qualifications.

An additional, and perhaps more serious problem, in terms of viewing college education as an economic equalizer and guaranteed pathway to success for low-income students, is the substantial number of students who enroll in college but don't leave with a degree. In terms of enrollment, the nation has made enormous progress in improving access to two- and four-year institutions for low-income youth from disadvantaged backgrounds. In fact, the number of students from the bottom income quintile who enrolled in college immediately following high school graduation reached a historic high of nearly 70 percent in 2016 (Cooper 2018).

Unfortunately, however, the rise in the number of high school graduates attending college has not been accompanied by an increase in the number who graduate from college. Furthermore, while colleges reap financial benefits from admitting large numbers of government-funded students, they are not held liable when a sizeable number drop out before receiving a degree. According to the National Center for Education Statistics (2022), only 67 percent of females and 60 percent of males who enrolled at a four-year degree-granting institution in the fall of 2014 had completed their degree six years later. Only 29 percent of students at public two-year degree-granting institutions and only 52 percent of students at private nonprofit two-year degree-granting institutions, who enrolled full time in the fall of 2017, attained a certificate or associate degree within three years.

The completion rates for minority students and those at the bottom of the income scale are even lower than the national averages. Many of these students drop out because of the financial constraints associated with limited individual and family resources, but lowering the costs of higher education is not enough to ensure their success. As Holzer and Baum (2017) explain, poor academic preparation in the K-12 years plays a significant role in the completion problem among disadvantaged students, as does a lack of social capital and familiarity with the academic world and what is required for success. Furthermore, many disadvantaged students have significant work and familial responsibilities that make it difficult to maintain their full-time student status.

Many of those who do complete a postsecondary degree find themselves in a precarious position. As the costs of attending college have risen more than four times the rate of inflation over the past several decades, students are forced to take on higher levels of debt to finance their education. Securing remunerative employment postgraduation, thus, becomes even more essential for graduates to maintain a satisfactory standard of living and avoid defaulting on their loans. Yet, data collected in recent years indicates that many college graduates, burdened by debt, have a difficult time finding stable, well-paying employment. More than half of college graduates in the United States face unemployment, underemployment, or employment in jobs that do not require a college degree (Weissman 2024).

Graduates who find themselves thousands of dollars in debt without the prospect of remunerative employment risk discovering that they are worse off financially than before they enrolled in school. Such a situation is particularly common among and detrimental for those who are already coming from an economically disadvantaged background. In fact, according to surveys of recent high school graduates, the cost of higher education combined with the growing educational skills gap, and the move to remote learning during the pandemic have all been major drivers of declining enrollment trends in recent years as fewer and fewer young people view traditional college enrollment as worth their time and money (Torry 2023).

Unemployment and Disconnection from Work

Another characteristic of poverty is failure to establish and maintain a consistent presence in the workforce. This could be due either to bouts of unemployment or what is referred to as disconnection from education and the workforce. Such disconnected individuals are called NEETs, individuals who are neither employed nor in education or training. These individuals are not included in unemployment rates, which refers only to those who are not currently employed but are participating in the labor force by actively seeking a job—sending out resumes, filling out applications, interviewing for positions, and so on. Thus, although the unemployment rate is customarily used to signify whether people who desire employment are able to find it, the rate is not always an accurate indicator since it does not include those who have decided to pursue other options, such as education or full-time parenthood or the percentage of disconnected individuals who have stopped looking for work altogether and who are not engaged in education or training to improve their chance of employment in the future.

The growing number of Americans in this latter category is a cause for concern. Since the 1990s, the nation has experienced steadily increasing rates of disconnection particularly among younger workers and prime working-age males between the ages of 25 to 54 (Social Capital Project 2021; Statista 2024).

The Covid-19 pandemic greatly accelerated this trend. Today, almost a third of prime working-age males are not in the labor force.

The pandemic and the government response to it caused immediate and significant increases in short-term unemployment, but even worse has been the longer-term effect on disconnection rates. While financial relief plans, stimulus checks, and extended unemployment benefits prevented many newly unemployed workers from falling into destitution, they also reduced the incentive to take advantage of available employment. Thus, even amid economic recovery, many of those who were physically able to join the workforce were disincentivized from doing so because they were bringing in more money from benefits than they would receive in wages (Hornstein et al. 2023). This was a chief cause of the ensuing labor shortage across multiple industries. In addition, while previous economic downturns have contributed to increases in enrollment in education and training, the Covid-19 recession had the opposite effect. The reduction in labor force participation combined with a decline in school enrollment contributed to a surge in disconnected youth (Crocket and Zhang 2023).

While unemployment rates vary depending on the vibrancy of the economy, the rising rates of disconnection mean that fewer people are employed or engaged in other productive pursuits (such as pursuing an education or caring for a child or family member) no matter how rosy the employment numbers may be or how well the broader economy appears to be doing. In the wake of the economic recovery from the pandemic for instance, drops in the unemployment rate were due in part to Americans giving up on working entirely.

Disconnection trends in America are ominous for several reasons. First, high rates of chronic unemployment and disconnection from the labor force produce personal economic harm and significant widespread negative economic consequences: these include lost earnings and economic potential, slower economic growth, fewer tax revenues, and increased government spending on social welfare and entitlement programs. While unemployment has an economically damaging effect at any age, it is particularly detrimental early in a person's professional career. Early periods of unemployment can stunt youths' transition into self-sufficiency and adulthood and are ultimately associated with long-term earning losses and joblessness.

The situation is even worse for youth who have undergone simultaneous gaps in labor force participation and education. Even when youth who have experienced such gaps eventually secure a job, they often suffer enduring harmful effects in comparison to others who have maintained continuous education and work histories. A large body of research now demonstrates that unemployment during the early years of an individual's professional life causes a pay and employment handicap for years to come. The longer the period of early unemployment, the bigger the negative scarring effect on potential lifetime earnings and employment potential. Although youth who face early bouts of involuntary unemployment are more likely to engage in short-term human capital development, such as work-related training as a catch-up response to mitigate possible setbacks, they still, on average, suffer a long-term negative impact on their earnings. According to a Brookings Institution memo, "A six-month bout of unemployment at age 22 would reduce wages by 8% in the following year" and would continue to reduce earnings over the next decade (Sawhill and Karpilow 2014). Some economists have projected that the earnings deficit of early periods of unemployment can persist for up to twenty years (Morsy 2012). Although youth with higher levels of education are less at risk of joblessness, their potential earning loss is further magnified by the debt they may have acquired to finance their education if they do experience unemployment.

While public assistance programs, including cash welfare payments and food and housing assistance, are designed to prevent youth from falling into poverty or turning to crime, they can further aggravate youth unemployment and disconnection by creating a lingering pattern of dependency. Harvey Golub (2013), former CEO of American Express, illustrates this danger by pointing out that if the wage premium from working is less than, equal to, or only slightly greater than the financial benefits provided by public assistance programs, the fear of losing benefits may create disincentives to work among youth—which further delays their entry into the labor market and achievement of employment potential. A phenomenon clearly demonstrated by the increase in government assistance during and following the Covid-19 pandemic.

While the detrimental economic effects of prolonged periods of unemployment and disconnection from the labor force are fairly well known, less frequently discussed are the psychological, physical, and social consequences. Research has shown that engaging in productive work, particularly work that serves and benefits others, contributes to long-term happiness and physical and mental well-being. On the other hand, long-term unemployment and a lack of productive work are strongly correlated to decreased happiness and mental and physical health issues.

After accounting for prior drinking behavior and psychological history, sociologist Krysia Mossakowski (2009) found that long periods of unemployment among young people were directly correlated to an increase in depressive symptoms. This correlation is particularly strong for youth who are neither working nor in education and training. Such youth are much more likely to have spent time in a mental hospital and to have received drug or alcohol treatment than their connected peers (Belfield, Levin, and Rosen 2012). They are also at increased risk of having suicidal thoughts and engaging in self-harm (Vogel 2015).

The deterioration of physical and mental well-being correlated with early bouts of unemployment and disconnection may be due in part to the financial stress and feeling of failure that frequently accompany joblessness, but it may also be a consequence of the prolonged idleness and social alienation associated with disconnection from education and the workforce. As political economist Nicholas Eberstadt (2016) observes in his book, *Men without Work*, this free time "can be devoted to recreation, reflection, and self-improvement as well as the pursuit of spirituality, and the arts, … [but it] can also be wasted or expended in ways that diminish the individual and his bonds to family and community."

A growing body of evidence suggests that the expendable time of those who are disconnected from education and the workforce in the United States is being spent in the latter way, particularly among disconnected males. A study by the National Bureau of Economic Research, for example, reveals that as the percentage of joblessness has increased among young males, most are not spending their free time in purposeful pursuits such as improving their social capital, volunteering, or building meaningful relationships, instead they are increasingly allocating their time to playing video games and other computer-related activities (Aguiar et al. 2017). Based on data from the Bureau of Labor Statistics annual American Time Use Survey, Eberstadt (2016) likewise reports that—whereas a large percentage of women who are not in education or in school are likely to be caring for children or other family members—only a small percentage of nonworking, disconnected men report that they are engaged in caring for children or other family members. Moreover, these men have very low levels of volunteer activity, community involvement, or religious attendance. Instead, they self-reported spending most of their day pursuing immediate sources of gratification, such as attending gambling establishments, using tobacco or illegal drugs, and watching movies or television. Even more troubling, many spend their expendable time in pursuit of criminal activities that are not only personally detrimental but socially harmful as well.

Among the most significant social costs imposed by chronic unemployment and disconnection is that they delay the achievement of key milestones, such as homeownership, and are associated with lower marriage and higher divorce rates (Lester 1996). When parents lose their jobs or experience long periods of disconnection, their children are less likely to do well in school and achieve remunerative employment themselves (Venator and Reeves 2013). Joblessness also has a stronger effect on violent crime than poverty itself in highly impoverished neighborhoods (Dollar, Donnelly, and Parker 2019).

Another social consequence of high levels of unemployment and disconnection is the disintegrating effect they have on the probability of social mobility, particularly if they occur in young adulthood. Harvey Golub (2013) explains that three factors determine whether individuals who are born into poverty are likely to rise out of poverty: finishing high school, avoiding becoming a teenage parent, and getting a full-time job. According to Golub, "Those who do all three have only a 2 percent chance of living in poverty and a 75 percent chance of joining the middle class." On the other hand, when large percentages of young people experience a weak start in the labor market and struggle to achieve economic sufficiency, the prospects of social mobility, both for themselves and for their children, are diminished (Mitnik and Grusky 2015).

Faced with intergenerational dependency and an inability to engage productively in the marketplace, youth risk becoming socially disconnected as well. The longer disconnection from the labor force persists, the more susceptible youth become to feelings of cynicism, disenfranchisement, and a lack of confidence in their own agency.

Basic Income Proposals

Factors producing poverty, inequality, stagnating mobility, and despair in America are influenced by, but also extend beyond, the performance of the labor market at any given time. Many of the causes are deep rooted and vary greatly by demographic, educational history, socioeconomic status, and geographical location. While a simple, universal solution to the unique and diverse causes of poverty and disconnection may not exist, a wide range of actors and organizations have sought to better understand the unique nature of poverty in modern America and have proposed a variety of solutions to address some of its underlying causes and mitigate its effects. The following sections will explore just a few of many proposals aimed at promoting widely shared growth, opportunity for all, and higher rates of intergenerational mobility.

During the Covid-19 pandemic, through multiple federal and state legislative acts, Americans received a slew of direct income payments. This brought renewed interest in taxpayer-funded basic income programs that have long been promoted by economic justice advocacy groups, left-leaning politicians, and tech billionaires as a means of alleviating poverty and financial distress (Napoletano 2022; Sadowski 2016). Basic income programs come in two forms: Universal Basic Income (UBI) programs involve universal cash payments to all individuals that recur consistently and unconditionally with no restrictions or strings attached, such as means tests or work requirements. Guaranteed Basic Income (GBI) programs are like UBI programs in that there are no strings attached to cash benefits, but unlike UBI programs, they only provide cash benefits to individuals whose income falls below a pre-determined threshold. In recent years, several state and local governments and nongovernmental organizations have begun to pilot small-scale basic income programs in targeted locations throughout the country.

While the outcomes of pilot programs pertaining to employment and changes in income have thus far produced mixed results, supporters of basic income programs contend that they reduce the wealth gap and thereby increase equity, especially considering the wage stagnation and automation that are affecting the employment prospects of America's lower and working classes (Okantey 2024). Even some devout free-market advocates and scholars have argued that government "income transfer payments" have reduced inequality in America (Gramm and Early 2021).

Others, however, have maintained that while transfer payments may reduce income inequality on paper, they do nothing to address the more pernicious problems caused by earned income inequality and the rapid concentration of assets in even fewer hands (Kotkin 2022). Opponents contend that the high costs and dependency created by expanded welfarism that is unconnected to productive work would sink the labor market and increase inflation, laying the ground for a further bifurcation between the affluent and the dependent classes. Their argument is that given the well-documented negative economic, psychological, physical, and social consequences of unemployment, disconnection, and idleness, proposals that elevate consumption at the same time they disincentivize production run the risk of exacerbating negative trends and furthering class divisions in American society—especially if they replace or are unaccompanied by policies aimed at restoring incentives and opportunities to engage in purposeful, productive, and gainful work.

Building a Less Bifurcated, More Productive American Economy

Instead of relying on basic income programs as a catch-all solution, lawmakers ought to consider policies narrowly tailored to improve immediate incentives and opportunities for Americans to engage in productive activities. An important first step might be to reevaluate and restructure social safety net programs, so they no longer discourage people from taking available jobs (Dolan 2022). For example, thanks to marginal tax rates in many states earning $1 too much can lead to thousands of dollars of loss in personal or family Medicaid benefits (Social Capital Project 2021). Today safety net programs are less targeted and the share of the working-age population receiving benefits has increased significantly over previous years—the threat of an immediate loss of benefits from working a job is thus a powerful disincentive for productive activity among working-age, capable individuals.

Removing Disincentives and Barriers to Work

A second step would be to remove some of the barriers that inhibit people from pursuing jobs and discourage employers from creating them. Over time, federal, state, and local policymakers from both major parties have proposed and adopted well-intentioned labor policies that thwart people's entry into the job market. Often such policies are adopted to benefit older, established workers with little regard for the negative effect they may have on the employment prospects of younger and other nonestablished workers. State and local occupational licensing requirements—laws that require workers to meet specific standards and obtain a government license before they are legally permitted to perform certain jobs—are one example. Though viewed as a means of protecting the public from injury at the hands of unskilled practitioners in fields like law and medicine, state licensing mandates extend far beyond the realm of public health and safety. In fact, over the past several decades, professional associations rather than consumer advocacy and public interest groups have been behind the rapid growth of state occupational licensing requirements, which impose significant restrictions on market entry and now extend to fields including cosmetology, interior design, computer repair, and tourism (Sanchez, Pohl, and Knepper 2022).

Furthermore, these regulations often include "grandparent provisions" exempting current practitioners from new requirements. As occupational licensing mandates are more frequently imposed to protect established businesses and professionals from competition, they serve as a substantial barrier to new market entrants and contribute to a decline in entrepreneurship. They, consequently, restrict people's ability to start their own businesses or pursue employment in certain industries, making it harder for them to put their skills to work and launch a career.

In the 2014 documentary, *Locked Out: A Mississippi Success Story*, director Sean Malone chronicles the struggles of Melony Armstrong, who fought to become the first professional African hair braider in Mississippi and to remove arbitrary regulations that stood in the way of other aspiring entrepreneurs seeking to enter the profession. As filmmaker Sean Malone explains, "For a lot of people, entrepreneurship—and even simply access to a variety of employment options—is the way to wealth and empowerment. Yet restrictions like the ones Melony faced push people into poverty, trap them in cycles of dependency, and prevent people from earning a good living doing something they actually want to do."

In recognition of this fact, some states have begun to lead the way in reform by recognizing out-of-state-licenses and by loosening market entry requirements for professions that do not pose serious health or safety risks (Gleason 2023). Considering that formerly incarcerated individuals make up a large percentage of disconnected prime-age workers, state occupational licensing boards have also been urged to consider—depending on the nature of the occupation—removing or revising legal bans on hiring individuals with a criminal record (National Conference of State Legislatures 2024).

Another potential reform that has been raised for discussion is to reframe labor regulations to allow employers to offer a range of work relationships—such as flexible schedules, telecommuting, and reduced hours—to employees with different priorities and life situations. While working from home is not for everyone, it allows those who want more time with their children, who are caregivers, or who have health conditions to continue to work. States and localities can support productive, entrepreneurial activity by those who struggle with traditional work relationships—for instance, because they are single parents, are mothers or fathers of young children, or have disabilities—by loosening oftentimes stringent home-based business zoning rules to allow for the operation of home-based businesses that do not negatively affect the local neighborhood (Dieterle and Weissman 2018).

Improving Real Wages and Opportunities for Gainful Employment

Another way to improve economic agency and engagement in the workforce is through the promotion of higher wages. Over the past several years, those calling for wage growth for American workers have primarily focused on laws mandating increases in federal, state, and local minimum wages. Proponents of raising mandated minimum wages contend that higher minimum wages boost the purchasing power of those struggling to get by and stimulate the economy by increasing productivity and consumer spending. Although the literature on wage laws is contested, the bulk of economic research now confirms that such laws have negative consequences, particularly for younger, low-wage, and low-skilled workers (Neumark and Shirley 2021). Employers faced with additional labor costs imposed by mandated wage increases generally react by hiring fewer low-skilled workers and relying more on labor-saving technology. By removing the incentive for companies to hire workers with few skills and little experience who are expensive to train, minimum-wage increases have the unintended effect of pushing the least-skilled and experienced employees, usually teenagers and minorities, out of the labor market altogether. When low-skilled and inexperienced workers are priced out of jobs through minimum-wage laws, they lose not only current compensation but also valuable job training opportunities, professional references, and so on that will allow them to demand higher wages in the future. In fact, most minimum-wage workers move on to higher-paying jobs within a year (Furchtgott-Roth 2016). In short, forcing wages upward by political mandate effectively restricts the ability of many people to prepare themselves for more lucrative work in the future and consequently reduces their lifetime earning potential.

One proposal to combat the negative effect that mandated wage hikes have on the employment prospects and long-term earning potential is to allow young people to work for a lower wage than older Americans. While some business owners are reluctant to hire young, inexperienced, and untested job applicants with few professional skills at higher wages, they might reconsider employing and training them if they are able to offer a lower wage for a short period. Opponents maintain, however, that allowing lower wages for young people is a form of age-based discrimination that could lead to exploitation (Mast 2024). Another alternative approach that has been proposed to increase wages without reducing labor demand is a government-funded direct hourly wage subsidy (Cass 2015). In contrast to a tax benefit paid out in a lump sum at the end of the fiscal year, such as the already existing earned-income tax credit, a wage subsidy is paid in real time as part of a regular paycheck for each hour worked. A direct wage subsidy has the distinct advantages of incentivizing work but is not without its challenges (Social Capital Project 2021). For example, employers could simply use the subsidy as an excuse to lower wages and let the government pay the difference. Additionally, unlike the earned-income tax credit, wage subsidies would not benefit equally those who work seasonally, part time, or as independent contractors.

Other suggestions for improving gainful employment opportunities for America's poor and working class include rethinking globalization and neoliberal trade policies and improving worker bargaining power through labor reform. In some ways globalization and loosening of international trade policies have greatly benefited ordinary Americans. Clothing and other household commodities are more affordable thanks to an influx of imported goods, and millions of Americans employed in the export-import industry. But globalization and financialization also severed the link between capital investment and domestic employment and production as corporate profits no were no longer dependent upon a domestic workforce or producing anything of value (Elsby, Hobijn, and Şahin 2013). Consequently, unrestricted trade and global markets have also disproportionately benefited shareholders in multinational industries and the wealthy and have exposed working-class Americans to massive trade deficits, competition from exploited cheap foreign labor, job losses, and decimated communities as entire industries shifted overseas.

Restoring America's productive capacities and domestic gainful employment opportunities will require careful consideration and potential adoption of policies designed to re-balance trade, foster large-scale industrial innovation, and impose constraints on competition from low-wage and exploited foreign labor. Improving American workers' bargaining power through labor reform and the restoration of less-politicized private sector unions that are better equipped to meet the unique needs of the twenty-first century, predominantly postindustrial workers might also prove a valuable means of enhancing stable employment, good working conditions, and higher wages (Social Capital Project 2021).

Expanding Access to Higher Education and Training

It is well established that the current generation of young people enrolled in Kindergarten through high school will have a difficult time achieving gainful employment, economic stability, and upward mobility without some level of postsecondary education or training, whether in the form of a traditional bachelor's degree, an associate's degree, or an occupational certificate. From grade school on, young people are likely to hear repeatedly from teachers, mentors, and guidance counselors that a college education is essential for future employability. Elected leaders across the political spectrum have additionally responded to this reality by offering various proposals to increase access to, enrollment in, and affordability of a traditional university education.

While those with more education in addition to work experience perform much better in the job market statistically, it is unclear whether increasing access to traditional four-year college degrees on its own is the best means of ensuring higher levels of employment and intergenerational income mobility. Poor students who do enroll in college are typically concentrated in less selective schools with low graduation and success rates. Many advocates for low-income youth have suggested measures to increase the percentage of those from disadvantaged backgrounds in the country's most elite institutions of higher learning by means of informational awareness, financial support, and admission preference (Holzer and Baum 2017).

Even with increased recruitment and assistance efforts, however, the number of low-income youth who are qualified and equipped for admission and success in the nation's most selective schools is statistically minimal. Aside from addressing systemic preparation gaps in K-12 education, real change will ultimately require effective practices and strategies to improve success rates at the vast majority of postsecondary schools attended by high percentages of low-income youth.

One of the biggest factors contributing to low rates of college success and completion among disadvantaged youth is their lack of a social or familial support system and working knowledge of how to manage time, prioritize tasks, effectively complete assignments, and otherwise thrive in an academic setting (Kuh et al. 2006). Thus, another commonly proposed approach for improving student success rates among those from disadvantaged backgrounds is to provide, and even require, a range of support services such as peer-learning communities, counseling, tutoring, and coaching. While a variety of intervention strategies have been implemented at schools across the country with mixed results, one practice that shows significant promise in improving college completion rates is the use of coaches as student mentors (Bettinger and Baker 2014).

While improving degree completion rates among those who enroll in postsecondary education will go a long way to improving youth employment prospects, significantly increasing graduates' potential for labor market success in remunerative skilled careers will require further bridging of the divide between skill supply and demand. Incidentally, institutions of higher learning could drastically improve the prospects of their graduates both by increasing students' opportunities for work-based applied learning experiences and by improving school ties with employers and local industries. One proposal for improving college affordability and ensuring that students have marketable work experience when they enter the labor market is to expand the number and reach of work colleges (Furchtgott-Roth and Meyer 2015). Work Colleges are accredited institutions of higher education that have a proven record of helping students of limited means—many of whom are first-generation college students—obtain a quality liberal arts college education, while developing transferable real-world professional skills without being burdened by debt.

Another way postsecondary institutions can encourage hands-on experiential learning and postgraduate employment success is through the support of internships and field projects. Students who participate in internships and classroom-based field projects can acquire real-world experience and develop valuable professional connections for future employment.

In recent years, a wide array of individuals have challenged the "college for all" mantra, arguing that it is inhibiting the expansion of valuable postsecondary education and training alternatives, particularly those tailored to meet the needs of poor and disadvantaged youth. Instead, they call for an exploration of the benefits of nontraditional constructive approaches to postsecondary education in addition to conventional four-year degrees. In fact, there are several other reliable and effective alternative paths to learning—outside of enrollment in traditional postsecondary programs—that can help youth obtain the skills, capacities, and experiences to thrive in the labor market and improve their postsecondary education outcomes should they eventually choose that route.

Among these promising routes to occupational success are apprenticeships and career and technical education beginning as early as high school. According to the Organization for Economic Co-operation and Development (2023), more than 40 percent of high school students in most developed countries other than the United States are enrolled in career pathways that emphasize technical training and direct work experience. Although middle-skill careers in fields that require technical training or apprenticeships—such as computer technology, high-skill manufacturing, service and healthcare technicians, construction, plumbing, and other fields—are often stigmatized as being filled by those who "are not college material," many of these jobs pay more than the median annual salary earned by those with a bachelor's degree (Manno 2020). Furthermore, while such middle-skill jobs account for more than half of the labor market, less than 45 percent of workers are sufficiently trained to fill them (Selingo 2017).

Enhancing Opportunity by Strengthening Families and Communities

Restoring higher rates of upward mobility and greater likelihood of achieving the American Dream among the American populace will ultimately require not just good economic policy, but also a reinvigoration of the familial and community support systems so essential to them. As discussed previously, family structures are highly correlated to poverty levels. Thus, W. Bradford Wilcox (2023), the director of the National Marriage Project at the University of Virginia, contends that the fragility of American family life, especially among the poor and working class, demands a strong public policy response. In turn, he suggests three legislative steps that he says taken together would improve the affordability and appeal of marriage and family life for ordinary Americans. First, he contends that the federal government should revise many of the means-tested programs and policies, such as Medicaid and the Earned Income Tax Credit (EITC), that penalize marriage, especially for working-class families earning between $25,000 and $50,000. One way that Congress could solve this problem is by doubling the income thresholds for these programs for married families compared to single-parent families.

Because children benefit from being raised in a home headed by their married parents with at least one parent engaged in the labor force, Watson secondly suggests that Congress strengthen the financial foundations of working families by allocating a permanent yearly financial benefit to families with at least $10,000 in earned income. Lastly, in an effort to overcome substantial cultural and social obstacles to marriage among young poor and working-class adults, Watson proposes federally funded grants to states and nonprofits to develop innovative public service campaigns and programs on behalf of the Success Sequence. The Success Sequence is based on evidence showing that 86 percent of young adults who get at least a high school degree, work full time in their 20s, and marry before having children reach the middle class or higher by their 30s, and 97 percent avoid poverty in adulthood. Such campaigns and programs, he maintains, could be modeled after previous campaigns aimed at steering social norms in a different direction, such as those related to drunk driving, teenage pregnancy, and smoking.

Others, such as Richard Reeves of the Brookings Institute, have suggested that "given that so many children are being raised in families of different sizes, and with different levels of stability and resources, a key goal for policy [should be] to reduce the impact of family instability, or lack of familial resources on the life chances of children" (Reeves 2018b). Such strategies to mitigate the effects of the family gap, Reeves contends, fall into three broad categories. The first is to enhance the material resources of single-parent, cohabitating, or unstable houses through transfer payments, tax credits, higher minimum wages, childcare support, or some combination of these. Like Wilcox, however, Reeves argues that care should be given to avoid structuring support in a way that reduces incentives for paid work and family formation. Second, Reeves advocates for policies and programs designed to improve parenting skills, especially among the less educated. Finally, Reeves calls for enhancing learning opportunities for children outside the home.

In addition to families, the communities in which children grow up play a significant role in their future well-being and success (Chetty et al. 2014). In his book on social alienation and poverty in communities across America, American Enterprise Institute fellow Timothy Carney (2019) points out the neighborhoods in which familial, civic, and religious ties and institutions are strong are far less likely to suffer from social alienation and physical and economic decline. Carney suggests that giving local governments and communities more control over their civic institutions, such as primary and secondary schools, and promoting policies that encourage rather than discourage the development of local charities, volunteerism, and involvement with local churches, synagogues, or mosques can go a long way toward strengthening the bonds of community. He additionally contends that local and state governments can play an important role in overcoming social alienation and isolation among their residents by rejecting policies, such as the extension of lavish tax breaks to shopping centers that help kill main street businesses or burden city budgets. They can also strive to build towns and cities in a way that is more conducive to walkability, neighborliness, and community building. Others, such as Brooking Institute scholars Martha Ross and Nicole Bateman (2020), have advocated incentivizing and expanding national services opportunities—such as those offered by AmeriCorps, YouthBuild, and Conservation Corps—as a means of decreasing social division, strengthening communities, and improving social capital among youth and young adults.

Conclusion

In contrast to earlier periods when economic growth was spread more evenly throughout the population, over the past several decades economic growth in America has been concentrated in the top-income quintile. Members of the country's professional and affluent classes increasingly live geographically and experientially segregated lives from low-income and working-class Americans who are more vulnerable to unemployment, ruinous medical expenses, and other drivers of poverty.

This is problematic for reasons that extend beyond economic hardship. As Wells King (2020) contends, the American Dream is about more than economic success or wage growth. Rather, for most Americans, "It is about sharing a common life within the families and communities that those wages support." In essence, it is about having the opportunity for a dignified way of life, one that for many requires the ability to have a good family life, achieve middle-class security, retire comfortably, and make valuable contributions to the community in which they live (Pew 2017). In this sense, the divide in America is not just economic, but social, moral, and cultural as well. Improving opportunities for Americans to thrive based on these goals will require engagement on all fronts but can ultimately begin with efforts to alleviate economic barriers to employment success and upward mobility, to equip Americans to thrive in the twenty-first-century marketplace through education reform, and to strengthen the bonds of family and communities as essential agents in the nurturing of productive and thriving citizens.

Bibliography

Aguiar, Mark, Mark Bliss, Kerwin Kofi Charles, and Eric Hurst. 2017. *Leisure Luxuries and the Labor Supply of Young Men*. Cambridge, MA: National Bureau of Economic Research. Accessed March 28, 2024. https://www.nber.org/papers/w23552.

American Compass. 2022a. "Where's the Growth?" March. Accessed March 1, 2024. https://americancompass.org/wp-content/uploads/2022/10/AC-Atlas-Wheres-the-Growth.pdf.

American Compass. 2022b. "A Guide to College-For-All." January 19. Accessed on March 25, 2024. https://americancompass.org/a-guide-to-college-for-all/.

Arnade, Chris. 2019. *Dignity: Seeking Respect in Back Row America*. New York: Penguin Random House.

Austen, Benjamin, Edward Glaeser, and Lawrence Summers. 2018. "Jobs for the Heartland: Place-based Policies in 21st Century America." *Brookings Papers on Economic Activity*. Spring: 151–255. Accessed March 24, 2024. https://www.brookings.edu/articles/saving-the-heartland-place-based-policies-in-21st-century-america/.

Azerrad, David, and Rea S. Hederman Jr. 2012. "Defending the Dream: Why Income Inequality Doesn't Threaten Opportunity." Special Report No. 119. *The Heritage Foundation*. September 13. Accessed March 8, 2024. https://www.heritage.org/poverty-and-inequality/report/defending-the-dream-why-income-inequality-doesnt-threaten-opportunity.

Bahney, Anna. 2024. "Homeownership Gap between Black and White Owners Is Worse Now than It Was a Decade Ago." *CNN*. February 20. Accessed March 19, 2024. https://www.cnn.com/2024/02/20/economy/black-white-homeownership-gap/index.html.

Belfield, Clive R., Henry M. Levin, and Rachel Rosen. 2012. "The Economic Value of Opportunity Youth." *Civic Enterprises*. January. Accessed March 28, 2024. https://files.eric.ed.gov/fulltext/ED528650.pdf.

Bettinger and Baker. 2014. "The Effects of Student Coaching: An Evaluation of a Randomized Experiment in Student Advising." *Educational Evaluation and Policy Analysis* 36 (1): 3–19.

Burkhauser, Richard V., Kevin C. Corinth, Bruce D. Meyer, Angela Rachidi, Matt Weidinger, and Scott Winship. 2021. "Addressing the Shortcomings of the Supplemental Poverty Measure." *American Enterprise Institute.* July. Accessed March 3, 2024. https://www.aei.org/research-products/report/addressing-the-shortcomings-of-the-supplemental-poverty-measure/.

Cannato, Vincent J. 2010. "A Home of One's Own." *National Affairs.* Spring. Accessed March 19, 2024. https://www.nationalaffairs.com/publications/detail/a-home-of-ones-own.

Carnevale, Anthony P. 2012. "The Great Sorting." *Chronicle of Higher Education.* July 2. Accessed March 25, 2024. https://www.chronicle.com/article/the-great-sorting/.

Carnevale, Anthony P., Nicole Smith, Martin Van Der Werf, and Michael C. Quinn. 2023. "After Everything: Projections of Jobs, Education, and Training Requirements through 2031." Georgetown University Center on Education and the Workforce. Accessed March 25, 2024. https://cew.georgetown.edu/wp-content/uploads/Projections2031-National-Report.pdf.

Carney, Timothy P. 2019. *Alienated America: Why Some Places Thrive While Others Collapse.* New York: HarperCollins.

Cass, Oren. 2015. "The Wage Subsidy: A Better Way to Help the Poor." *The Manhattan Institute for Policy Research*, Issue Brief 37. August. Accessed April 3, 2024. https://media4.manhattan-institute.org/sites/default/files/ib_37.pdf.

Center for Poverty and Inequality Research. 2017. "How Is Poverty Measured in the United States." *UC Davis.* Accessed on March 1, 2024. https://poverty.ucdavis.edu/faq/how-poverty-measured-united-states.

Chang, Alvin. 2023. "How Fining a Home in America Became so Absurdly Expensive." *The Guardian.* May 10. Accessed March 19, 2024. https://www.theguardian.com/us-news/2023/may/10/us-housing-market-prices-increasing.

Chetty, Raj, Nathaniel Hendren, Patrick Kline, and Emmanuel Saez. 2014. "Where Is the Land of Opportunity? The Geography of Intergenerational Mobility in the United States." *Quarterly Journal of Economics* 129 (4): 1553–623.

Chetty, Raj, David Grusky, Maximilian Hell, Nathaniel Hendren, Robert Manduca, and Jimmy Narang. 2017. "The Fading American Dream: Trends in Absolute Income Mobility since 1940." *Science* 356 (6336): 398–406.

Childers, Chandra. 2023. "The Expiration of Pandemic-Era Public Assistance Measures Fueled Poverty Increases in the Majority of States." *Working Economics Blog.* Economic Policy Institute. September 28. Accessed March 1, 2024. https://www.epi.org/blog/the-expiration-of-pandemic-era-public-assistance-measures-fueled-poverty-increases-in-every-state/#:~:text=When%20using%20the%20more%20comprehensive,Credit%20were%20allowed%20to%20expire.

Collins, Michael. 2023. "The Post-Industrial Service Economy Isn't Working for the Middle Class." *Industry Week.* August 11. Accessed March 22, 2024. https://www.

industryweek.com/the-economy/data-and-statistics/article/21271497/the-post-industrial-service-economy-isnt-working.

Congressional Budget Office (CBO). 2023. "The Distribution of Household Income in 2020." November 1. Accessed March 7, 2024. https://www.cbo.gov/system/files/2023-11/59509-household-income_2019-2020.pdf.

Cooper, Preston. 2018. "College Enrollment Surges among Low Income Students." *Forbes*. February 26. Accessed March 26, 2024. https://www.forbes.com/sites/prestoncooper2/2018/02/26/college-enrollment-surges-among-low-income-students/?sh=ddaa327293b9.

Crocket, Anna, and Xiaohan Zhang. 2023. "Young Adults Are Disconnected from Work and School Due to Long-term Labor Force Trends." *Federal Reserve Bank of Dallas*. April 6. Accessed March 28, 2024. https://www.dallasfed.org/cd/communities/2023/2303#:~:text=This%20percentage%2C%20called%20the%20disconnection,the%20onset%20of%20the%20pandemic.

Curry, Benjamin. 2023. "What Happens When the Fed Raises Interest Rates?" *Forbes*. June 21. Accessed March 19, 2024. https://www.forbes.com/advisor/investing/fed-raises-interest-rates/.

Desilver, Drew. 2017. "U.S. Academic Achievement Still Lags That of Their Peers in Many Other Countries." *Pew Research Center*. February 15. Accessed May 9, 2024. https://www.pewresearch.org/short-reads/2017/02/15/u-s-students-internationally-math-science/.

Dieterle, C. Jarrett, and Shoshana Weissman. 2018. "When the City Comes for Your Home Based Business." *The Wall Street Journal*. July 15. Accessed April 3, 2024. https://www.wsj.com/articles/when-the-city-comes-for-your-home-based-business-1531691394.

Dolan, Ed 2022. "Work Disincentives Hit the Near-Poor Hardest: Why and What to Do about It." *Niskanen Center*. May 5. Accessed April 2, 2024. https://www.niskanencenter.org/work-disincentives-hit-the-near-poor-hardest-why-and-what-to-do-about-it/.

Dollar, Cindy Brooks, Ellen A. Donnelly, and Karen F. Parker. 2019. "Joblessness, Poverty, and Neighborhood Crime: Testing Wilson's Assertions of Jobless Poverty." *Social Currents* 6 (4): 343–60.

Douglass, Frederick. 1872. "Self-made Men." Accessed March 8, 2024. https://teachingamericanhistory.org/document/self-made-men/.

Dynarski, Mark. 2018. "Is the Highschool Graduation Rate Really Going Up?" *Brookings*. May 3. Accessed March 25, 2024. https://www.brookings.edu/articles/is-the-high-school-graduation-rate-really-going-up/.

Eberstadt, Nicholas. 2016. *America's Invisible Crisis: Men without Work*. West Conshohocken, PA: Templeton Press.

Economic Innovation Group (EIG). 2016. "New Map of Economic Growth and Recovery." May. Accessed March 22, 2014. https://eig.org/wp-content/uploads/2016/05/recoverygrowthreport.pdf.

Economic Innovation Group (EIG). n.d. "Distressed Communities Index." Accessed March 22, 2024. https://eig.org/distressed-communities/?geo=states&lat=26.45&lon=-48.7&z=2.88.

Edin, Kathrin, and Maria Kafalas. 2005. *Promises I Can Keep: Why Poor Women Put Motherhood before Marriage*. Berkeley, CA: University of California Press.

Elejalde-Ruiz, Alexia. 2017. "Report Says Youth Unemployment Chronic, Concentrated and Deeply Rooted." *Chicago Tribune.* January 2017. Accessed March 20, 2018. http://www.chicagotribune.com/business/ct-youth-unemployment-data-0129-biz-20170127-story.html.

Elsby, Michae W.L., Bart Hobijn, and Ayşegul Şahin. 2013. "The Decline of U.S. Labor Share." Washington, DC: Brookings Institution. Accessed April 3, 2024. https://www.brookings.edu/wp-content/uploads/2016/07/2013b_elsby_labor_share.pdf.

Fischer, Karin. 2013. "The Employment Mismatch." *The Chronicle of Higher Education.* March 4. Accessed March 26, 2024. https://www.chronicle.com/article/the-employment-mismatch/.

Fischer, Karin. 2016. "Engine of Inequality." *Chronicle of Higher Education.* January 17. Accessed March 25, 2024. https://www.chronicle.com/article/engine-of-inequality/.

Fisher, Gordon M. 1992. "The Development and History of the Poverty Thresholds." *Social Security Bulletin* 55 (4): 3–14.

Florida, Richard. 2017. "The Class Geography of New York City." *Bloomberg.* March 28. Accessed March 22, 2024. https://www.bloomberg.com/news/articles/2017-03-28/a-class-portrait-of-new-york-s-tale-of-two-cities.

Frankfurt, Harry G. 2015. *On Inequality*. Princeton, NJ: Princeton University Press.

Furchtgott-Roth, Diana. 2016. "Raising the Minimum Wage Lowers Employment for Teens and Low Skill Workers." *PBS*. December 16. Accessed April 3, 2024. https://www.pbs.org/newshour/economy/column-minimum-wage-lowers-employment-teens-low-skill-workers.

Furchtgott-Roth, Diana, and Jared Meyer. 2015. *Disinherited: How Washington Is Betraying America's Youth*. New York: Encounter Books.

Gleason, Patrick. 2023. "Barriers to Employment Fall in Some States Thanks to Licensing Reform." *Forbes*. March 21. Accessed April 1, 2024. https://www.forbes.com/sites/patrickgleason/2023/03/21/barriers-to-employment-fall-with-the-rise-of-out-of-state-occupational-license-recognition/?sh=2b053bcf64a9.

Golub, Harvey. 2013. "The Tragedy of Teenage Unemployment." *Real Clear Markets.* December 5. Accessed March 27, 2024. https://www.realclearmarkets.com/articles/2013/12/05/the_tragedy_of_teenage_unemployment_100777.html.

Gramm, Phil, and John Early. 2021. "Incredible Shrinking Income Inequality." *The Wall Street Journal*. March 23. Accessed April 1, 2024. https://www.wsj.com/articles/incredible-shrinking-income-inequality-11616517284.

Gramm, Phil, and John Early. 2023. "Another Wrong Way to Measure Poverty." *Wall Street Journal*. December 5. Accessed March 1, 2024. https://www.wsj.com/articles/another-wrong-way-to-measure-poverty-welfare-biden-fd9018b1.

Gramm, Phil, Robert Ekelund, and John Early. 2022. *The Myth of American Inequality: How Government Biases Policy Debate*. Lanham, MD: Rowman & Littlefield.

Greenstone, Michael, and Adam Looney. 2012. "The Marriage Gap: The Impact of Economic and Technological Change on Marriage Rates." *Brookings*. February 3. Accessed March 23, 2024. https://www.brookings.edu/articles/the-marriage-gap-the-impact-of-economic-and-technological-change-on-marriage-rates/.

Guryan, Jonathan, and Jens Ludwig. 2014. "Why Half of Urban Kids Drop Out." *CNN*. March 12. Accessed March 25, 2024. https://www.cnn.com/2014/03/12/opinion/ludwig-guryan-chicago-education/index.html.

Hansen, Michael. 2021. "The U.S. Education System Isn't Giving Students What Employers Need." *Harvard Business Review*. May 18. Accessed March 26, 2024. https://hbr.org/2021/05/the-u-s-education-system-isnt-giving-students-what-employers-need.

Hederman, Rea, and David Azerrad. 2012. "Defending the Dream: Why Income Inequality Doesn't Threaten Opportunity." *The Heritage Foundation*. September 13. Accessed March 6, 2024. https://www.heritage.org/poverty-and-inequality/report/defending-the-dream-why-income-inequality-doesnt-threaten-opportunity.

Hoffman, Liz, and Jennifer Maloney. 2020. "For Many Big Businesses, 2020 Was a Surprisingly Good Year." *The Wall Street Journal*. December 18. Accessed March 18, 2024. https://www.wsj.com/articles/for-many-big-businesses-2020-was-a-surprisingly-good-year-11608310791.

Holzer, Harry J., and Sandy Baum. 2017. *Making College Work: Pathways to Success for Disadvantaged Students*. Washington, DC: Brookings Institution Press.

Hornstein, Andreas, Marios Karabarbounis, André Kurmann, Etienne Lalé, and Lien Ta. 2023. "Disincentive Effects of Unemployment Insurance Benefits." *Federal Reserve Bank of Richmond*. Accessed May 9, 2024. https://www.richmondfed.org/-/media/RichmondFedOrg/publications/research/working_papers/2023/wp23-11.pdf.

Horowitz, Juliana M., Ruth Igielnik, and Rakesh Kochhar. 2020. "Trends in Income and Wealth Inequality." *Pew Research Center*. January 9. Accessed March 16, 2024. https://www.pewresearch.org/social-trends/2020/01/09/trends-in-income-and-wealth-inequality/.

Institute for Policy Studies. 2024. "Total U.S. Billionaire Wealth: Up 88 Percent over Four Years." March 18. Accessed March 20, 2024. https://inequality.org/great-divide/updates-billionaire-pandemic/.

Isaacs, Julia B., Isabel V. Sawhill, and Ron Haskins. *Getting Ahead or Losing Ground: Economic Mobility in America*. Washington, DC: The Brookings Institution.

Katz, Lily. 2024. "Investors Bought 26 Percent of the Country's Most Affordable Homes in the Fourth Quarter—The Highest Share on Record." *Redfin*. February 14. Accessed March 19, 2024. https://www.redfin.com/news/investor-home-purchases-q4-2023/.

Kearney, Melissa S. 2017. "What Does Culture Have to Do with the American Dream?" *Institute for Family Studies*. May 22. Accessed March 23, 2024. https://ifstudies.org/blog/what-does-culture-have-to-do-with-the-american-dream.

Kearney, Melissa S. 2023. "The Two-parent Privilege. How American's Stopped Getting Married and Started Falling Behind." Chicago, IL: University of Chicago Press.

Kent, Ana Hernández, and Lowell R. Rickets. "Disparities by Race, Ethnicity, and Education Underlie Millennials' Comeback in Wealth." *Federal Reserve Bank of St. Louis*. April 1. Accessed March 18, 2024. https://www.stlouisfed.org/on-the-economy/2021/april/disparities-race-ethnicity-education-millennials-comeback-wealth#.

King, Wells. 2020. "American Scream." *First Things*. May. Accessed March 15, 2024. https://www.firstthings.com/article/2020/05/american-scream.

King, Wells. 2021. "The Rich Get Richer, the Middle Class Shrinks, and Conservatives Must Act." *The Daily Caller*. April 20. Accessed March 16, 2024. https://dailycaller.com/2021/04/20/king-income-inequality-endangers-america/.

Kochhar, Rakesh, and Stella Sechopoulos. 2022. "COVID-19 Pandemic Pinches Finances of America's Lower- and Middle-income Families." *Pew Research Center*. April 20. Accessed March 18, 2024. https://www.pewresearch.org/social-trends/2022/04/20/covid-19-pandemic-pinches-finances-of-americas-lower-and-middle-income-families/.

Kotkin, Joel. 2014. "Where Inequality Is Worst in the United States." March 20. Accessed March 22, 2024. https://www.forbes.com/sites/joelkotkin/2014/03/20/where-inequality-is-worst-in-the-united-states/?sh=5765f023327c.

Kotkin, Joel. 2019. "The End of Aspiration." *Quillette*. April 10. Accessed March 15, 2024. https://quillette.com/2019/04/10/the-end-of-aspiration/.

Kotkin, Joel. 2020. *The Coming of Neo-Feudalism: A Warning to the Global Middle Class*. New York: Encounter Books.

Kotkin, Joel. 2022. "There Is Nothing Progressive about a Universal Basic Income." *Spiked*. October 11. Accessed April 1, 2024. https://www.spiked-online.com/2022/10/11/there-is-nothing-progressive-about-a-universal-basic-income/.

Kramer, Stephanie. 2019. "U.S. Has the World's Highest Rate of Children Living in Single-Parent Households." *Pew Research Center*. December 12. Accessed March 23, 2024. https://www.pewresearch.org/short-reads/2019/12/12/u-s-children-more-likely-than-children-in-other-countries-to-live-with-just-one-parent/.

Kuh, George D., Jillian Kinzie, Jennifer A. Buckley, Brian Bridges, and John C. Hayek. 2006. "What Matters to Student Success: A Review of the Literature." Commissioned

Report for the National Symposium on Postsecondary Student Success: Spearheading a Dialog on Student Success. *National Postsecondary Education Cooperative* (July). Accessed May 12, 2024. https://nces.ed.gov/npec/pdf/kuh_team_report.pdf.

Kuhfeld, Megan, Jim Soland, Karyn Lewis, and Emily Morton. 2022. "The Pandemic Has Had Devastating Impacts on Learning. What Will It Take to Help Students Catch Up?" *Brookings*. March 3. Accessed March 15, 2024. https://www.brookings.edu/articles/the-pandemic-has-had-devastating-impacts-on-learning-what-will-it-take-to-help-students-catch-up/.

Lester, David. 1996. "The Impact of Unemployment on Marriage and Divorce." *Journal of Divorce and Remarriage* 25 (3–4): 151–3.

Lindsay, Jay. 2023. "Research Indicates Foreign Investment in Real Estate Has Underappreciated Impacts." *Federal Reserve Bank of Boston*. November 14. Accessed March 19, 2024. https://www.bostonfed.org/news-and-events/news/2023/11/china-massive-us-real-estate-investment-housing-shock-major-impacts-leslie-shen-boston-fed.aspx.

Locked Out: A Mississippi Success Story. 2014. Directed by Sean W. Malone. Honest Enterprise.

Lowrey, Annie. 2021. "Why Millennials Can't Grow Up." *The Atlantic*. May 13. Accessed March 10, 2024. https://www.theatlantic.com/ideas/archive/2021/05/millennial-grandparents-unequal-generation/618859/.

Lutton, Linda. 2019. "The Middle Class Is Shrinking Everywhere—In Chicago It's Almost Gone." *WBEZ Chicago*. February 19. Accessed March 1, 2024. https://www.wbez.org/stories/the-middle-class-is-shrinking-everywhere-in-chicago-its-almost-gone/e63cb407-5d1e-41b1-9124-a717d4fb1b0b.

Manno, Bruno V. 2020. "A Social Capital Approach to Education Reform." *National Affairs*. Fall. Accessed April 2, 2024. https://www.nationalaffairs.com/publications/detail/a-social-capital-approach-to-education-reform.

Massey, Douglas S., Jonathan Rothwell, and Thurston Domina. 2009. "The Changing Bases of Segregation in the United States." *The Annals of the American Academy of Political and Social Science* 626: 74–90.

Mast, Nina. 2024. "Youth Subminimum Wages and Why They Should Be Eliminated." *Economic Policy Institute*. January 8. Accessed May 12, 2024. https://www.epi.org/blog/youth-subminimum-wages/.

Mastrangelo, Dominick. 2022. "We're Using 1960s Guidance to Measure Poverty in 2022." *The Hill*. November 8. Accessed March 3, 2024. https://thehill.com/opinion/finance/3724866-were-using-1960s-guidance-to-measure-poverty-in-2022/.

McElwee, Sean. 2014. "Absolute and Relative Mobility, A Short Primer." *Demos*. January 23. Accessed March 15, 2024. https://www.demos.org/blog/absolute-and-relative-mobility-short-primer.

McLanahan, Sara, and Isabel Sawhill. 2015. "Marriage and Child Wellbeing Revisited: Introducing the Issue." *Future of Children* 25 (2): 3–9.

Mervosh, Sarah, and Francesca Paris. 2024. "Why School Absences Have 'Exploded' Almost Everywhere." *New York Times*. March 29. Accessed April 1, 2024. https://www.nytimes.com/interactive/2024/03/29/us/chronic-absences.html?action=click&block=storyline_top_links_recirc&module=styln-us-schools&pgtype=Article&region=MAIN_CONTENT_1&state=default&variant=show.

Meyer, Bruce D., and James X. Sullivan. 2017. "Annual Report on U.S. Consumption Poverty: 2017." University of Notre Dame. Accessed March 3, 2024. https://www3.nd.edu/~jsulliv4/2017%20Consumption%20Poverty%20Report%20Meyer%20Sullivan%20final.pdf.

Michaelson, John. 2018. "America's Lost Decade." *City Journal*. Winter. Accessed March 26, 2024. https://www.city-journal.org/article/americas-lost-decade#:~:text=The%20economic%20legacy%20of%20the,America%20is%20incredibly%20resilient.

Mitnik, Pablo A., and David B. Grusky. 2015. "Economic Mobility in the United States." *Pew Charitable Trusts*. July. Accessed March 28, 2024. https://www.pewtrusts.org/en/research-and-analysis/reports/2015/07/economic-mobility-in-the-united-states.

Mohammed, Omar. 2023. "Housing Crisis Could Be the Death Knell for America's Middle Class." *Newsweek*. December 12. Accessed March 19, 2024. https://www.newsweek.com/housing-crisis-could-death-knell-americas-middle-class-1848936.

Morsy, Hana. 2012. "Scarred Generation." *Finance and Development* 49 (1): 15–17.

Mossakowski, Krysia. 2009. "The Influence of Past Unemployment Duration on Symptoms of Depression among Young Women and Men in the United States." *American Journal of Public Health* 99: 1826–32.

Napoletano, E. 2022. "An Unexpected Outcome of the Covid-19 Pandemic: A Slew of Universal Income Programs." *Forbes*. May 12. https://www.forbes.com/advisor/personal-finance/universal-basic-income-programs/.

National Assessment of Educational Progress. 2024. "Results from the 2019 Mathematics and Reading Assessments at Grade 12." Accessed March 25, 2024. https://nces.ed.gov/nationsreportcard/.

National Association of Realtors (NAR). 2021. "Student Loan Debt Holding back Majority of Millennials from Home Ownership." September 14. Accessed March 19, 2024. https://www.nber.org/papers/w28388.

National Center for Education Statistics. 2022. "Undergraduate Graduation Rates." Accessed March 26, 2024. https://nces.ed.gov/fastfacts/display.asp?id=40.

National Center for Education Statistics. 2023. "Public High School Graduation Rates." Accessed March 25, 2024. https://nces.ed.gov/programs/coe/indicator/coi/high-school-graduation-rates.

National Conference of State Legislatures. 2024. "Barriers to Work: Increasing Access to Licensed Occupations for Individuals with Criminal Records." Accessed April 2,

2024. https://www.ncsl.org/labor-and-employment/barriers-to-work-improving-employment-in-licensed-occupations-for-individuals-with-criminal-records.

Neumark, David, and Peter Shirley. 2021. "Myth or Measurement: What Does the New Minimum Wage Research Say about Minimum Wages and Job Loss in the United States?" Working Paper 28388, National Bureau of Economic Research. May. Accessed April 3, 2024.

Ney, Jeremy. 2023. "The Surprising Poverty Levels across the U.S." *Time*. October 4. Accessed March 1, 2024. https://time.com/6320076/american-poverty-levels-state-by-state/.

Obama, Barack. 2013. "Remarks by the President on Economic Mobility." December 4. Accessed March 6, 2024. https://obamawhitehouse.archives.gov/the-press-office/2013/12/04/remarks-president-economic-mobility.

O'Donnell, Tim. 2020. "Fed Survey Shows almost 40 Percent of American Households Making Less than $40,000 Lost a Job in March." *The Week*. May 13. Accessed March 18, 2024. https://theweek.com/speedreads/914236/fed-survey-shows-almost-40-percent-american-households-making-less-than-40k-lost-job-march.

Offenheiser, Ray. 2022. "Inequality, Dignity, and Despair." Keough School of Global Affairs, University of Notre Dame. November 3. Accessed March 15, 2024. https://keough.nd.edu/inequality-dignity-and-despair/#:~:text=It%20was%20the%20Golden%20Age,parks%2C%20education%2C%20and%20health.

Okantey, Beth. 2024. "Are Universal and Guaranteed Basic Income Programs Effective in the United States? A Review." *Research on Social Work Practice* 34 (4): 384–401.

Opportunity Insights. 2024. "How Can We Amplify Education as an Engine of Mobility." Accessed March 25, 2024. https://opportunityinsights.org/education/.

Organization for Economic Co-operation and Development (OECD). 2023. "Vocational Training Will Be Key to Meeting Increasing Demands for Skilled Workers and Adapting to a Changing Labor Market." December 9. Accessed April 2, 2024. https://www.oecd.org/education/vocational-training-will-be-key-to-meeting-increasing-demands-for-skilled-workers-and-adapting-to-a-changing-labour-market.htm.

Ovide, Shira. 2021. "How Big Tech Won the Pandemic." *New York Times*. April 30. Accessed March 18, 2024. https://www.nytimes.com/2021/04/30/technology/big-tech-pandemic.html.

Paris, Francesca. 2024. "What Data Says about Pandemic School Closures, Four Years Later." *New York Times*. March 19. Accessed March 25, 2024. https://www.nytimes.com/2024/03/18/upshot/pandemic-school-closures-data.html?action=click&block=storyline_top_links_recirc&module=styln-us-schools&pgtype=Article&region=MAIN_CONTENT_1&state=default&variant=show.

Parker, Kim, Juliana Menasce Horowitz, and Anna Brown. 2020. "About Half of Lower-Income Americans Report Household Job or Wage Loss due to COVID-19." *Pew Research Center*. April 21. Accessed March 18, 2024. https://www.pewresearch.org/

social-trends/2020/04/21/about-half-of-lower-income-americans-report-household-job-or-wage-loss-due-to-covid-19/.

Pascus, Brian. 2023. "Who Turned the American Dream of Homeownership into a Nightmare?" *Commercial Observer*. December 11. Accessed March 19, 2024. https://commercialobserver.com/2023/12/who-turned-american-dream-single-family-housing-nightmare/.

Pew Research Center. 2017. "Few See 'Becoming Wealthy' as Essential to Their View of the American Dream." October 31. Accessed February 10, 2024. https://www.pewresearch.org/short-reads/2017/10/31/most-think-the-american-dream-is-within-reach-for-them/ft_17-10-31_americandream_definitions/.

Price, Carter C., and Kathryn A. Edwards. 2020. "Trends in Income from 1975 to 2018." Santa Monica, CA: Rand Corporation. Accessed March 15, 2024. https://www.rand.org/pubs/working_papers/WRA516-1.html.

Putnam, Robert D. 2015. *Our Kids: The American Dream in Crisis*. New York: Simon and Schuster.

Rank, Mark R. "From Rags to Riches to Rags." *New York Times*. April 18. Accessed March 7, 2024. https://www.nytimes.com/2014/04/20/opinion/sunday/from-rags-to-riches-to-rags.html.

Reeves, Richard V. 2014. "Saving Horatio Alger: Equality, Opportunity, and the American Dream." Washington, DC: Brookings Institute.

Reeves, Richard V. 2018a. *Dream Hoarders: How the American Upper Middle Class Is Leaving Everyone Else in the Dust, Why That Is a Problem, and What to Do about It*. Washington, DC: Brookings Institution Press.

Reeves, Richard V. 2018b. "Where's the Glue?: Policies to Close the Family Gap" in Naomi R. Cahn, ed. *Unequal Family Lives: Causes and Consequences in Europe and the Americas*. New York: Cambridge University Press: 216–59.

Reeves, Richard V., and Christopher Pulliam. 2020. "Middle Class Marriage Is Declining and Likely Deepening Inequality." *Brookings*. March 11. Accessed March 23, 2024. https://www.brookings.edu/articles/middle-class-marriage-is-declining-and-likely-deepening-inequality/#:~:text=One%20potential%20explanation%20for%20the,before%20having%20their%20first%20child.

Ross, Martha, and Nicole Bateman. 2020. "National Service Can Connect America's Young People to Opportunity and Community—And Promote Work of Real Social Value." *The Brookings Institution*. December 9. Accessed May 13, 2024. https://www.brookings.edu/articles/national-service-can-connect-americas-young-people-to-opportunity-and-community-and-promote-work-of-real-social-value/.

Sadowski, Jathan. 2016. "Why Silicon Valley Is Embracing Universal Basic Income." *The Guardian*. June 22. Accessed April 2, 2024. https://www.theguardian.com/technology/2016/jun/22/silicon-valley-universal-basic-income-y-combinator.

Sanchez, Kathy, Elyse Smith Pohl, and Lisa Knepper. 2022. "Too Many Licenses? Government 'Sunrise' Reviews Cast Doubt on Barriers to Work." *Institute for Justice*. Accessed March 29, 2024. https://ij.org/report/too-many-licenses/.

Sanders, Bernie. 2022. Accessed May 9, 2024. https://justfacts.votesmart.org/public-statement/1594275/tweet-when-we-talk-about-oligarchy-in-america-we-are-talking-about-700-billionaires-who-became-nearly-2-trillion-richer-during-the-pandemic-pay-a-lower-tax-rate-than-a-nurse-while-the-child-poverty.

Sassler, Sharon, and Amanda Miller. 2017. *Cohabitation Nation: Gender, Class, and the Remaking of Relationships.* Oakland, CA: University of California Press.

Sawhill, Isabel. 2014. "The Economics of Marriage and Family Breakdown." *Brookings.* July 15. Accessed March 24, 2024. https://www.brookings.edu/articles/the-economics-of-marriage-and-family-breakdown/.

Sawhill, Isabel. 2020. "Social Capital: Why We Need It and How We Can Create More of It." Washington, DC: Brookings Institution. July. Accessed March 7, 2024. https://www.brookings.edu/wp-content/uploads/2020/07/Sawhill_Social-Capital_Final_07.16.2020.pdf.

Sawhill, Isabel, and Quentin Karpilow. 2014. "Youth Unemployment Is a Problem for Social Mobility." *Brookings.* March 5. Accessed March 27, 2024. https://www.brookings.edu/articles/youth-unemployment-is-a-problem-for-social-mobility/#:~:text=The%20Most%20Disadvantaged%20Are%20Hit,have%20implications%20for%20social%20mobility.

Selingo, Jeffrey J. 2017. "Wanted: Factory Workers, Degree Required." *New York Times.* January 30. Accessed April 2, 2024. https://www.nytimes.com/2017/01/30/education/edlife/factory-workers-college-degree-apprenticeships.html.

Simon, Ruth. 2021. "COVID-19's Toll on U.S. Business? 200,000 Extra Closures in Pandemic's First Year." *The Wall Street Journal.* April 16. Accessed March 18, 2024. https://www.wsj.com/articles/covid-19s-toll-on-u-s-business-200-000-extra-closures-in-pandemics-first-year-11618580619.

Siripurapu, Anshu. 2022. "The U.S. Inequality Debate." *Council on Foreign Relations.* April 20. Accessed March 5, 2024. https://www.cfr.org/backgrounder/us-inequality-debate.

Social Capital Project. 2021. "Reconnecting Americans to the Benefits of Work." SCP Report No. 5021. U.S. Congress Joint Economic Committee. Accessed March 28, 2024. https://www.jec.senate.gov/public/_cache/files/5ac0a254-ff00-4a18-baf0-bdfedb9bb154/connections-to-work.pdf.

Statista. 2024. "Male Civilian Labor Force Participation Rate in the United States from 1990 to 2023." Accessed March 28, 2024. https://www.statista.com/statistics/191725/us-male-civilian-labor-force-participation-rate-since-1990/.

Stokes, Bruce. 2017. "Public Divided on Prospects for Next Generation." *Pew Research Center.* June 5. Accessed March 16, 2024. https://www.pewresearch.org/global/2017/06/05/2-public-divided-on-prospects-for-the-next-generation/.

Stone, Chad, Danilo Trisi, Arloc Sherman, and Jennifer Beltrán. 2020. "A Guide to Statistics on Historical Trends in Income Inequality." January 13. Washington, DC: Center on Budget and Policy Priorities. Accessed March 16, 2024. https://www.cbpp.org/research/poverty-and-inequality/a-guide-to-statistics-on-historical-trends-in-income-inequality.

Strain, Michael R. 2020. "The American Dream Is Not Dead: But Populism Could Kill It." Conshohocken, PA: Templeton Press.

Tomasky, Michael. 2022. *The Middle Out: The Rise of Progressive Economics and a Return to Shared Prosperity*. New York: Doubleday.

Torry, Harriet. 2023. "More High-School Grads Forgo College in Hot Labor Market." *The Wall Street Journal*. May 29. Accessed March 25. 2024. https://www.wsj.com/articles/more-high-school-grads-forgo-college-in-hot-labor-market-c052c773.

U.S. Bureau of Labor Statistics. 2021. "Projections Overview and Highlights, 2020–30." October 21. Accessed March 4, 2024. https://www.bls.gov/opub/mlr/2021/article/projections-overview-and-highlights-2020-30.htm.

U.S. Bureau of Labor Statistics. 2024. "Employment Status of Civilian Population 25 Years and Older by Educational Attainment." Accessed March 25, 2024. https://www.bls.gov/news.release/empsit.t04.htm.

U.S. Census Bureau. 2022. "Measuring America: How the U.S. Census Bureau Measures Poverty." June. Accessed March 1, 2024. https://www.census.gov/library/visualizations/2021/demo/poverty_measure-how.html.

Valdez, Roger. 2009. "A Poor Measure of Poverty." *Sightline Institute*. August 31. Accessed March 3, 2024. https://www.sightline.org/2009/08/31/a-poor-measure-of-poverty/.

Vedder, Richard, Christopher Denhar, and Jonathan Robe. 2013. *Why Are Recent College Graduates Underemployed? University Enrollments and Labor-Market Realities*. Washington, DC: Center for College Affordability and Productivity. Accessed March 25, 2024. https://files.eric.ed.gov/fulltext/ED539373.pdf.

Venator, Joanna, and Richard V. Reeves. 2013. "Parental Unemployment Hurts Kids' Futures and Social Mobility." *Brookings*. November 25. Accessed March 27, 2024. https://www.brookings.edu/articles/parental-unemployment-hurts-kids-futures-and-social-mobility/.

Vogel, Peter. 2015. *Generation Jobless? Turning the Youth Unemployment Crisis into Opportunity*. New York: Palgrave Macmillan.

Wax, Amy. 2011. "Diverging Family Structure and 'Rational' Behavior: The Decline in Marriage as a Disorder of Choice" in Lloyd R. Cohen and Joshua D. Wright, eds. *Research Handbook on the Economics of Family Law*. Cheltenham: Edward Elgar: 15–71.

Weber, Lauren. 2024. "62% of Americans Lack a College Degree. Can They Solve the Labor Shortage?" *The Wall Street Journal*. February 16. Accessed March 25, 2024. https://www.wsj.com/lifestyle/careers/employers-open-more-doors-to-workers-without-degrees-but-few-are-getting-in-732f1098.

Weissman, Sara. 2024. "More than Half of Recent 4-Year College Grads Underemployed." *Inside Higher Ed*. February 22. Accessed March 26, 2024. https://www.insidehighered.com/news/students/academics/2024/02/22/more-half-recent-four-year-college-grads-underemployed#:~:text=More%20than%20half%20of%20 recent%20four%2Dyear%20college%20graduates%2C%2052,requires%20a%20four%2Dyear%20degree.

Whitney, Peyton. 2024. "More than 42 Million U.S. Households Were Cost Burdened in 2022." Harvard University: Joint Center for Housing Studies. January 19. Accessed March 19, 2024. https://www.jchs.harvard.edu/blog/more-42-million-us-households-were-cost-burdened-2022#:~:text=In%20total%2C%2042.0%20million%20households,year%20before%20the%20pandemic%20started.

Wilcox, W. Bradford. 2023. "Programs Should Family First." *American Compass*. June. Accessed April 4, 2024. https://americancompass.org/rebuilding-american-capitalism/supportive-communities/programs-should-put-family-first/.

Wilcox, W. Bradford, and Wendy Wang. 2017. "The Marriage Divide: How and Why Working-Class Families Are More Fragile Today." Research brief for Opportunity America-AEI-Brookings Working Class Group. September. Accessed March 24, 2024. https://www.aei.org/wp-content/uploads/2017/09/The-Marriage-Divide.pdf?x85095.

Wilcox, W. Bradford, Joseph P. Price, and Angela Rachidi. 2016. "Marriage, Penalized: Does Social-Welfare Policy Affect Family Formation?" AEI and Institute for Family Studies. Accessed March 24, 2024. https://ifstudies.org/ifs-admin/resources/marriage-penalty-hep-2016.pdf.

Wilcox, W. Bradford, Wendy Wang, and Alysse ELHage. 2022. "Life without Father': Less College, Less Work, and More Prison for Young Men Growing up without Their Biological Father." *Institute for Family Studies*. June 17. Accessed March 24, 2024. https://ifstudies.org/blog/life-without-father-less-college-less-work-and-more-prison-for-young-men-growing-up-without-their-biological-father.

Wilkins, Brett. 2022. "'Obscene,' Says Sanders After CBO Reports Richest 1% Now Owns over 1/3 of U.S. Wealth." *Common Dreams*. September 28. Accessed March 7, 2024. https://www.commondreams.org/news/2022/09/28/obscene-says-sanders-after-cbo-reports-richest-1-now-owns-over-13-us-wealth.

Williams, Joan. 2016. "What So Many People Don't Get about the U.S. Working Class." *Harvard Business Review*. November 10. Accessed April 2, 2024. https://hbr.org/2016/11/what-so-many-people-dont-get-about-the-u-s-working-class.

Worstall, Tim. 2015. "Poverty and Inequality Are Not the Same Thing so Let's Try Not to Confuse Them." *Forbes*. March 19. Accessed March 7, 2024. https://www.forbes.com/sites/timworstall/2015/03/19/poverty-and-inequality-are-not-the-same-thing-so-lets-try-not-to-confuse-them/?sh=1d6c7499483f.

Wyman, Nicholas. 2015. *Job U: How to Find Wealth and Success by Developing Skills Companies Actually Need*. New York: Crown Business.

MODES
EDGE FINDER
S750 M3
NIKE

3

Perspectives

Introduction

This chapter includes five essays written by authors from a variety of perspectives and professional backgrounds on a range of topics related to the issue of poverty in America. The chapter opens with an essay by Oren Cass, executive director at American Compass, which describes itself as a think tank dedicated to highlighting the plight of modern American workers and promoting economic development that sustains the social institutions vital to the country's liberty and prosperity. Cass's essay "The Culture War on Work" addresses the harmful social and economic effects of culturally devaluing blue-collar work. While waiters, truck drivers, clerks, plumbers, and secretaries fill roles that are crucial to the community, public honor is generally reserved for those working high-paying, white-collar jobs in major metropolitan areas. Cass makes a case for restoring cultural admiration for those who do hard, unglamorous, but valuable work, for limited pay—thereby raising the social wages of such work.

The second and third essays are written by sociology professor and former Child Protective Services (CPS) investigator Sarah A. Font and politics and judicial studies professor Thora Giallouri, respectively. In her essay, "Child Neglect and Child Poverty—Connections and Distinctions," Font examines the charge that most child neglect investigated by the government through

---

The Jane Addams Resource Corporation, a nonprofit organization, offers job skills training and support services for lower-income and unemployed workers to help them achieve self-sufficiency. Participants acquire skills that are in demand in the construction and manufacturing sectors. (Maryland GovPics via Flickr, Creative Commons License CC BY-SA 2.0 DEED)

CPS is merely poverty. Font demonstrates that while the standard definition of neglect could be applied to children whose needs are unmet solely for reasons of poverty, it is well established that cases of neglect typically center on unique psychosocial problems such as parental substance abuse, mental illness, and domestic violence that are not immediately remedied by poverty alleviation and that contribute to a greater likelihood of adverse life outcomes in children who experience them than is typical of children who experience material deprivation alone. Font believes comprehensive strategies extending beyond poverty relief are necessary to adequately respond to most cases of child neglect.

In the essay "Reneging on *Gideon*: Public Defender Fees as Poverty Penalties," Giallouri assesses the current application of *Gideon v. Wainwright*, the 1963 Supreme Court decision that ordered state governments to provide free legal counsel to all those accused of a felony who could not afford counsel of their own. Giallouri demonstrates that, more than sixty years after the decision, public defender fees in most states still pose a barrier to equal justice and due process for the nation's poor.

In the fourth essay, "A Lack of Finances or a Lack of Financial Knowledge? Examining Veteran Poverty," Rebecca Burgess, a consultant on civil-military affairs and veterans policy, exposes some of the myths surrounding military veterans and poverty. She points out that though conventional opinion holds that military veterans are disproportionately affected by poverty, an abundance of research and quantitative analysis has shown that US military veterans and their families consistently achieve higher standards of living than the general public—due in part to the federal and state veteran-specific benefits, skills training, social connections, and labor market opportunities that their service gives them access to. Nevertheless, veterans and those in active military services, especially among younger post-9/11 generations, are not immune from financial hardship and stress. Burgess demonstrates that such difficulties among veterans are typically caused not by a lack of finances, but by a lack of financial literacy and skills.

The final essay, "Democrats, Republicans, and the Populist Moment," written by political science professor Scot J. Zentner, traces the rise of modern American populism, shifting political coalitions, and Donald Trump's controversial leadership of the Republican Party to the deteriorating economic and social conditions among the working class in the twenty-first century.

The Culture War on Work

Oren Cass

Debates about poverty often pit "economics" against "culture." One side argues that economic conditions and incentives, influenced by the structure of anti-poverty programs, play the leading role in creating poverty or helping people out of it. The other side attributes the problem to cultural forces that encourage or discourage various behaviors and argue that only with cultural change can poverty's root causes be addressed. But when it comes to work, which most people on all sides see as a central concern, the dichotomy is a false one. Work's rewards are social as well as financial, determined by both culture and economics. American culture increasingly devalues the work on the lower rungs of the economic ladder, which can have a deleterious effect every bit as severe as a pay cut.

Take, for instance, the fashionable bourgeois self-criticism that Americans start conversations with "so, what do you do?" In some tellings, the question's offense lies in its implication that what you do defines who you are. In others, it represents a thinly veiled attempt to determine how much someone earns or where he ranks in society. But while one's vocation conveys a lot of personal information and thus invites judgment, the nature of the judgment—the way the information is evaluated—depends on culture.

Waiters, truck drivers, retail clerks, plumbers, secretaries, and others all spend their days helping the people around them and filling roles crucial to the community. They do hard, unglamorous work for limited pay to support themselves and their families. Why shouldn't they be eager to share this information with their conversation partners? Surely their replies would compare favorably with those of the derivatives trader, white-collar defense lawyer, premium-alcohol social media manager, or professor of comparative literature. If blue-collar replies instead are cause for embarrassment, or an invitation to the listener to feel superior, then something is amiss.

We are perfectly capable of awarding respect and status on the basis of sacrifice and social contribution for soldiers and police officers, teachers, and nurses. What we lack is recognition that just about any job fits these criteria, and that work is inherently deserving of respect. Through our public policy and our culture, we have spent decades devaluing the basic act of doing a job that supports a family and contributes to a community. The idea that people "work to live" has been replaced by one that everybody should "live to work," leaving behind the vast majority for whom a job is not an end unto itself but rather a means to fulfilling obligations and building a good life.

Look at the stories told by popular culture. In the 1970s and 1980s, the Emmy Award for Outstanding Comedy Series routinely went to shows with blue-collar characters, such as *All in the Family, Taxi, Cheers*, and *The Wonder Years*. An especially famous *Wonder Years* episode, "My Father's Office," told the story of Kevin learning about his father's career path from loading-dock worker to distribution manager and that he had dreamed of being a ship's captain. "You can't do every silly thing you want in life," Mr. Arnold told his son. "You have to make your choices. You have to try to be happy with them. I think we've done pretty well, don't you?"

But for twenty-five years, beginning in 1992, the Emmy went almost every time to a show about white-collar adults working in Los Angeles, Seattle, Boston, New York, or Washington, few of whom were raising children. The one exception is *The Office*, about paper salesmen in Scranton, but its primary vein of humor was the evidently miserable lives and meaningless jobs of its provincial subjects (none of whom seemed to have a family, either). In 2017, the seven nominations went to shows about an ad executive and his family in Los Angeles, professionals and their families in Los Angeles, an actor in New York, a young woman restarting her life as a nanny in New York, political operatives in New York and Washington, nerds in Silicon Valley, and rappers in Atlanta. Has a lineup starring characters male and female; gay and straight; Black, white, and Hispanic, ever looked so little "like America" in terms of representing poor and working-class Americans?

This does not just reflect market demand for what people want to see. In the drama category, for instance, alongside the usual fare about crime, politics, dystopian science fiction, fantasy, and the British aristocracy, a show called *This Is Us* appeared in 2017. It followed a blue-collar family in Pennsylvania; the dad worked construction and struggled with alcoholism. That story was told through flashbacks to the 1970s and 1980s; in the modern-day segments, the now-grown-up kids are a singer, an actor, and a businessman, all working in New York City or Los Angeles. Likewise, *The Goldbergs*, which ran from 2013 to 2023, was about a suburban Pennsylvania family where the father is a furniture salesman, the mom is a homemaker, and the kids learn to value their father's commitment to working every day in a job he doesn't like to provide for them. It too was set in the 1980s. Hollywood seems to think these things happened only in prior generations.

Similar messages have bombarded Americans on all sides from the cultural heights. The belief that everyone needed college came accompanied by one that other tracks were for losers, and also the popularization of the term "dead-end job." In his iconic 2005 commencement address, Steve Jobs analogized between jobs and lovers. "You've got to find what you love," Jobs explained. "And, like any great relationship, it just gets better and better as the years roll on." "So," he continued, "keep looking until you find it. Don't settle." A venture capitalist can earn plaudits in the *New York Times* for his "sincerity and sophistication" when observing unashamedly that "I think it's a bad use of a human to spend 20 years of their life driving a truck back and forth across the United States. That's not what we aspired to do as humans—it's a bad use of a human brain."

Simultaneously, as these new criteria for "good" work have been added, the old criteria that most jobs could meet have been stripped away. Taking pride in providing for a family becomes much harder when the government's package of safety-net benefits offers to do so almost as well as most blue-collar occupations. For men, especially, the idea that they provide a critical function by working to support their families can be hard to square with lived experience in a community of broken families where single-mother-headed households are the norm.

The accumulation and internalization of ideas and experiences like these can be very real and painful—a "respect cut" to accompany the decades-long stall in paycheck growth. Intuitively, work seems far from the domain of cultural concerns. It occurs in the marketplace, purportedly in rational response to economic incentives. But culture includes the norms and expectations against which a society's members understand themselves to be measured, and so it defines the nonmonetary rewards and penalties—in terms of status and respect, pride, and shame—that people earn through their behavior.

The social wages of work derive from cultural recognition of the obligation to provide for a self-sufficient family and make positive contributions to the larger community. If that obligation—and the enormous value of its fulfillment—is widely recognized, then work can bring with it affirmation and the pride of success. Those rewards should not hinge on the type of work, its glamour, or its salary. If anything, people who do harder jobs for lower wages deserve the greatest admiration.

Idleness, meanwhile, should bring a sense of failure and some measure of shame—that is, one reason to work might be to avoid the social cost of not working. That is not a pleasant message to send. But if individuals, their families, and their communities benefit from their engagement in work, lessening the social distinction between idleness and productive activities is not an enhancement of freedom but rather a form of deprivation. Work may have large benefits, but it's also often hard, and we need to maximize the reward for pursuing it. People have no problem appreciating this dynamic in their own lives and applying it to the expectations they establish for their own children. The challenge is to make those beliefs public.

At our hypothetical party, a possibility always exists that the person asked, "what do you do?" in fact does nothing at all. The moment might be quite awkward for him—maybe for the questioner too. All the more reason to go ahead and ask.

Oren Cass is the executive director of American Compass and author of "The Once and Future Worker: A Vision for the Renewal of Work in America."

Child Neglect and Child Poverty—Connections and Distinctions

Sarah A. Font

"It's time to stop confusing poverty for neglect," declared Jerry Milner and John Kelly, then of the US Children's Bureau, in 2020. The premise of their argument—that the vast majority of what the government, through the Child Protection System (CPS), investigates as child neglect is merely poverty—has been asserted so frequently by parental rights and anti-poverty activists that it is now conventional wisdom. But is it true? Or have we moved from assertion to axiom without meaningful assessment and debate?

The "neglect or poverty" debate sits within a larger conversation about the reach and impact of CPS. It is reasonable—and necessary—to reduce the scope of CPS. An estimated 28 to 37 percent of US children, and up to half of Black children, encounter CPS by age eighteen (Kim et al. 2017; Putnam-Hornstein et al. 2021). The system lacks the funding, capacity, or ability to adequately serve so many children, at least some of whom could be protected and supported through less intrusive systems.

The stakes, both of over- and under-responding to alleged child neglect, are extraordinarily high. To require those accused of neglect to participate in parenting classes and counseling, often coerced with court orders and the threat or actuality of child removal (Pelton 2016), when all that is needed is something as simple and unintrusive as money to pay the electric bill, is wasteful and cruel. In this scenario, struggling but loving parents are labeled perpetrators; they are vilified but not helped. Moreover, CPS has neither the staffing nor resources to respond to child poverty, which is experienced by roughly 11 million children each year (Dawson 2023).

And yet, to ignore the harms inflicted by neglect is equally unconscionable. Neglect is present in an overwhelming majority of known child maltreatment-related deaths (U.S. Department of Health and Human Services 2023) and it is associated with developmental and social delays (Manly et al. 2013a; 2013b), academic failure, teen parenthood (Font and Maguire-Jack 2020), delinquency (Font and Kennedy 2022), and an array of other social problems. Children who experience neglect are also far more likely to later experience physical or sexual abuse (Palmer et al. 2023). These associations between neglect and adverse life outcomes are not fully explained by poverty. In true cases of neglect, failing to intervene, or intervening solely with economic supports, leaves children vulnerable to lifelong impairment.

So, what is neglect? And does CPS know how to distinguish neglect from poverty? Drawing on my varied experiences, including a few years as a CPS investigator, I could give infinite examples of neglect. The parent who left her six children, ages 1 through 8 years, unbathed, unclothed, and alone all day in an apartment without food or an emergency contact while she went to a salon. The parent who continued to leave her child in the care of her boyfriend even after the child disclosed that the boyfriend was molesting her. The parents who would regularly physically assault and threaten one another while their child hid, crying, in a closet. In each of these cases, the family was also living in or near poverty, but few would argue that money alone would protect the children from further harm.

But, akin to the problem of distinguishing obscenity from art, it is easier to give examples of neglect than a clear and concise definition. The standard definition of neglect is the "failure of a parent or other person with responsibility for the child to provide needed food, clothing, shelter, medical care, or supervision to the degree that the child's health, safety, and well-being are threatened with harm" (CWIG 2022). A child who is not provided with shelter could be a member of a family experiencing homelessness, and that family could be experiencing homelessness for any number of reasons, including parental illness or job loss—conditions that may or may not stem from parental negligence. It is therefore possible that the standard definition of neglect could be applied to children whose needs are unmet solely for reasons of poverty. State legislators would be wise to clarify that a finding of neglect requires evidence of either (1) parental culpability in the form of recklessness or intent, or (2) incapacity or unwillingness to rectify the conditions of neglect despite access to services.

In practice, CPS has a great deal of discretion in determining whether and how to intervene with families. It is well established that neglect cases frequently center on parental substance use (U.S. GAO 1994; 1998), mental illness, and domestic violence (Palmer et al. 2022). That is, CPS generally investigates parents who have psychosocial problems likely to interfere with parenting, not merely parents with economic problems (Barth et al. 2021; Jonson-Reid, Drake, and Kohl 2009).

But, one might wonder, wouldn't parents be better positioned to address psychosocial problems if their basic needs were met? Might mental illness, drug use, or domestic violence be the result of or exacerbated by economic stress? Observational and experimental research finds that poverty-related stress can impact decision-making (Haushofer and Fehr 2014), health (Wolfe et al. 2012), and parenting behavior. Providing pathways out of poverty would undoubtedly improve the quality of family life for innumerable children and may also reduce CPS contact (Pac et al. 2023).

And yet, three points of clarification are crucial to make. First, prevention and cure are not the same. A flu shot does not cure influenza. Putting on a bike helmet does not reverse brain damage after a crash. In this same way, providing financial support alone, in the absence of other treatment services, is unlikely to reverse substance use disorders, serious mental illness, domestic violence, or the other psychosocial problems conducive to the neglect of children. And, unfortunately, voluntary parenting and other noneconomic support services are typically declined or not completed by parents at risk for child neglect (Putnam-Hornstein, Prindle, and Hammond 2021; Smokowski et al. 2018).

Second, episodic poverty and chronic poverty are distinct phenomena. When Americans experience a brief period of poverty due to job loss, family structure change, or illness, many are able to draw on family and governmental support and then rebound to a state of relative self-sufficiency. However, chronic poverty is distinctive—it is geographically concentrated both in isolated rural areas and racially segregated inner cities and often reproduced intergenerationally. Consequently, a chronically poor individual is less able to rely on both economic and social resources from family and community. In addition to economic deprivation, individuals raised in chronic poverty experience higher rates of social adversities, such as abuse and parental absence, that compromise their future economic prospects, mental and physical health and, yes, parenting capacity. For those individuals, poverty relief—an infusion of money or goods from government or charity—will indeed provide relief but is unlikely to reverse the effects of a lifetime of adversity (Van Ryzin, Fishbein, and Biglan 2018). In short, even if one believes that the root cause of neglect is poverty, the proximal causes—substance abuse, mental illness, domestic violence, and other psychosocial and behavioral circumstances—are neither ignorable nor immediately remedied by poverty alleviation. Comprehensive strategies that seek to address comorbid psychosocial, behavioral, and physical health issues alongside economic needs, such as those being implemented to address chronic homelessness (Center on Budget and Policy Priorities 2016), are highly relevant to the CPS-involved population.

Too much of the current media and academic discourse focuses on a false binary. It is nonsensical to assert that neglect must be either poverty or behavioral, either structural or individual. Child neglect is a complex social problem. Oversimplifying this reality is a disservice to children and parents.

Sarah A. Font is Associate Professor of Sociology and Public Policy and Associate Director of the Graduate Program in Sociology at Pennsylvania State University.

References

Barth, Richard P. et al. 2021. "Research to Consider while Effectively Re-designing Child Welfare Services." *Research on Social Work Practice* 32 (October 18): 10497315211050000. Accessed December 1, 2023. https://doi.org/10.1177/10497315211050000.

Center on Budget and Policy Priorities. 2016. "Supportive Housing Helps Vulnerable People Live and Thrive in the Community." May 31. Accessed December 1, 2023. https://www.cbpp.org/research/housing/supportive-housing-helps-vulnerable-people-live-and-thrive-in-the-community.

CWIG (Child Welfare Information Gateway). 2022. "Definitions of Child Abuse and Neglect." Washington, DC: U.S. Department of Health and Human Services. Accessed December 1, 2023. https://www.childwelfare.gov/topics/systemwide/laws-policies/statutes/define/.

Dawson, Ben. 2023. "The State of America's Children 2023—Child Poverty." *Children's Defense Fund* (blog). Accessed December 1, 2023, https://www.childrensdefense.org/the-state-of-americas-children/soac-2023-child-poverty/.

Font, Sarah A., and Kathryn Maguire-Jack. 2020. "It's Not 'Just Poverty': Educational, Social, and Economic Functioning among Young Adults Exposed to Childhood Neglect, Abuse, and Poverty." *Child Abuse & Neglect* 101 (March 1). Accessed December 1, 2023. https://doi.org/10.1016/j.chiabu.2020.104356.

Font, Sarah A., and Reeve Kennedy. 2022. "The Centrality of Child Maltreatment to Criminology." *Annual Review of Criminology* 5 (1): 371–96. Accessed December 1, 2023. https://doi.org/10.1146/annurev-criminol-030920-120220.

Haushofer, Johannes, and Ernst Fehr. 2014. "On the Psychology of Poverty." *Science* 344 (6186): 862–7. Accessed December 1, 2023. https://doi.org/10.1126/science.1232491.

Jonson-Reid, Melissa, Brett Drake, and Patricia L Kohl. 2009. "Is the Overrepresentation of the Poor in Child Welfare Caseloads due to Bias or Need?" *Children and Youth Services Review* 31: 422–7. Accessed December 1, 2023. https://doi.org/10.1016/j.childyouth.2008.09.009.

Kim, Hyunil et al. 2017. "Lifetime Prevalence of Investigating Child Maltreatment among US Children." *American Journal of Public Health* 107 (2): 274–80.

Manly, Jody Todd et al. 2013a. "Child Neglect and the Development of Externalizing Behavior Problems: Associations with Maternal Drug Dependence and Neighborhood Crime." *Child Maltreatment* 18 (1): 17–29.

Manly, Jody Todd et al. 2013b. "The Impact of Neglect on Initial Adaptation to School." *Child Maltreatment* 18 (3): 155–70.

Milner, Jerry, and David Kelly. 2020. "It's Time to Stop Confusing Poverty with Neglect." *Chronicle of Social Change* (blog). January 17. Accessed December 1, 2023. https://chronicleofsocialchange.org/child-welfare-2/time-for-child-welfare-system-to-stop-confusing-poverty-with-neglect/40222.

Pac, Jessica et al. 2023. "The Effects of Child Poverty Reductions on Child Protective Services Involvement." *Social Service Review* 97 (1): 43–91. Accessed December 1, 2023. https://doi.org/10.1086/723219.

Palmer, Lindsey et al. 2022. "What Does Child Protective Services Investigate as Neglect? A Population-Based Study." *Child Maltreatment* 29 (July 13): 8–13, 10775595221114144. Accessed December 1, 2023. https://doi.org/10.1177/10775595221114144.

Palmer, Lindsey et al. 2023. "Lifetime Rates and Types of Subsequent Child Protection System Contact Following a First Report of Neglect: An Age-stratified Analysis." *PLOS ONE* 18 (4): e0283534. Accessed December 1, 2023. https://doi.org/10.1371/journal.pone.0283534.

Pelton, Leroy H. 2016. "Separating Coercion from Provision in Child Welfare: Preventive Supports Should Be Accessible without Conditions Attached." *Child Abuse & Neglect* 51 (1): 427–34.

Putnam-Hornstein, Emily et al. 2021. "Cumulative Rates of Child Protection Involvement and Terminations of Parental Rights in a California Birth Cohort, 1999–2017." *American Journal of Public Health* 111 (6): 1157–63.

Putnam-Hornstein, Emily, John Prindle, and Ivy Hammond. 2021. "Engaging Families in Voluntary Prevention Services to Reduce Future Child Abuse and Neglect: A Randomized Controlled Trial." *Prevention Science* 22 (August 27): 856–65. Accessed December 1, 2023. https://doi.org/10.1007/s11121-021-01285-w.

Smokowski, Paul et al. 2018. "Addressing Barriers to Recruitment and Retention in the Implementation of Parenting Programs: Lessons Learned for Effective Program Delivery in Rural and Urban Areas." *Journal of Child and Family Studies* 27 (9): 2925–42. Accessed December 1, 2023. https://doi.org/10.1007/s10826-018-1139-8.

U.S. Department of Health and Human Services. 2023. "Child Maltreatment 2021." Accessed December 1, 2023. https://www.acf.hhs.gov/sites/default/files/documents/cb/cm2021.pdf.

U.S. General Accounting Office (GAO). 1994. "Foster Care Parental Drug Abuse Has Alarming Impact on Young Children" (April). Accessed December 1, 2023. https://www.gao.gov/assets/hehs-94-89.pdf.

U.S. General Accounting Office (GAO). 1998. "Foster Care: Agencies Face Challenges Securing Stable Homes for Children of Substance Abusers." Accessed December 1, 2023. https://www.gao.gov/assets/230/226295.pdf.

Van Ryzin, Mark J., Diana Fishbein, and Anthony Biglan. 2018. "The Promise of Prevention Science for Addressing Intergenerational Poverty." *Psychology, Public Policy, and Law* 24 (1): 128–43. Accessed December 1, 2023. https://doi.org/10.1037/law0000138.

Wolfe, Barbara et al. 2012. "The Income and Health Effects of Tribal Casino Gaming on American Indians." *Demography* 49 (2): 499–524. Accessed December 1, 2023. https://doi.org/10.1007/s13524-012-0098-8.

Reneging on *Gideon*: Public Defender Fees as Poverty Penalties

Thora Giallouri

Every decade since 1963, legal academics and practitioners mark with speeches and celebrations the anniversary of *Gideon v. Wainwright*, the Supreme Court decision that ordered state governments to provide free legal counsel to all those accused of a felony who could not afford counsel of their own. The reason for the Court's decision seems obvious; how could a non-lawyer navigate complicated and arcane processes *and* successfully defend themselves without any knowledge of court procedure or legal statute? To paraphrase Justice Black's famous sentence from *Gideon*, someone who cannot afford a lawyer is too ill-equipped to handle the American adversarial criminal justice system, to the point that they are being denied a fair trial (344). It was the simple conclusion that justice (or due process in American jurisprudential parlance) could not be ensured in a society where, for the same crime and circumstances, a person of means can be exonerated, whereas a poor person is convicted. After all, Justice Black was only providing a straightforward interpretation of the Sixth Amendment's provision that "in all criminal prosecutions, the accused shall enjoy the right . . . to have the Assistance of Counsel for his defense." This right was too fundamental, too important for the American scheme of justice to leave its implementation to chance. Accordingly, in 1967, the Supreme Court expanded the right of indigent (a more polite word for "poor") defendants to public-expense counsel to juveniles (*In re Gault*), and in 1972 to misdemeanor cases (*Argersinger v. Hamlin*).

In most jurisdictions before *Gideon*, the criminally accused who lacked financial means would routinely find themselves alone and helpless in court, imprisoned or fined, regardless of the merit of the charges against them. *Gideon* and its accompanying cases forced state governments to create new public defender services or drastically expand those already offered. It makes sense, therefore, that the decision was embraced as a beacon of hope toward eradicating the *de facto* double-standard system of criminal justice based on wealth. This year, we are "celebrating" sixty years of *Gideon*, and as in previous years, we take stock of the failures of state governments and courts alike to deliver on its promise.

In courtrooms across the country, public defenders are met with the same image; accused persons sit around and wait their turn to talk to a court clerk who will assess the fees to pay for being provided with public defender services. Many court clerks will ask defendants to pay a fee up-front to evaluate whether they qualify for such services, regardless of final determination (Middlewood 1997, 18). And most of these defendants will not actually be able to afford the \$40–200 (depending on the jurisdiction) application fee to have their case considered for public defender services because they earn less than that per week and still have to secure necessities like food. Many will be initially assigned a public defender, and, upon conclusion of their case or plea agreement, they will be ordered by the judge to pay "statutory fees" for services rendered, which range from hundreds to thousands of dollars depending on the severity of the offense and the length of court proceedings, even over protestations by public defenders themselves (Levine 2007).

In addition, that courtroom image increasingly consists of defendants declining counsel for themselves and parents declining counsel for their juvenile children, because they know they will never be able to repay these public defender fees (Gourdie 2021). After all, sometimes, spending time in prison or a juvenile facility may cost less than the alternatives imposed upon those who do not repay "recuperation fees," as courts and county governments dub them—or "criminal justice debt," as most others do.

In a society whose culture exalts lawyers, due process, and the rule of law, this surely must be a rare image! Yet, the more astonishing statistic is that up to 90 percent of individuals facing criminal charges in the United States cannot in fact afford private counsel. From those, only the poorest qualify for public-expense counsel, as states and different counties within states determine cut-off income limits, which usually fall a little over/under the federal poverty level. Of course, these are becoming stricter, as observed in states like Florida, Wisconsin, and even California before the latter repealed all public defender fees in 2021 (Shimura 2011). Nevertheless, the National Legal Aid and Defense Association (NLADA), in the most comprehensive study of public defender fees in decades, found that "in 42 states and the District of Columbia, laws authorize courts to impose public defense system fees—both upfront application or administrative fees, and fees recouping the cost of counsel—on people who are represented by court-appointed attorneys" (Beeman et al. 2022, 1). While the states recoup less than 5 percent of public defense costs via those fees, the debts that indigent defendants incur hamper any meaningful attempt at a fair and efficient experience with the criminal justice system, further penalizing the indigent for being poor.

But what is the nature and extent of poverty penalties imposed upon indigent defendants when they cannot pay the public defense fees assessed to them? When indigent defendants cannot pay, their debt usually transfers to some private collection agency that contracts with the county and the court. Those who end up in "collections" have their assets seized, assuming these exist, their wages garnished, their tax returns intercepted, and their credit ruined, which translates to further obstacles in finding employment, securing housing, purchasing a car, or being granted any other type of loan. Unpaid public defender fees can be the reason why in some jurisdictions, like Iowa or Oklahoma, indigents cannot have their license or registration renewed, and why in thirty states they can have their probation revoked. Thus, they end up serving a prison sentence, which a person of means facing the same punishment would not have to serve. Public defender debt also carries the possibility that a bench warrant will be issued for the arrest of the debtor, with either threatened or actual incarceration as a result.

As NLADA reports, public defender debt can indeed tether the individual to the criminal justice system for a very long time, leading to a never-ending cycle of recidivism (4). Research shows that between 60 and 70 percent of those who use public defender services never make any repayment of fees (Beckett et al. 2008; Laisne et al. 2017; Shade 2020; Ward et al. 2020). Moreover, Rafael and Mai (2022, 16) find that repayment becomes less and less likely as time goes on, even for very low amounts of debt associated with less serious offenses. To clarify, defendants who use public defender services can petition the judge to waive any or some of those fees due to inability to pay, but there is no uniformity as to who qualifies for the waiver because the decision is *ad hoc* without prior rules for guidance; the process is as arbitrary as it gets (Miller 2023).

Public defender agencies routinely recover only 1 to 3 percent of operational costs through fees, while these have the tendency to cause undue harm to adults and juveniles entangled in the criminal justice system. It, therefore, begs the question why they still exist in most jurisdictions. Just like criminal fines have a disproportionate impact upon the poor, public defender fees signal another poverty penalty. Scholars and experts remind us that public defender fees are the natural outcome of a combination of political indifference and outright warfare against the poor (Galbraith et al. 2023; Gourdie 2021; Middlewood 1997).

Seasoned by decades of tough-on-crime and benefits-freeloader rhetoric, a good portion of the public has learnt to deem anyone who faces criminal charges as automatically guilty, and anyone poor as unworthy of society's sympathy, making many voters unlikely allies in pushes for reform. In the quest for more votes, legislators enact statutes that allow the assessment of public defender fees with one hand, while they cut public defender budgets with the other. Decades of voting behavior research have shown us that the poor and the criminally accused vote at a significantly lower rate than high-socioeconomic status Americans (Campbell et al. 1960; Verba and Nie 1972) and legislators know that. The three states (Weill-Greenberg 2023) that just abolished public defender fees may pose hope that reform is not out of reach, but the preponderance of states (and evidence) points more toward the difficulty of currently celebrating *Gideon* with a straight face.

Thora Giallouri is Assistant Professor of Political Science at California State University, San Bernardino. She teaches courses in law, courts and public policy, and American politics.

References

Argersinger v. Hamlin. 1972. 407 U.S. 25.

Beckett, Katherine, Alexes Harris, and Heather Evans. 2008. "The Assessment and Consequences of Legal Financial Obligations in Washington State." *Washington State Minority and Justice Commission Research Report*. Accessed December 16, 2023. https://media.spokesman.com/documents/2009/05/study_LFOimpact.pdf.

Beeman, Marea, Kellianne Elliott, Rosalie Joy, Elizabeth Allen, and Michael Mrozinski. 2022. *At What Cost? Findings from an Examination into the Imposition of Public Defense System Fees*. Washington, DC: National Legal Aid & Defender Association.

Campbell, Angus, Philip Converse, Warren Miller, and Donald Stokes. 1960. *The American Voter*. New York: Wiley.

Galbraith, Jean, Latifa AlMarri, Lisha Bhati, Rheem Brooks, Zachary Green, Margo Hu, and Noor Irshaidat. 2023. "Poverty Penalties as Human Rights Problems." *American Journal of International Law* 117 (3): 397–440.

*Gideon v. Wainwright.*1963. 372. U.S. 335.

Gourdie, Hannah. 2021. "The Guiding Hand of Counsel, for a Price: Juvenile Public Defender Fees and Their Effects." *William & Mary Law Review* 62 (3): 999.

In re Gault. 1967. 387 U.S. 1.

Laisne, Mathilde, Jon Wool, and Christian Henrichson. 2017. *Past Due: Examining the Costs and Consequences of Charging for Justice in New Orleans*. Brooklyn, NY: Vera Institute of Justice.

Levine, Kate. 2007. "If You Cannot Afford a Lawyer: Assessing the Constitutionality of Massachusetts's Reimbursement Statute." *Harvard Civil Rights-Civil Liberties Law Review* 42: 191.

Middlewood, Erin. 1997. "Pay Per Plea." *The Progressive* 61: 18–20.

Miller, Nicholas. 2023. "You Have the Right to an Attorney, but It Might Cost You." *The Nation*. Accessed December 16, 2023. https://www.thenation.com/article/society/public-defender-fees/.

Rafael, Maria Katarina, and Chris Mai. 2022. "Understanding the Burden of Legal Financial Obligations on Indigent Washingtonians." *Social Sciences* 11 (1): 17.

Shade, Damion. 2020. *Reducing Oklahoma's Court Fines and Fees Is Police Reform*. Tulsa, OK: Oklahoma Policy Center.

Shimura, Tomoya. 2011. "Public Defenders Increase Attorney Fees." *Daily Press*. Accessed December 16, 2023. https://www.vvdailypress.com/story/news/2011/07/10/public-defenders-increase-attorney-fees/37104022007/.

Verba, Sidney, and Norman Nie. 1972. *Participation in America: Political Democracy and Social Equality*. New York: Harper and Row.

Ward, Jeffrey, Nathan Link, and Andrew Christy. 2020. "Imposition and Collection of Fines, Costs, and Restitution in Pennsylvania Criminal Courts." *Philadelphia: ACLU of Pennsylvania.*

Weill-Greenberg, Elizabeth. 2023. "New Jersey Took a Big Step toward Eliminating Public Defender Fees. But Some Costs Remain." *The Appeal.* Accessed December 16, 2023. https://theappeal.org/new-jersey-public-defender-fees/

A Lack of Finances or a Lack of Financial Knowledge? Examining Veteran Poverty

Rebecca Burgess

Around half of Americans who see a homeless man panhandling on a street corner believe that he is a military veteran—and yet 90 percent of the time they are wrong in that estimation (Burgess and Schmitt 2017). Americans for decades now have persisted in viewing veterans as "broken heroes," and in thinking that veterans are more likely than non-veterans to be unemployed, undereducated, homeless, and experiencing mental health issues (Tivald and Kawashima-Ginsberg 2015). This helps to explain the equally widespread misperception among the American public that veterans as a group are in straightened circumstances financially, experiencing poverty at higher rates than their civilian peers. In reality, as a wealth of research and quantitative analysis has repeatedly uncovered, over the past forty years US military veterans and their families have consistently achieved higher standards of living than non-veterans.

This does not, of course, mean that some veterans do not experience poverty or that they never encounter financial hardships, or that there are currently no veterans living at or under the poverty level in the United States. But upon closer examination of the landscape of those veterans and their families who are experiencing financial hardship, an unexpected story emerges: It may be that financial stress among especially younger (Post-9/11) veterans is connected with a lack of a financial skill set, and with low financial literacy among veterans and members of the Armed Forces more generally.

The inaccurate, even negative perception of active-duty service members and veterans being disproportionately affected by poverty is influenced by several social, cultural, and political factors that have had a long-lasting resonance. These include the Vietnam War era backlash in the 1960s against anything perceived to be military connected; the reality of a conscript military for nearly four decades where basic pay was below labor market wages; and the well-publicized scandals, low-quality recruits and performance, and bad morale that plagued especially the US Army in the first decade of the transition to an all-volunteer force model (Griffith Jr. 1997; Rostker 2006).

The widening civil-military "gap" or divide in evidence especially since the post-9/11 attacks and America's twenty-year-long military responses in Afghanistan and Iraq is another contributing factor: as fewer Americans serve in uniform (currently less than 1 percent of all American adults), fewer simply know anyone in the military or anything about the reality of military service (Schafer 2017; Schake and Mattis 2016). Thus long-repeated assumptions and tropes about soldiers and veterans, which may once have had some basis in fact, have persisted if not metastasized beyond the realm of accuracy in the age of mass media.

Fifty years of an All-Volunteer Force where successful recruitment has relied on payrates commensurate with the civilian labor market, in addition to increasingly generous benefits, have helped to steady the financial situation of veterans and military connected families (Burgess 2023). Additionally, most members of the military now come from middle-class neighborhoods, with the middle three quintiles for household income being overrepresented among enlisted recruits (Council on Foreign Relations 2020). According to an extensive report compiled by the Military Family Advisory Network about military family financial readiness, service members were less likely than US adults overall to be at risk of material hardship (Military Family Advisory Network 2023). And once out of the service, studies of even those veterans with a Department of Veterans Affairs (VA) designated service-connected disability (SCD) have revealed that SCD veterans typically fair better economically than their disabled civilian peers, thanks to the package of (most often) untaxed VA benefits at their disposal, and their ability to simultaneously hold employment and receive the SCD benefits (London, Landes, and Wilmoth 2023).

As the Pew Research Center reported in a 2019 analysis of US Census Bureau data, while both veteran and non-veteran households have experienced income growth since 1980, in 2017, the median annual income for veteran households was around $88,700. This was compared to about $76,100 for non-veteran households, representing an over $12,000 difference. This gap is even more pronounced in households headed by racial or ethnic minority veterans, as well as those with lower levels of education, where the differential is even more significant—with the former making $20,000 more than their non-veteran peers.

In the specific economic measurement of poverty, civilian households fare *worse* than veteran ones: the civilian household poverty rate was 6.4 percentage points higher than the veteran household rate (13.0 versus 6.6 percent). However, that rate of poverty has been creeping upward for even veteran households since 1980 (from 4.4 percent to 6.6 percent). Nevertheless, in 2022 the Census Bureau estimated that less than 10 percent (7.5 percent, around 1.2 million) of all veterans have income below the poverty level. Additionally, the veteran population has a lower unemployment rate than non-veterans (2.8 versus 3.6 percent). The number of homeless veterans has also decreased by over 55 percent in the last twelve years, to an estimated 33,139 homeless veterans in 2022 (USAFacts 2023).

Researchers credit the "military capital effect" (the benefits of military service that may include health-promoting activities via physical training; the establishment of social networks that broaden ties to the community and labor market opportunities; development of social and translatable occupational/technical skills; and access to a broad range of DoD and VA benefits, including education, healthcare, and home-loan guaranty benefits) for these positive financial outcomes for veterans (London, Landes, and Wilmoth 2023). But this does not mean that veterans, especially young post-9/11 veterans, are completely immune from experiencing financial hardship and stress.

Young veterans, who may have joined the military immediately upon their high school graduation, have not necessarily learned how to manage bills and budgeting by the time they exit the service. According to the Bush Center's "Advancing Veteran Employment, Education & Health and Well-being" Report, 35 percent of post-9/11 veterans reported difficulty paying bills the first few years post-service. Similarly, 53 percent of all post-9/11 veteran respondents to the 2021 Military Family Lifestyle Survey indicated that they were experiencing financial stress, with 30 percent citing excessive credit-card debt (D'Aniello Institute for Veterans and Military Families 2022). Frequently linked with the financial stress and the excessive credit-card debt is spouse underemployment or unemployment (24 percent) and student loans (22 percent).

It turns out that to the extent that veterans may be more likely to end up homeless than their civilian peers, the cause most frequently lies in having poor financial skills, according to the *American Journal of Public Health.* When veterans lack familiarity with household budgeting, they are also more likely to be the targets for predatory lenders and to lack money managing know-how (Shane 2013). The extent to which veteran homelessness has decreased since the 2010s can thus be seen as a positive outcome of both public and private efforts to provide more robust opportunities for those both currently in the military and recently separated from it to learn how to build their financial skillsets.

Military veterans and those in active military service today suffer from widespread misconceptions and outright myths about both who they are and what their true challenges are. The reality is that veterans benefit both economically and financially over their life course from their military service and the continuing federal and state veteran-specific benefits their service gives them access to, but these benefits do not render veterans immune from either financial hardship or financial stress. And one of the greatest aids to preventing them from falling into a deleterious pathway of financial hardship is to provide active-duty members, veterans, and their families with a greater breadth and depth of financial literacy tools.

Rebecca Burgess is Senior Fellow at the Yorktown Institute and a consultant on civil-military affairs and veterans policy.

References

Bennett, Jesse. 2019. "Veteran Households in U.S. Are Economically Better Off than Those of Non-veterans." *Pew Research Center*. December 9. Accessed December 15, 2023. https://www.pewresearch.org/short-reads/2019/12/09/veteran-households-in-u-s-are-economically-better-off-than-those-of-non-veterans/.

Burgess, Rebecca. 2023. "Saluting Those Who Freely Serve." *Law & Liberty*. August 22. https://lawliberty.org/features/saluting-those-who-freely-serve/.

Burgess, Rebecca, and Gary J. Schmitt. 2017. "What We Don't Know about Veterans." *The Wall Street Journal*. June 13. Accessed December 15, 2023. https://www.wsj.com/articles/what-we-dont-know-about-veterans-1497307334.

Council on Foreign Relations. 2020. "Demographics of the U.S. Military." *cfr.org*. July 13. Accessed December 15, 2023. https://www.cfr.org/backgrounder/demographics-us-military.

D'Aniello Institute for Veterans & Military Families. 2022. "Financial Literacy Month: Military Financial Readiness and Resources." Syracuse University. Accessed

December 15, 2023. https://ivmf.syracuse.edu/2022/04/26/military-financial-readiness-and-resources/.

Griffith, Jr., Robert K. 1997. *The U.S. Army's Transition to the All-Volunteer Force, 1968–1974.* Washington, DC: U.S. Army Center of Military History.

London, Andrew S., Scott D. Landes, and Janet M. Wilmoth. 2023. "Service-Connected Disability and Poverty among US Veterans" in Robyn Lewis Brown, Michelle Maroto, and David Pettinicchio, eds., *The Oxford Handbook of the Sociology of Disability.* New York: Oxford University Press: 441–67.

Military Family Advisory Network. 2023. "Research Review: Military & Veteran Family Financial Readiness." *Military Family Advisory Network, Inc.* January. Accessed December 15, 2023. https://www.mfan.org/research-reports/?doctype=full-report.

Rostker, Bernard D. 2006. *I Want You! The Evolution of the All-Volunteer Force.* Santa Monica, CA: The Rand Corporation.

Schafer, Amy. 2017. "Generations of War: The Rise of the Warrior Caste and the All-Volunteer Force." *CNAS.* May 8. Accessed December 15, 2023. https://www.cnas.org/publications/reports/generations-of-war.

Schake, Kori, and Jim Mattis, eds. 2016. *Warriors & Citizens: American Views of Our Military.* Stanford, CA: Hoover Institution Press.

Shane, Leo. 2013. "Study: Lack of Financial Literacy May Trigger Vets' Homelessness." *Stars and Stripes.* October 22. Accessed December 15, 2023. https://www.stripes.com/news/study-lack-of-financial-literacy-may-trigger-vets-homelessness-1.248524.

Tivald, Julia, and Kei Kawashima-Ginsberg. 2015. "America's Greatest Assets: How Military Veterans Are Strengthening Our Communities." *2015 Veterans Civic Health Index.* National Conference on Citizenship, 2015. Accessed December 15, 2023. chrome-extension://bdfcnmeidppjeaggnmidamkiddifkdib/viewer.html?file=https://ncoc.org/wp-content/uploads/2016/08/VetsCHI_2015_FINAL.pdf.

USAFacts. 2023. "How Is the Standard of Living Changing for Veterans?" *usafacts.org.* November 10. Accessed December 15, 2023. https://usafacts.org/articles/who-are-our-nations-veterans-and-how-is-their-standard-of-living-changing/.

Democrats, Republicans, and the Populist Moment

Scot J. Zentner

Economic inequality is a perennial problem of political life. Traditional political science encouraged the development of a middle class in order to blunt the extreme differences between the rich and the poor. In this way, the public good, the good of the whole, would be preserved. The Founders of the United States aimed to do something similar by creating a commercial republic, in which economic interests would be numerous and the poor relatively few in number, thereby making a strident class-based majority less likely to occur. Nevertheless, American politics has always manifested to some extent the traditional class division. One of the major political parties usually fashions itself as the more populist or democratic of the two. This often was the case with the Democratic Party. But deteriorating economic and social conditions in the twenty-first century have shaken the old order, evidenced most notably by the rise of Donald Trump's controversial brand of populism and his leadership of the Republican Party.

The Democrats reached the zenith of their power during the New Deal and the Great Depression, when economic issues were paramount. After the Second World War and the resulting economic boom, the Party began to move away from traditional majoritarian populism, the concerns of the "common man," and pursued policies aimed at aiding racial and social minorities (Gerring 1998). This shift coincided with the Democrats' traditional populist message of aiding the disadvantaged, but with an emphasis on aggregating multiple discrete groups in opposition to a common center. In a well-known thesis, analysts John Judis and Ruy Teixeira (2004) argued that immigration and increasing cultural liberalism had led to an "emerging Democratic majority." Barack Obama's election in 2008 as the first Black president seemed to confirm the strength of this multicultural coalition. The conservative shift toward free markets and low taxes during the 1980s appeared to present no serious impediment to the rise of the new majority.

However, there were difficulties with the Democratic coalition. The first problem was the alienation of social conservatives, which helped Republicans eventually become the dominant party in the South (Shafer and Claggett 1995). But over time, more intractable economic issues emerged. Free trade became less obviously a good thing when capital became dramatically more mobile: since computers and the internet allowed factories with cheap labor abroad to be managed from home, there was less incentive or need for businesses to remain tied to their countries of origin (Baldwin 2016). The result was a loss of manufacturing jobs, especially in the Midwest, but with fewer new compensating opportunities in old, declining communities. Free market Republicans offered little in response to this issue. But the rhetorical shift to minority populism, with its globalizing dimension, became problematic for the Democrats as well.

More generally, the move away from a traditional, majoritarian populism began to marginalize the Democratic Party in significant ways. Judis and Teixeira now lament that the Democratic Party is abandoning its populist roots.

They detail how the Party has become more aligned with many wealthy interests, government employees, and global corporations, and focuses on matters such as climate change, transgenderism, and racial conflict (Judis and Teixeira 2023). In other words, factors that were central to the emerging Democratic majority—support of mass immigration, globalism, and cultural liberalism—have left the impression, right or wrong, among portions of the working-class electorate that the Party is now insufficiently concerned with bread-and-butter issues like declining wages, the lack of well-paying blue-collar jobs, and the social despair that comes with such economic decline. This has occurred despite the fact that Democrats are more supportive of minimum wage hikes, labor unions, and redistributive tax policies than Trump and that many of the GOP's touted economic policies remain oriented toward the interests of corporate investors and high earners.

In 2016, the electorate was primed for a return to a more traditional form of populism. In his presidential campaign, Donald Trump shrewdly focused on immigration restriction, trade protectionism, and a less interventionist foreign policy. His positions on these issues played particularly well in the "Rust Belt" states of the upper Midwest. Trump's agenda was aimed, as he said, at transforming the Republicans into the party of the American "worker," the "forgotten man and woman." That is, he appeared to be concerned with the issues that had animated the old Democratic Party. The bluster surrounding Trump's candidacy tended to obscure this fact. Edward Luttwak (2017) argued that the "major cause" of Trump's election had

> remained mostly unexplored, even undiscovered. That is not due to intellectual laziness, but rather reflects the refusal of almost all commentators to contend with the political economy that determined the outcome of the election. Long-term processes of income redistribution from working people to everyone else, non-working welfare recipients as well as the very rich, had been evident for at least two decades.

The slow economic growth during the Obama presidency no doubt contributed to this underlying dissatisfaction of many ordinary voters, who eventually would support Trump.

Trump's signature issue, of course, was immigration. The continual flow of low-skilled immigrant laborers, many in the country illegally, left the general impression that elite policymakers favored the interests of foreigners more than that of ordinary Americans. Judis and Teixeira believe that Trump's views on immigration were "laced with bigotry," but they admit that the Democrats' embrace of open borders serves to "drive down wages and undermine unions" (2023, 220, 205). That is, they recognize that, from their own point of view as Trump opponents, there is among many Democratic elites a serious disconnect between claims to care about the working class and their actual policies on immigration, trade, environmental regulation, and polarizing cultural issues.

To be sure, some Democratic leaders saw the problem facing their party. The popularity of Vermont Senator Bernie Sanders's campaign for the 2016 Democratic presidential nomination reflected in part the new anxieties of the working class. Like Trump, he seemed to realize that long-term economic stagnation was a main concern of voters. But while Sanders argued for better trade deals and railed against Wall Street, he did not focus on anything like Trump's "America First" program. He had voted in 2007 to kill an immigration reform bill in the US Senate, which he argued would harm American workers. But as Hillary Clinton criticized him for this during the nomination fight, Sanders moved off the immigration issue (Phillips 2016). Clinton's lax immigration policy during the primaries likely made her that much more vulnerable to Trump in the general election. Moreover, both Clinton and Sanders continued, like President Obama, to present climate change, not immigration's effect on the economy, as the greater problem for the nation. Clinton even said she was going to put coal miners out of work, a comment which was used repeatedly by Trump to show her indifference to the plight of the working class.

Trump also triggered a fight within his own party. His attacks on "establishment" Republicans, including even personal insults of his rivals, appeared calculated to highlight the new division. Republicans had long emphasized unrestricted free markets and major business interests affiliated with the Party favored cheap immigrant labor and even cheaper labor offshore. But an intellectual movement emerged in favor of a "Trumpian" reorientation of the Republican Party. These populist elements argued that there is a single "political class" that includes leaders of both parties and serves the interests of financial and cultural elites rather than ordinary Americans (Codevilla 2010). Whether it was accurate or not, Trump was able to capitalize on the perception that the two parties were more akin to a "uniparty," essentially sharing the same goals, especially a more liberal immigration policy (Hanson 2019).

However accurate this characterization of the parties may be, there is no doubt that Trump drew fire from every quarter of elite institutions in America, including the media, government bureaucracies, and the intelligence agencies.

His presidency, it goes without saying, was tumultuous. And as of this writing, he is under indictment on dozens of felony counts in state and federal courts. Yet, remarkably, as *New York Times* columnist Thomas B. Edsall and others have noted, polls indicate that his following remains strong and is even growing slightly among demographics classified as working class—even as such voters remain somewhat ambivalent about the Republican Party as a whole (Edsall 2024; Ruffini 2023). It is impossible to predict what will happen under these unprecedented circumstances. But it is well worth considering that the essential problems that gave rise to the populist moment—declining economic opportunity for many and a widespread sense of despair about the future—remain. In other words, Trump is perhaps more a symptom than a cause of political dysfunction in the Union States.

As intimated above, a healthy republic requires a healthy middle class, a society in which ordinary people are able to achieve a modicum of self-sufficiency. Without that self-sufficiency, the people become unfree, dependent on one kind of patron or another. Therefore, the basic interests of the people, such as an economic environment where meaningful and remunerative work is available, ought to be addressed by the political system. As James Madison argued, "the public good, the real welfare of the great body of the people, is the supreme object to be pursued" by the government (Hamilton et al. 2003, 286). The upheavals of recent years, and the consequent distrust of the political order, perhaps indicate that the government has not fulfilled that duty.

Scot J. Zentner is Professor of Political Science at California State University, San Bernardino, and co-author of "Party and Nation: Immigration and Regime Politics in American History."

References

Baldwin, Richard. 2016. *The Great Convergence*. Cambridge, MA: Belknap Press of Harvard University Press.

Codevilla, Angelo. 2010. *The Ruling Class: How They Corrupted America and What We Can Do about It*. New York: Beaufort Books.

Edsall, Thomas B. 2024. "One Thing Keeping Democrats Up at Night." *New York Times*. March 20. Accessed May 6, 2024. https://www.nytimes.com/2024/03/20/opinion/biden-trump-black-hispanic-voters.html.

Gerring, John. 1998. *Party Ideologies in America, 1828–1996*. Cambridge: Cambridge University Press.

Hamilton, Alexander, James Madison, and John Jay. 2003. *The Federalist Papers*, ed. Clinton Rossiter. New York: New American Library.

Hanson, Victor Davis. 2019. *The Case for Trump*. New York: Basic Books.

Judis, John B., and Ruy Teixeira. 2004. *The Emerging Democratic Majority*. New York: Lisa Drew/Scribner-Simon & Schuster.

Judis, John B., and Ruy Teixeira. 2023. *Where Have All the Democrats Gone?: The Soul of the Party in the Age of Extremes*. New York: Henry Holt and Company.

Luttwak, Edward. July 24, 2017. "Why the Trump Dynasty Will Last Sixteen Years." *Times Literary Supplement*. Accessed November 25, 2023. https://www.the-tls.co.uk/articles/public/trump-dynasty-luttwak/.

Phillips, Amber. March 10, 2016. "Yes, Bernie Sanders Voted to Kill Immigration Reform in 2007. But It's Complicated." *Washington Post*. Accessed November 25, 2023. https://www.washingtonpost.com/news/the-fix/wp/2016/03/10/yes-bernie-sanders-voted-to-kill-immigration-reform-in-2007-but-its-complicated/?utm_term=.89a437749afb.

Ruffini, Patrick. 2023. "The Emerging Working-Class Republican Majority." *Politico*. November 4. Accessed May 6, 2024. https://www.politico.com/news/magazine/2023/11/04/new-republican-party-working-class-coalition-00122822.

Shafer, Byron E., and William J.M. Claggett. 1995. *The Two Majorities: The Issue Context of Modern American Politics*. Baltimore: Johns Hopkins University Press.

natural
100%
Apple Juice

4

Profiles

Introduction

There are currently thousands of governmental and nonprofit organizations and individuals working in various capacities to serve children, young adults, families, and the elderly affected by poverty in the United States. This chapter highlights the work of some key national and local organizations, including government-sponsored entities, policy and research institutions, faith-based groups, and other private nonprofits. These organizations and initiatives are dedicated to providing direct services to the poor, equipping individuals for social and economic mobility, better understanding the nature and causes of poverty, compiling and maintaining data, improving anti-poverty policy, and promoting more effective short- and long-term solutions to reduce impoverishment in America. The chapter concludes with a few profiles of historic and present-day individuals who have brought public attention to the issue of poverty in America and who have shaped the policy debate over its causes and solutions.

Government-Sponsored Agencies, Organizations, and Programs

Administration for Children and Families

Housed in the United States Department of Health and Human Services, the Administration for Children and Families (ACF) was created in 1991 to merge several major agencies. Today, the department bears primary responsibility for funding state, territory, local, and tribal organizations to provide family assistance

---

The US Department of Agriculture's Food and Nutrition Service Meals to You program responded to the school closures during the Covid-19 pandemic, partnering with food companies and logistics companies to distribute food boxes to children in rural locations multiple times per week. (USDA Media by Lance Cheung)

(welfare benefits), child support, foster care, adoption assistance, childcare, early childhood education, and other programs related to promoting the economic and social well-being of children, families, individuals, and communities. Several of the agency's major departments and programs are highlighted below.

Children's Bureau

The Children's Bureau is the most senior department within ACF. Created by President William H. Taft in 1912, it was the first federal agency in the United States (and in the world) to focus exclusively on improving the lives of children and families.

Today, the Children's Bureau partners with federal, state, tribal, and local agencies to advance the overall well-being of our nation's children and families. Its efforts primarily focus on improving child abuse prevention, foster care, and adoption. The Bureau, which operates an on annual budget of nearly $10 billion, is composed of eight divisions and teams and participates in a variety of projects that provide guidance on federal law, policy, and program regulations; fund essential services, helping states and tribes operate every aspect of their child welfare systems; support innovation through competitive, peer-reviewed grants for research and program development; offer training and technical assistance to improve child welfare service delivery; monitor child welfare services to help states and tribes achieve positive outcomes for children and families; and share research to help child welfare professionals improve their services.

Family and Youth Services Bureau

Established in 1974, the Family and Youth Services Bureau (FYSB) is tasked with administering programs and supporting organizations that work to promote youth well-being, and combat youth homelessness, adolescent pregnancy, and domestic violence. The bureau is home to three major grant programs. The first, the Runaway and Homeless Youth program, is the main national provider of shelter services to homeless youth. The grants administered under the program fund four major initiatives. Basic Center Programs support the provision of emergency shelter, food, clothing, and medical care for up to twenty-one days, along with counseling, education and employment assistance, and after-care services. Transitional Living Programs fund grants for community-based, adult-supervised group homes, family homes, and apartments for youth ages sixteen to twenty-two years who cannot safely live with their own families. Maternity

Group Home Programs fund homes through the Transitional Living Program that are specifically designed to meet the needs of pregnant and parenting youth and their young families. Finally, Street Outreach Programs fund prevention and intervention services to runaway, homeless, and street youth, who have been subjected to, or are at risk of being subjected to, sexual abuse, human trafficking, or sexual exploitation.

The FYSB's second major grant program, the Adolescent Pregnancy Prevention Program, funds efforts to reduce rates of teenage pregnancy and the transmission of sexually transmitted diseases. The third grant program, the Family Violence Prevention and Services Program, provides funding for emergency shelters, counseling, and a national domestic violence hotline.

The FYSB additionally funds the National Runaway Safeline, a nationwide crisis hotline for runaway youth, and the National Clearinghouse on Runaway and Homeless Youth, a repository for information and research related to runaway or homeless youth. The agency also works collaboratively with the Departments of Agriculture, Education, Housing and Urban Development, Justice, and Labor on projects related to its mission.

Office of Family Assistance

The Office of Family Assistance (OFA) is the agency responsible for administrating Temporary Assistance for Needy Families (TANF), the nation's primary welfare program which replaced Aid to Families with Dependent Children (AFDC) in 1997. TANF is a federal block grant that provides nearly $17 billion annually to states, territories, Washington DC, and federally recognized Indian Tribes to provide income support and other services (such as work-related activities, childcare, and refundable tax credits) to low-income families with children.

The OFA additionally administers the Native Employment Works (NEW) program, the Tribal TANF-Child Welfare Coordination grants, and the Healthy Marriage and Responsible Fatherhood (HMRF) initiative. The NEW program provides annual funding to organizations sponsoring work-related activities to support job readiness, placement, and retention for Native Americans. The Tribal TANF-Child Welfare Coordination grants provided funding to eight tribes and tribal organizations to demonstrate models of effective coordination of Trible TANF and children welfare services given to tribal families at risk of child abuse and neglect. The demonstration period allotted for these grants was from September 30, 2020, through September 29, 2025. Finally, the HMRF initiative is a discretionary grant program that was authorized in 2005 to support community-based efforts aimed at promoting strong, healthy family formation and maintenance; responsible fatherhood and parenting; and reentry opportunities for fathers returning from incarceration.

Other ACF Departments and Programs

ACF is home to a host of additional Departments and Programs relating to the issue of poverty in America. Among these are the Administration for Native Americans (ANA), which was founded to promote the goal of self-sufficiency and cultural preservation for Native Americans by providing social and economic development opportunities; the Office of Child Care (OCC), which works to help low-income families improve access to affordable, high-quality early care and after-school care and supports childcare research, demonstration, and evaluation activities; the Office of Head Start (OHS), which oversees agencies operating Head Start early childhood education programs; and the Office of Refugee Resettlement (ORR), which provides resources for refugees, asylum seekers, and other new arrivals to the United States to assist with their integration into their new community.

Department of Housing and Urban Development

In 1965, President Lyndon Johnson signed the Housing and Urban Development Act. The act promoted the Housing and Home Finance Agency (which administered the Federal Housing Administration [FHA] along with public housing and urban renewal programs) to a cabinet level department. This newly elevated department was officially renamed the Department of Housing and Urban Development (HUD). In 1968, HUD was tasked with enforcing housing laws and encouraging neighborhood desegregation. Following criticism of previous federal public housing construction and urban renewal efforts, the Section 8 program was created in 1974. The program allowed HUD to utilize private developers and landlords to create housing for the poor, both through new construction and financial assistance to renters of existing units. During the Reagan administration, federally funded construction was phased out and Section 8 was transformed into a voucher program that subsidized the rent of low-income tenants.

Today, through its individual offices and programs, HUD administers affordable housing and homelessness programs; manages federal funding for public housing and housing vouchers; enforces federal laws against housing discrimination; overseas the Federal Housing Administration's federal loan insurance program for moderate-income home buyers; directs federal community development programs such as urban renewal and Community Development Block Grants; and conducts research on housing needs, market conditions, existing programs, and community development.

Federal Work Study

Originally established under the Economic Opportunity Act of 1964, the Federal Work Study program was modeled after the Depression-era National Youth Administration program that provided federally funded work opportunities to low-income high school and college students who needed earnings to remain in school. Today, the program continues to fund part-time employment for college students with financial need by subsidizing the wages of eligible students. Student participants may be employed by educational institutions, government agencies, or private nonprofit and for-profit organizations if they meet the legal requirements established by law. According to Department of Education regulations, participating institutions and employers must also use at least 7 percent of their Work Study allocation to fund students engaged in community service jobs such as tutoring or emergency preparedness and response.

The program maintains the three-pronged goal of helping students earn money to subsidize their education costs, providing students with work experience relevant to their chosen major or career field, and improving relations between institutions of higher education and the surrounding community.

Food and Nutrition Services

Housed within the United States Department of Agriculture (USDA), Food and Nutrition Services (FNS) is the federal agency responsible for administering the federal government's domestic food and nutrition assistance and education programs. FNS was officially launched as a separate agency within the USDA in 1969, but its roots trace back to several Depression-era food assistance programs and the Supplemental Nutrition Assistance Program (formerly known as the

Food Stamp Program). Most FNS-funded programs are administered by state, local, territorial, and tribal governments that determine details regarding the distribution of food benefits and eligibility of participants.

Today, more than one in five Americans benefit from products and services funded by FNS's domestic nutrition assistance programs. Two of the most prominent FNS programs are the Supplemental Nutrition Assistance Program (SNAP), which provides food purchasing assistance to low-income individuals and families to help them avoid food insecurity, and Women, Infants, and Children (WIC), which provides federal grants to the states to provide low-income pregnant and postpartum women and children up to age five with supplemental foods, healthcare referrals, and nutrition education. A few additional major FNS grant programs include the Farmers Market Nutrition Program, which provides coupons to low-income seniors and SNAP and WIC beneficiaries to buy locally grown fruits, vegetables, honey, and herbs from eligible farmers, farmers markets, and roadside stands; the Child and Adult Care Food Program, which provides reimbursement for food provided to eligible children and adults enrolled at participating childcare centers, daycare homes, and adult daycare centers; the Fresh Fruit and Vegetable Program, which funds the introduction of a variety of produce to elementary school students; the School Breakfast Program and the Special Milk Program, which provide breakfast and milk to children in schools and childcare institutions; the Summer Food Service Program, which reimburses program operators who serve no-cost meals and snacks to children and teens at summer sites in low-income communities; and the Emergency Food Assistance Program, which provides emergency food assistance through distribution agencies.

Job Corps

First enacted under the Economic Opportunity Act of 1964, the Job Corps program aims to provide disadvantaged youth with intensive social, academic, career, and technical education and service-learning opportunities through contractor organizations, including nonprofit and for-profit entities as well as the US Department of Agriculture's Forest Service. To qualify for Job Corps, participants must be low-income and face specific barriers to employment, such as basic skill deficiency, pregnancy or teen parenthood, homelessness, or involvement in the foster-care system. Job Corps is one of the only employment programs geared toward youth that provides residential centers, where participants can live, receive healthcare, childcare, and other services. While supporters of the program typically contend that Job Corps has helped youth from troubled backgrounds turn their life around, critics have pointed out the exorbitant costs for each enrollee and the fact that less than 50 percent of participants complete the program or find jobs related to their training.

Joint Economic Committee

In 1946, Congress passed and President Truman signed the Employment Act of 1846, creating the President's Council of Economic Advisors (CEA) and the Joint Economic Committee (JEC) to review economic conditions and recommend improvements in economic policy. The JEC is one of four permanent joint committees in the US Congress, which are made up of members from both the House and the Senate. The committee was originally assigned three primary duties: to monitor the subjects included in the president's Yearly Economic Report, to identify ways to coordinate federal government programs, and to produce a yearly report in response to the President's Economic Report. The JEC's responsibilities were eventually expanded to require the issuance of a monthly publication of economic indicators and a report to the House and Senate Budget Committees analyzing the short- and medium-term goals contained within the President's Economic Report.

The JEC is currently made up of ten members from the House and ten members of the Senate. The partisan distribution of the committee is based roughly on the overall percentage of seats the majority and minority parties hold in each chamber. Chairmanship of the Committee alternates between the Senate and the House at the start of each new Congress. The JEC does not have legislative jurisdiction. It is authorized, however, to perform research, advise members of Congress, and hold hearings to receive testimony from Members of Congress, government agencies, and the public. Recent hearings have focused on topics such as policy approaches to increase affordable housing, empowering older workers, connecting people to work, and improving family stability, and wealth gaps and economic inequality.

In 2017, Senator Mike Lee (R-UT) founded the JEC's Social Capital Project to study the state of social capital in America and to make policy recommendations for its improvement. Social capital refers to an individual's network of relationships and level of social connectedness—including informal ties to relatives, friends, and neighbors as well as formal ties to civic associations, volunteer or professional organizations, and religious and educational institutions. These connections and relationship networks can help individuals successfully navigate society and its institutions. The Social Capital Project maps communities by social and demographic indicators such as the rate of unwed childbearing and marriage, along with civil engagement measures, such as churchgoing, volunteering, and voting. It also advises Congress on policies to increase social capital through reconnecting Americans to work, improving investment in youth, making it more affordable to raise a family, increasing family stability, and rebuilding civil society.

National Service Programs

Dating back to the Depression-era's Civilian Conservation Corps, national service programs are federally established institutions that serve the community, while providing experience and training to youth participants. These programs generally create full-time, year-long public service positions—financed by public and private resources—that provide participants with a minimal stipend and healthcare and childcare benefits. National service programs additionally offer financial awards to participants who complete a term of service that can be used to finance higher education, career training, or student loans. National service programs are not designed to replace long-term careers, but they can help prepare difficult-to-employ young adults and recent college graduates for future employment in the private or public sector. Although Congress has at times questioned the effectiveness of such programs, studies sponsored by the Corporation for National and Community Service Programs have found that youth who participate in volunteer service programs experience an increased likelihood of future gainful employment following their service—this is especially true for participants who lack a high school diploma.

The federal government currently funds national service opportunities for youth through a variety of programs and focus areas.

AmeriCorps

AmeriCorps is the largest national service program in the country. Created by federal law in 1993, AmeriCorps provides grants to state and national organizations, including nonprofits, colleges, government agencies, and faith-based groups, to provide recent college graduates, veterans, and at-risk youth with direct service opportunities. Most service opportunities are designed to respond to critical community needs in the areas of education, public health and safety, and environmental protection. One major aim of AmeriCorps' programs is to create a pathway for young adults to enter public service careers that might otherwise experience substantial workforce shortages.

In July 2013, the Corporation for National and Community Service, which oversees AmeriCorps, announced the launch of the president's Task Force on Expanding National Service. This Task Force led to the creation of several collaborative programs between federal agencies and the private sector designed to provide service opportunities for vulnerable youth. One of these programs, Youth Opportunity AmeriCorps, established in 2014 under the Justice Department's Office of Juvenile Justice and Delinquency Prevention, creates opportunities for formerly incarcerated youth to reconnect to society by enrolling in direct service activities throughout the nation.

Also founded in 2014, ServiceWorks is a collaborative program sponsored by AmeriCorps, The Citi Foundation, and the international non-profit Points of Light, which aims to help low-income youth in ten major cities across the United States to develop the skills they need to prepare for college and careers while engaging in service. Participants first receive training courses taught by field professionals in twenty-first-century leadership and workplace skills. Then, under the guidance of a mentor, they participate in and lead volunteer service projects. Additional partnerships have been established with the US Forest Service and US Department of Transportation to provide opportunities for youth and veterans to work to protect and restore the nation's forest and grasslands or to improve state and regional transportation.

The National Association of Service and Conservation Corps (NASCC)

The National Association of Service and Conservation Corps (NASCC), also known as the Corps Network, directs and supports a network of nearly 150 locally based organizations that engage youth, aged sixteen to twenty-five, and veterans up to the age of thirty-five, in various service and conservation projects involving infrastructure, public lands, and disaster response. The Corps Network is supported in part by AmeriCorps funding and in part by private donations—including sizable contributions from the Ford, Hewlett, and Mott Foundations. Participants or "Corps members" are compensated with a stipend, while participating in work activities designed to preserve and improve the nation's public lands, such as building and enhancing rails, increasing access to public lands and waters, creating and maintaining urban parks, removing invasive species, and restoring communities and resources following disasters. Corps members also receive education, training, and certification in skills such as wildland firefighting, carpentry, HAZMAT remediation, and heavy equipment operation. Many also work simultaneously on completing their GED or high school diploma.

Volunteers in Service to America (VISTA)

Volunteers in Service to America (VISTA), originally founded in 1965 as the domestic version of the Peace Corps, was incorporated into AmeriCorps in 1993 and renamed AmeriCorps VISTA. The program funds and deploys volunteers to assist nonprofits focused on addressing the economic challenges of the long-term poor living in low-income communities. Volunteers are tasked with recruiting additional volunteers, raising funds, developing new programs, and building community partnerships.

Youth Conservation Corps

Youth Conservation Corps is an eight-to-ten-week summer employment program for youth, aged fifteen through eighteen. Participants are paid minimum wage to work alongside federal employees in national parks, forests, wildlife refuges, and fish hatcheries. Assignments may include projects such as building and maintaining trails and fences, cleaning campgrounds, improving wildlife habitat, environmental education planning, and historical building preservation.

YouthCorps

YouthCorps is a network of services programs focused on recruiting youth, aged sixteen to twenty-four, who are not in the labor force and not in school and are economically, physically, or educationally disadvantaged. YouthCorps programs encourage participants to earn a General Educational Development high school equivalency, while they acquire job-related skills through service projects in energy conservation, human services, and urban construction.

Office of Apprenticeship

Operating under the Department of Labor, the federal Office of Apprenticeship (OA) administers the National Apprenticeship Act, which authorizes the federal government in cooperation with independent State Apprenticeship Agencies (SAAs) to manage the nation's apprenticeship system. The primary function of OA is to oversee and set guidelines for the federal Registered Apprenticeship programs. Registered Apprenticeships are programs that have been certified by the Department of Labor's Office of Apprenticeship or by a State Apprenticeship Agency because they meet specified standards. As part of its oversight responsibilities, the OA oversees program approval and registration, sets standards for training quality and worker health and safety, ensures equality of access, and issues nationally recognized certificates of completion. The OA directly administers the Registered Apprenticeship program in twenty-five states and it delegates operational authority to independent State Apprenticeship Agencies (SAAs) in twenty-five states and in Washington DC.

To qualify to participate in the OA Registered Apprenticeship program, an occupation must involve skills that are customarily learned in a practical way through supervised on-the-job training. Registered Apprenticeships generally last between one and six years and require the completion of at least 2,000 hours of on-the-job learning in addition to 144 annual hours of supplemental classroom instruction in technical subjects related to the occupation. Today, thousands of employers and companies in a variety of industries—including construction, manufacturing, information technology, healthcare, the military, and others—offer Registered Apprenticeship training opportunities to nearly half a million apprentices.

In June 2017, President Donald Trump signed an Executive Order calling for the expansion of available apprenticeships under the Department of Labor's Registered Apprenticeship Program. The order also shifted the role of developing and issuing guidelines for government-funded apprenticeship programs from the OA to private entities—such as companies, labor unions, and industry groups—pending Department of Labor approval.

Reentry Employment Opportunities Program

The Reentry Employment Opportunities program is designed to provide job training and other services for individuals with a criminal record. While

Congress never explicitly authorized this program, the Department of Labor has appropriated funding for its operation under the Workforce Investment and Opportunity Act and the Second Chances Act. Through the allocation of grants to community-based organizations, school districts, and state departments of correction, the youth component of the program aims to increase employment opportunities and educational services for youth who have been involved with the juvenile justice or criminal justice system or who are at risk of dropping out of school and becoming involved with the justice system. Services provided under the program include pre-release mentoring, housing, and employment services.

United States Interagency Council on Homelessness

The United States Interagency Council on Homelessness (USICH) was first established as an independent agency in the executive branch under Title II of the Homeless Assistance Act of 1987. The agency, which was most recently reauthorized under the Homeless Emergency Assistance and Rapid Transition to Housing Act in 2009, is the only federal agency with the sole mission of preventing and ending homelessness in America. The Council, which includes the heads of 19 federal member agencies, is charged with the development and implementation of a coordinated federal strategic response to homelessness. Pursuant to this charge, the USICH creates partnerships at every level of government and with the public and private sector service providers to improve federal spending outcomes for homelessness; to reduce federal bureaucracy and competing priorities; to develop an effective portal to federal programs and initiatives; to efficiently implement local plans to end homelessness; to monitor, evaluate, and recommend improvements and disseminated best practices in serving those experiencing homelessness; and to provide professional and technical assistance to states, local governments, and other public and private nonprofit organizations.

YouthBuild

First established under the Cranston-Gonzalez National Affordable Housing Act of 1992, YouthBuild was administered by the Department of Housing and Urban Development until it was transferred to the Department of Labor in 2007. YouthBuild is a competitive grant program intended to engage disadvantaged, low-income youth in employment and other activities related to housing and construction. YouthBuild participants are generally taught construction skills while working on community service projects, such as building parks and community centers and improving low-income housing and schools. Participants are required to spend at least 40 percent of their time in work and skill development activities and at least 50 percent of their time in education or activities designed to meet their educational needs, including training in industry rules and requirements.

Youth Workforce Investment Activities Program

The Youth Workforce Investment Activities Program, also referred to as the Youth Activities Program, is a formula grant program that allocates funding to state and local workforce development boards to provide year-round employment opportunities and other services to youth. Although most federally funded youth employment and training programs accept participants only from low-income backgrounds, the Youth Activities Program accepts those who are not low-income if they have dropped out of high school. Workforce development boards are required to provide a variety of different services to participants, including mentoring services, tutoring, study skills training, alternative secondary school services or dropout recovery services, and paid and unpaid work experiences—which could include summer employment, pre-apprenticeships, or internships.

Non-Governmental Organizations and Programs

American Compass

American Compass is a policy think tank founded to reorient the typical conservative/libertarian economic consensus, which elevates unhampered free markets and emphasizes economic growth as the standard of national prosperity. In contrast, American Compass is working to build a new economic agenda which highlights the plight of modern American workers and focuses on economic development that sustains the social institutions vital to the country's liberty and prosperity: the family, community, and industry. On the policy front, American Compass scholars work to help policymakers navigate the limitations and strengths of both markets and the government in promoting the general welfare and the nation's security. The organization aims to sustain and develop three pillars: productive markets, supportive communities, and responsive politics.

Based on the belief that unrestricted free markets do not always benefit American workers, their families, and communities, American Compass seeks to promote public policy that aims at productive markets which align individual self-interest with the public interest. In this area, American Compass scholars focus particularly on the parallel trends of globalization and financialization, which they contend generate profit, but undermine the nation's prosperity.

American Compass additionally rejects the market fundamentalism, which reduces the complexities of the modern market to trade between autonomous individuals and defines capitalism as nothing more than "economic freedom." Instead, American Compass scholars seek to highlight and strengthen the range of institutions and supportive communities operating prior to, alongside, and within the market, which shape and are shaped by market outcomes. Among these institutions and communities are families, schools, and labor unions.

Finally, in the realm of policy, American Compass scholars work to identify and promote politically the values and quality of life concerns that Americans hold dear but that are ignored by markets focused solely on increased consumption. In conjunction with its policy work, American Compass, alongside the Ethics and Public Policy Center, publishes "The Edgerton Essays: Perspectives from the Working Class." This series—named after Jim Edgerton, the subject of a famous Norman Rockwell painting—is a collection of two dozen essays by working-class Americans answering in their own words the question, "What do you wish policy makers knew about the challenges facing your families and communities?"

America Works

America Works was founded in 1984 by Peter Cove, after he had spent two decades working in several of the programs implemented to reduce poverty during President Lyndon B. Johnson's "War on Poverty." He was soon joined by his wife Dr. Lee Bowes, one of the nation's leading experts on policies related to welfare-to-work and prison-to-work workforce development. He served as a consultant before becoming the CEO of America Works in 1987.

Based on his first-hand experience working in poor relief and his review of available research, Cove concluded that extended education and job training programs had not proved an effective means of securing long-term employment or a path out of poverty for welfare recipients. Instead, Cove determined that the most effective approach to helping people out of poverty is by assisting them in finding immediate employment. He founded America Works to put this theory into action. America Works was designed as a for-profit employment service that works with state and local welfare agencies to place welfare recipients and other candidates in jobs quickly and then to invest in the human capital and training services to advance the already employed individual up in wages and position.

Alongside his role at America Works, Cove developed and promoted prisoner reentry initiatives and advocated for second-chance legislation that successfully reintegrates ex-offenders into communities using a work-first model. During the 1990s, Cove and Bowes worked to educate members of both political parties on the merits of implementing a national "Work First" welfare policy. In 1996, they were invited by President Bill Clinton and House Speaker Newt Gingrich to help craft welfare reform legislation.

Today, America Works uses a blended model that includes work readiness training, vocational training, career placement, career advancement, and employment retention services. The first step involves a four-week job-readiness training program in which clients are taught universally applicable skills such as verbal and written communication, customer service, computer literacy, and more. Next America Works matches their clients' career goals and work history with available opportunities, utilizing connections with local employers to help their clients get right to the interview stage. Once clients are hired, case managers provide continued mentoring and support services, ensuring that clients establish a positive routine and transition effectively into the workplace. America Works' staff then provide clients with access to training, certification, and educational opportunities that will help them advance within their chosen company or field or move to another opportunity.

America Works reports that it has helped more than two million people achieve gainful, long-term employment including military veterans, welfare and SNAP recipients, teens aging out of the foster care system, criminal justice involved and homeless individuals, and persons with disabilities.

Asset-Based Community Development Institute

The Asset-Based Community Development Institute (ABCD) was cofounded by former social activist and Northwestern professor John L. McKnight and his long-time colleague and collaborator in community research, John P. Kretzmann.

Today, the institute is at the center of a growing movement that challenges the traditional approach to solving urban problems by focusing service providers and funding agencies on the needs and deficiencies of neighborhoods. Instead, the ABCD approach considers local assets—including the skills of residents, the resources and supportive functions of local associations, the history and culture of a neighborhood, and the physical infrastructure and space in a community—as the key building blocks in sustainable urban and rural community revitalization and development.

The institute is currently partnered with and housed in the Steans Center for Community-Based Service Learning and Community Service Studies at DePaul University in Chicago, Illinois. Thanks to the growing and widespread interest in the principles and practice of building community capacity, ABCD now has over seventy-five faculty, made up of highly skilled practitioners, who engage directly with community groups to support their asset-based community development efforts. Faculty lead training workshops throughout the year to introduce the principles of ABCD to students, community groups, educators, civic leaders, non-profits, and churches. Affiliated faculty have additionally created a library of community building workbooks, published scholarly articles, developed training curricula, provided examples of asset-mapping tools, and promoted community stories so that community groups and organizations can learn from the experiences of others engaged in asset-based community development work.

Black Male Initiative

In 2004, the City University of New York (CUNY) launched the Black Male Initiative to increase the educational and employment attainment of young Black males. The initiative initially provided funding to the campuses in the CUNY system to establish demonstration projects. These projects include mentorship opportunities, academic support, and career counseling to Black males and other disadvantaged youth, as well as support geared specifically to formerly incarcerated individuals. The program was designed to provide a model for other universities and colleges around the country, and similarly styled initiatives have since been adopted by several additional schools.

Brookings Institution

The Brookings Institution, one of the oldest and most influential think tanks in the United States, is a nonprofit public policy organization based in Washington

DC that seeks to conduct quality, in-depth research and analysis and to influence policy debates with proposals firmly rooted in observed facts, empirical evidence, and experience rather than political ideology. Its scholars conduct research on a variety of issues related to domestic and foreign policy, many of which are related to the topic of poverty in America. Several institute fellows, including Martha Ross, Isabel V. Sawhill, Ron Haskins, and Julia B. Isaacs, have produced substantial, groundbreaking research and analysis on topics related to social and economic mobility, employment trends, and improving educational options and career pathways for low-income or low-skilled workers.

In 2006, the Brookings Institution launched an economic policy initiative titled "The Hamilton Project," which is administered by an advisory council of academics, business leaders, and former public policymakers. The project provides a platform for economic thinkers to develop innovative and pragmatic policy options. The project is named after Alexander Hamilton, the nation's first treasury secretary, who, as an immigrant born into poverty, symbolizes the American values of opportunity and mobility that motivated the project's work. Over the past decade, the Hamilton Project has produced thoughtful analysis of the long-term effects of the Great Recession on America's Youth and improving economic opportunity for low-income youth.

Center for Advancing Opportunity

The Center for Advancing Opportunity (CAO), a research and education initiative headquartered in Washington DC, was founded after Johnny C. Taylor, the former president and CEO of the Thurgood Marshall College Fund (TMCF), heard Charles Koch, the CEO of Koch Industries and cofounder of the Koch Foundation, give a television interview about removing barriers to opportunity. Taylor sent Koch a letter proposing a partnership between Koch Industries and TMCF, which led to the establishment of CAO shortly thereafter. Thanks to a more than $25 million grant from the Koch Foundation, CAO now financially supports faculty and students at Historically Black Colleges and Universities (HBCUs) and other postsecondary institutions to research barriers to opportunity for those living in fragile urban, rural, and suburban communities and to develop research-based solutions to challenging issues in education, criminal justice, and entrepreneurship. The center defines fragile communities as areas in the United States characterized by high proportions of residents struggling in their daily lives and possessing limited opportunities for social mobility. In addition to faculty and student research, CAO additionally sponsors an annual State of Opportunity in America Summit to examine and discuss the latest findings and best practices regarding the problems in fragile communities.

CAO-sponsored research adopts a different approach than much of the previous research conducted on poverty-stricken urban and rural communities. Whereas most research is conducted by academics who view themselves as responsible for solving the problems of those they study, CAO seeks to include those living in impacted communities as active participants in the problem-solving. In an effort to gain insight into the lives and experiences of individuals living in fragile communities nationwide, CAO partnered with Gallup to conduct a comprehensive six-month qualitative and quantitative survey of thousands of residents from low-income areas in Birmingham, Alabama; Cleveland, Ohio; Fresno, California; and Chicago, Illinois. The survey sought to reveal residents' feelings, opinions, and perceptions on education, criminal justice, entrepreneurship, optimism, and self-efficacy.

The CAO established three research hubs at HBCU's in 2018: the Center for the Study of Economic Mobility at Winston-Salem State University in North Carolina, the Center for Criminal Justice Research at Texas Southern University, and the Center for Educational Opportunity at Albany State University in Georgia.

Christian Community Development Association

The Christian Community Development Association (CCDA) describes itself as a network of Christians committed to seeing people and underprivileged communities holistically restored spiritually, emotionally, physically, economically, and socially.

The roots of the CCDA date back to 1960, when founder John Perkins and his wife Vera May relocated their family to the poverty-stricken community of Mendenhall, Mississippi, to live and work with the people there. For the next thirty-five years, they engaged in community development in the areas in both Mississippi and California, leaving behind ministries headed by local leaders. In 1989, they officially established the CCDA and hosted their first annual conference in Chicago with the goal of training, educating, connecting, and inspiring like-minded individuals committed to reclaiming, restoring, and empowering poor communities.

Today, Christian Community Development (CCD) Practitioners commit to living in a poor or under-resourced neighborhood for a minimum of ten years. CCD Practitioners dedicate themselves to several components of Christian community development. These include relocation, living among the people with whom they work and sharing in their suffering and pain; reconciliation, reconciling individuals to God and connecting them to church fellowship; redistribution, investing resources in the community; leadership development, raising local leaders who will remain in the community to live and lead; listening to the community, taking into account the ideas, dreams, and thoughts of community residents rather than outsiders; and empowerment, empowering community members with the training and resources to improve their own lives and communities.

Cristo Rey Network

The Cristo Rey Network is a network of thirty-five Catholic work-preparatory high schools that exclusively serve underprivileged students. The network was established in 2000 to increase the number of schools modeled after Cristo Rey Jesuit School, which was founded in 1996 in Chicago. Network schools adopt an effective and innovative approach to inner-city education designed to equip students from underserved, economically disadvantaged communities to develop their minds and become lifelong contributors to society. It is the only network of high schools in the country that integrates four years of rigorous college preparatory academics with four years of professional work experience through its Corporate Work Study Program. This program operates as a temporary employment agency within the schools. Throughout the academic year each student is employed in an entry-level, professional job five days a month. Work experiences are offered in a variety of fields including law, finance, healthcare, and technology. Students typically earn $18 an hour in education support and are able to use their earnings to defer most of their education expenses.

In 2009, the network established a University Partners program to forge collaborative relationships between select colleges and Cristo Rey schools and students. University partners commit to supporting, mentoring, and recruiting Cristo Rey students, many of whom are first-generation college students. This partnership not only benefits students, it also benefits university partners by providing them with access to a national pipeline of diverse, motivated, and well-prepared students. Although the average Cristo Rey student begins about two grade levels behind their peers, the school has been successful at catching students up academically and 90 percent of graduates enroll in college.

Conrad N. Hilton Foundation

The Conrad N. Hilton Foundation is a nonprofit charitable foundation established and funded by the late hotel entrepreneur Conrad N. Hilton with the mission to "relieve the suffering, the distressed, and the destitute." In March 2012, the Foundation Board approved the launch of the first phase of the organization's Foster Youth Strategic Initiative Strategy. The goal of the initiative is to support one of the nation's most challenged populations, foster youth between the ages of sixteen and twenty-four, and to work with partners to ensure that as these youth age out of the foster system they are able to become self-sufficient and thriving adults. The Strategic Initiative aims to achieve its vision in a variety of ways, but the core focus is to bring about systemic policy change by developing and advocating a new framework for addressing the unique needs of "transition age youth" (TAY) and by creating new education and career pathways to ensure their success. According to the initiative report, research and frontline experience have demonstrated that expanding knowledge, skills, and opportunities in career pathways have the most significant impact on a young person's ability to become self-sufficient. Between 2012 and 2017, the foundation invested $53.5 million and joined with community partners and other investors in New York and Los Angeles to move public child welfare systems and policies away from a one-size-fits-all approach that narrowly focuses on foster TAY's safety and basic needs toward an approach that emphasizes TAY's potential to succeed in education, careers, and life. The partnerships have spurred policy reform and the successful passage of more than 120 new state and local legislative proposals in Los Angeles County and New York City that expand educational and career services for older youth in foster care.

Economic Policy Institute

The Economic Policy Institute is a liberal leaning think tank funded in part by labor unions. The institute was founded in 1986 by several economists to assess current economic policies and propose new policies aiming to address economic inequalities and to protect and improve the living standards of low- and middle-income workers. Areas of research and analysis include education, immigration, public investment, raising wages, trade and globalization, and unions and labor standards. Every year the institute publishes a flagship manual, *The State of Working America,* which examines the US economy's impact on wages, employment, wealth, and poverty.

Employment Policies Institute

The Employment Policies Institute is a conservative leaning think tank that publishes research conducted by independent economists on employment-related issues. Of central concern to the institute is the impact particular policies have on employment growth and entry-level employment. Institute-sponsored research largely aims to quantify the effects of minimum wage mandates, healthcare mandates, and employment taxes credits on low-wage labor markets and the degree to which higher labor costs inhibit job creation.

Homeboy Industries

Homeboy Industries is a nonprofit community organization based in Los Angeles, California, that provides support and employment training to formerly gang-involved and previously incarcerated men and women. It was originally started in 1988 as a small jobs program in one of the most gang-ridden parishes in Los Angeles by a Jesuit priest, Father Greg Boyle, who recognized the need to provide community support, jobs, and education as an alternative to gangs. It has since grown to become one of the largest, most comprehensive, and most successful gang intervention, rehabilitation, and reentry programs in the country.

The organization offers services including educational courses, tattoo removal, substance abuse treatment, legal assistance, and job placement services to more than 1,000 members of the community each month. It also provides full-time employment to more than 200 men and women at a time through an eighteenth-month program designed to help participants reidentify who they are in the world and develop workplace skills that enable them to redirect their lives and become contributing members of the community. Since its inception, the organization has inspired the establishment of more than forty other organizations across the country based on similar models.

Jim Casey Youth Opportunity Initiative

A branch of the Annie E. Casey Foundation, the Jim Casey Youth Opportunity Initiative works to promote practices and policies that help foster youth (aged fourteen to twenty-six) successfully transition to adulthood. The Initiative sponsors the Opportunity Passport, a program designed to build the financial capability of foster youth by providing financial literacy training, a bank account, and matched-savings-program to help them pay for assets such as a car, books for school, and initial housing-related costs. Foster youth who purchase these assets through the matched-savings programs more than double their chances of having a full-time job.

Jobs for America's Graduates

Jobs for America's Graduates (JAG) is a national nonprofit network dedicated to helping at-risk-youth graduate from high school and either enroll in postsecondary education or secure a quality entry-level job with career advancement potential. Originally founded in Delaware in 1980 by former state governor Pete du Pont, the network now includes thirty-four state organizations and over a thousand program affiliates, including middle schools, high schools, community colleges, and government agencies. The state-based organizations and affiliates work together to provide youth who face serious barriers to graduation and employment with mentoring, dropout recovery services, employability skills development, and career and academic counseling—including one-on-one assistance with finding and keeping a job after graduation.

Jobs for the Future

Based in Boston, Washington DC, and Oakland, California, Jobs for the Future (JFF) is a leading national workforce and education nonprofit that provides expert consulting and analysis to transform workforce and education systems to create economic advancement opportunities for low-income young adults who face significant barriers in the labor market, especially as automation and technology reshape the economy. JFF works with key stakeholders in a community—including employers, system leaders, youth leaders, community-based organizations, schools, and postsecondary institutions—to help them develop collaborative career pathways that will enable young adults to prepare effectively to transition into occupational training programs that lead to skilled jobs with advancement potential or into degree-granting postsecondary programs of study. For the past fifteen years, JFF has additionally convened the Postsecondary State Network to advance policies and practices that hasten community college completion rates and career advancement through guided career pathways.

Manhattan Institute

The Manhattan Institute (MI) is a leading free-market policy think tank that aims to develop and disseminate new ideas that foster economic choice and individual responsibility. MI recruits experts that work to shape public discourse and influence policy in a variety of areas—including economic growth, education, energy and the environment, healthcare, race, and urban policy—by authorizing reports, essays, and books; testifying at government hearings; and communicating directly with citizens through op-eds, podcasts, and television interviews. MI often collaborates directly with cities and public officials to put policy prescriptions into practice. For example, in 2007, the institute partnered with Newark, New Jersey's mayor Cory Booker to implement a new approach to prisoner reentry based on the "work-first" strategy of connecting ex-offenders with paid work immediately upon release (a long-standing research area of the institute). In 2017, the institute launched a project to identify ways to expand funding to New York charter schools and enable them to educate more students.

MENTOR: The National Mentoring Partnership

MENTOR: The National Mentoring Partnership is a national network committed to increasing the quantity and quality of mentoring relationships for disconnected youth and those who are at risk of disconnection. The organization dates back to 1990 when Wall Street financiers Geoffrey Boisi and Raymond Chambers cofounded One-to-One partnership to serve as a resource for mentors and mentoring networks nationwide and to advocate for the expansion of mentoring. In 1991, they produced the first edition of the manual *The Elements of Effective Practice for Mentoring.* Now in its fourth edition, the manual outlines national-adopted standards that serve as guide to assist organizations in starting and operating quality mentor programs.

One-to-One partnership was officially rebranded MENTOR in 1997, after the organization received a $4 million grant from the federal Office of Juvenile Justice and Delinquency Prevention for a juvenile mentoring program. Today, MENTOR oversees, advises, and provides infrastructure for more than 2,000 mentoring program partners across the country and continues its commitment to ensuring that at-risk youth have access to caring adults who will help them overcome personal and institutional obstacles as they pursue their interests and work to develop their skills. MENTOR additionally supports mentor recruitment and connects volunteers to these local programs by operating the Mentor Connector, the only national database of quality mentoring programs across the country that allows volunteers to search for a local program that meets their criteria. Every year, MENTOR convenes the National Mentoring Summit in Washington, DC, which brings together more than 1,000 practitioners, researchers, philanthropists, government and civic leaders, and youth-serving organizations from across the country to discuss and share emerging research, program models, and innovative practices. MENTOR additionally engages with elected and public officials to advocate for policy that supports positive youth development and mentoring relationships as a solution to community challenges.

National Youth Employment Coalition

The National Youth Employment Coalition (NYEC) is a national membership network of organizations—including nonprofit service providers, city agencies, local workforce development boards, and research entities—that work with, study, and advocate for disconnected youth. NYEC's primary mission is to improve the effectiveness of organizations and systems that seek to help disconnected youth become productive citizens. To advance this mission, NYEC engages in four kinds of activities. First, NYEC keeps the field up to date on recent innovations in practice and the latest research on best practices and service models. Second, NYEC builds its members' capacities to effectively serve opportunity youth by providing professional development services and working to help organizations implement best practices, expand their reach, and adapt to changing policy contexts. Third, NYEC serves as a unique line of communication between practitioners and policymakers and regularly solicits the views of members on how policy affects their service to youth. Based on this information, NYEC analyzes policy developments that affect disconnected youth, such as workforce development and K-12 and higher education reform. NYEC then uses these analyses to inform policy recommendations at the federal, state, and local levels. Finally, NYEC promotes the establishment and expansion of models based on research findings.

Network for Teaching Entrepreneurship

The Network for Teaching Entrepreneurship (NFTE) is an international nonprofit that seeks to activate an entrepreneurial mindset and build entrepreneurial skills in low-income urban youth. Founded by business executive and entrepreneur Steve Mariotti, a former public high school teacher in New York City's South Bronx neighborhood, NFTE provides schools and partners with high-impact, award-winning entrepreneurship curriculum and teacher training and support. NFTE materials—which include versions for middle school, high school, and young adult students—can be implemented in semester or year-long courses in schools, in after-school programs, and in summer business camps. Over 1,000 schools and organizations across the country currently use NFTE's program, and more than 400 educators have joined NFTE's Teacher Corps, which provides training on how to effectively deliver project-based learning and the NFTE curriculum.

Besides providing schools and nonprofit organizations with high-quality curriculum that helps students work through the process of creating, refining, and implementing an original business concept, NFTE hosts two-week intensive summer BizCamps for at-risk students between the ages of thirteen and eighteen, which include daily course work, guest speakers, and field trips. At the end of the camp, students present their business plan in competitions for cash awards. NFTE also sponsors regional business competitions that lead up to a yearly national competition. Winning students receive an all-expense paid trip to the annual awards dinner in New York City and a grant that can be applied toward establishing a business or college tuition.

Opportunity America

Opportunity America is a Washington-based think tank that aims to restore and advance economic mobility for poor and working Americans through the promotion of work, careers, ownership, and entrepreneurship. The organization works to advance equal opportunity and economic mobility by influencing state and federal policymakers and encouraging civic engagement by workers and employers alike. Primary activities include research, policy development, dissemination of policy ideas, and working to build consensus around policy proposals. In recent years, Opportunity America has published a volume on new ways of thinking about poverty and economic mobility, and several reports on improving community colleges, workforce education, and high school career and technical education.

Opportunity America additionally sponsors the Opportunity America Jobs and Careers Coalition, a Washington-based business coalition focused on drawing attention to the need for workforce training, changing national perceptions of technical careers and career training, and highlighting successful state initiatives. Members include employers and employer associations from a broad range of industries—such as IT, manufacturing, construction, and hospitality—that are currently experiencing skills mismatches and worker shortages.

Opportunity Insights

Opportunity Insights (OI), formerly the Equal Opportunity Project, is a Harvard-based research lab spearheaded by economist and social scientist Raj Chetty, renowned for his cutting-edge research on social, economic, and geographical mobility. The center is codirected by economists John Friedman and Nathaniel Hendren. Chetty, Friedman, and Hendren work alongside a team of researchers and policy analysts to identify barriers to economic opportunity and to develop scalable solutions that will improve economic mobility and empower families and individuals to achieve better life outcomes. The center is currently focused on several ongoing initiatives and programs. The Creating Moves to Opportunity (CMTO) project is a collaboration of academic researchers and public housing authorities seeking to answer the question of why most of the 2.2 million families receiving housing vouchers under the United States Housing Choice Voucher Program continue living in high-poverty, low-opportunity neighborhoods. The aim is to use this information to identify strategies that will increase access to high-opportunity areas. Pursuant to this goal, OI partnered with the Seattle and King County Public Housing Authorities starting in April 2018 to test a new program designed to reduce the barriers that families face in moving to higher opportunity neighborhoods. The program provided housing search assistance, connections to landlords, and financial support to voucher recipients. A randomized evaluation of the program's impact showed that the housing mobility services provided in Seattle and King County dramatically increased the percentage of families who moved to high-opportunity areas. Given the success of the program, OI is looking to apply the same model in other communities across the country.

The Charlotte Opportunity Initiative is a collaborative project between OI and local community leaders in Charlotte, North Carolina. Through this initiative, OI seeks to understand why Charlotte has one of the lowest rates of upward mobility among the largest fifty metropolitan areas in the country and to support data-driven systems and policies to increase upward mobility in the city.

OI additionally spearheads the Collegiate Leaders in Increasing MoBility (CLIMB) Initiative. This initiative is a partnership between leading higher education economists, policymakers, and a diverse set of US colleges and universities working to understand which colleges act as engines of economic mobility and how schools and policymakers can help larger numbers of low-income students reach the middle class.

Opportunity Nation

Opportunity Nation is a bipartisan coalition of more than 350 organizations and individuals—including employers, educational institutions, nonprofits, philanthropies, policymakers, and young Americans—seeking to reduce the opportunity gap by expanding economic mobility. Opportunity Nation maintains an opportunity index to measure factors that contribute to upward mobility and opportunity at both the state and county level and seeks to promote bipartisan policy approaches to increase access to education, tackle the skills gap, and expand opportunity for young adults. Opportunity Nation recently published the pamphlet, "We Got This: A Call to Action for Youth Unemployment," outlining how private and public groups and individuals can collaborate and form cross-sector partnerships to connect young people to meaningful, seamless education and career pathways.

Prison Entrepreneurship Program

The Prison Entrepreneurship Program (PEP) was established in Texas in 2004 in response to the state's vast prison population and the reduced prospects that individuals with a previous record of incarceration have for securing legitimate work that pays livable wages. Based on the goal of preparing inmates with the tools, skills, and support structure they need to successfully reintegrate into society and pursue healthy, fulfilling, and productive lives, PEP has developed a series of rehabilitative programs focused on character and career development, including entrepreneurship training and mentorship, that begin in the prison system prior to release and continue after release.

PEP's program starts with a rigorous selection process that begins when the Texas Department of Criminal Justice provides PEP with a list of approximately 10,000 eligible inmates. PEP then sends information to these inmates inviting them to apply. On average, 2,000 candidates return the nearly twenty-page application. PEP staff selects the top 1,500 candidates, to whom they send a study packet, including the AP Writing Style Guide, a list of PEP's Ten Driving Values, and a Basic Business Vocabulary reference. Two weeks after sending the study packets, PEP recruiters visit prisons to interview candidates. Each candidate who scores higher than 70 percent on the test moves on to a personal interview, in which PEP staff determine whether the candidate has the work ethic and commitment to succeed in the program. At this stage, the top 450 to 500 candidates are selected for a final round of interviews with the program manager and several recently released graduates.

Once inmates are accepted into the program, they are transferred to one of two prison facilities where PEP operates, either the Estes Unit south of Dallas or the Cleveland Correctional Facility outside of Houston. The program begins with a three-month character development and leadership program called the Leadership Academy, where participants work through curriculum in "The Quest for Authentic Manhood" series. Mentors work with participants to help them live out PEP's Ten Driving Values: Integrity, Accountability, Wise Stewardship, Love, Fun, Fresh Start Outlook, Servant-Leader Mentality, Innovation, Execution, and Excellence.

Following the Leadership Academy is a six-month in-prison "mini-MBA" boot camp, in which PEP staff and business executives teach businesses courses on topics related to their areas of expertise. Participants additionally work through a college textbook titled *Entrepreneurship: A Small Business Approach*, and several Harvard and Stanford Business School case studies. During this time, each student is required to research and develop a business plan for the Business Plan Competition. Participants additionally complete a financial literacy course, an employment workshop, a business etiquette course, and a Toastmasters class. Finally, after completing the in-prison program, participants graduate in a cap-and-gown ceremony attended by family and friends. PEP often financially subsidizes the travel costs of family members who wish to attend the graduation. In recognition of the intensity of the program, the Baylor University Hankamer School of Business provides each graduate with a Certificate of Entrepreneurship.

In addition to coordinating the in-prison program, PEP provides extensive post-release support to its participants. Upon release, PEP alumni are supported with a variety of reentry services, including case management, transition housing, and assistance in finding employment and connecting to social services.

The PEP model has proven remarkably successful at preventing recidivism and maximizing self-sufficiency. To date, the program has helped nearly 1,500 prisoners reintegrate into society with a less than 7 percent three-year recidivism rate, compared to an average recidivism rate of 50 to 70 percent in Texas. A study conducted by researchers at Baylor University found that PEP outperformed all nine other rehabilitation programs in Texas in reducing recidivism rates. Moreover, PEP graduates have launched over 200 businesses, and almost 100 percent are employed within ninety days of their release and continue to be employed after twelve months. The Baylor study concluded that every dollar donated to PEP produces a 340 percent return on investment due to avoided incarceration, increased child support payments, and reduced reliance on government assistance.

Project CRAFT

Project CRAFT (Community, Restitution, and Apprenticeship-Focused Training) was established in 1994 after the Home Builders Institute (HBI), the workforce development and educational arm of the National Association of Home Builders, received a Youth Offender demonstration grant from the US Department of Labor's Employment and Training Administration. Project CRAFT aims to improve educational levels, teach vocational skills, and reduce recidivism among court adjudicated youth, while simultaneously addressing the home-building industry's ongoing shortage of entry-level workers.

The Project CRAFT model includes ten main components: outreach and recruitment, assessment and screening; individualized development plans; case management services; industry-validated, trades-related training; building industry-related academics; community service; academic preparation and substance abuse treatment; employability and life skills training; and community transition and long-term follow-up. Most youth participants are initially referred to a Project CRAFT site by their state departments of juvenile justice or by juvenile judges or probation officers. Once accepted, student participants engage in 840 hours of pre-apprenticeship training and industry-approved curriculum over a six-month period. About 75 percent of this time is spent engaged in hands-on construction projects, many of which involve service to the community, while the remaining time is spent receiving classroom instruction in the use of tools, safety, work habits, and trades-related mathematics in addition to field-specific education on topics such as electrical wiring, carpentry, plumbing, and landscaping. Before they are eligible for graduation, participants must demonstrate a mastery of several skills related to the building industry. Upon completion of the program, participants are given an industry-recognized certificate and a personal set of hand tools. Program staff additionally work with participants to connect them with steady employment or additional training or career advancement opportunities following graduation. Thus far, the program has shown remarkable success in reducing juvenile recidivism and providing at-risk youth with the opportunity for economic mobility and career success.

Project CRAFT currently serves around 400 youth annually and operates at nine sites in Florida, Tennessee, New Jersey, and Mississippi funded in large part by state departments of juvenile justice.

Project Quest

Project Quest is a workforce training program founded in San Antonio in 1992 in response to the acute skills mismatch that developed as the city's economic base began to shift from manufacturing to service and technology-driven fields. At the same time that several thousand manufacturing jobs were eliminated, nearly 20,000 new high-paying jobs were created in other fields. Yet, the skills and expertise required for the newly available positions were in short supply among San Antonio's low-income residents. Project Quest thus grew out of a grassroots effort to implement training programs that would enable San Antonio residents to acquire the skills necessary for the professional, high-paying jobs available in growing sectors of the local economy.

Project Quest provides comprehensive support and resources—including financial assistance, remedial instruction, counseling, life skills courses, and job placement assistance—to help individuals complete occupational training programs at local community colleges, pass certification exams, and obtain jobs in targeted industries. Project Quest training programs, which are funded in large part by the Casey Foundation and are conducted primarily through local community colleges, are based on four principles: the program is jobs driven, the program focuses on training and careers that offer family wages and advancement opportunities, the program incorporates intensive support services to help participants overcome financial aid and personal barriers to skill acquisition, and the program leverages the training resources already operational in the community. Since its inception, Project Quest has helped more than 6,000 job seekers complete training. A six-year evaluation of the program conducted by the Economic Mobility Corporation revealed that program strategies and services have been successful at lifting low-income workers out of poverty. The evaluation found that Quest participants work more consistently, earn higher hourly wages, and experience larger increases in their pay overtime than people in the control group. In fact, average annual earnings of graduates grew from $11,400 when they first entered the program to more than $38,000 by the final year of the controlled trial. According to the Economic Mobility Corporation study, few workforce development programs have created this kind of mobility. Furthermore, 96 percent of Quest participants were still living in Texas and 85 percent remained in the San Antonio area six years after enrollment.

Over the years, Project Quest's workforce development model has been replicated by other organizations in cities throughout Texas and outside of Texas in Monroe, Louisiana; Tucson and Phoenix, Arizona; and Des Moines, Iowa to meet the employment needs of their communities.

This Way ONward

In 2007, Gap Inc. launched This Way ONward (previously called This Way Ahead), a life skills and paid internship program, to help teens and young adults from low-income communities gain access to life-changing first job experiences at Gap Inc. stores—Old Navy, Gap, and Banana Republic.

This Way ONward participants are first recruited by urban nonprofits and are then enrolled in two months of in-person and online job training and coaching. After this initial training period, participants are eligible to apply for paid internships at one of the Gap Inc. stores. During the internship period, participants receive ongoing support from nonprofit job coaches, store managers, and fellow employees.

To date, thousands of youth have participated in and graduated from the This Way ONward program, and GAP Inc. reports that they eventually hire nearly 75 percent of program interns. This Way ONward participants also tend to stay with the company and more engaged than young employees who did not participate in the program. Gap Inc. expects that 20,000 young people will participate in the program by 2025, and the company aims to hire 5 percent of its entry-level store employees from the program.

True Charity Initiative

The True Charity Initiative is a national organization dedicated to equipping individuals, churches, and nonprofits to compassionately serve and assist the poor without creating long-term dependence. The roots of the coalition date back to the summer of 2000 when Founder and CEO James Whitford and his wife opened Watered Gardens Rescue Mission, an outreach to the poor, in Joplin, Missouri. The outreach eventually expanded to multiple campuses which sheltered, fed, clothed, and ministered to people who were hurting, addicted, homeless, and poor. After seeing very little change in the long-run situations of those whom they were serving, Whitford decided to shift from a focus on immediate crisis relief to a model designed to help the poor become a part of their own solutions through relationships and accountability and to provide them with the tools and motivation to improve their long-term situation. One example was the establishment of a social enterprise "Worth Shop," where participants could earn a week's worth of food by engaging in an hour's worth of creative, skill-building work alongside volunteers. Although the number of individuals interested in services declined following implementation of accountability and relational requirements, those who continued to participate in the Whitfords' programs saw a marked long-term improvement in their housing, employment, education, and relationships.

This experience inspired the formation of the True Charity Network, a national coalition designed to provide members churches and nonprofits with practical resources and connections that will enable them to address poverty more effectively through personalized, relationship-building solutions at the local level. The coalition specifically provides members with access to webinars, workshops, and model action plans, which provide detailed guidance on how to implement and operate innovative support programs such as mentoring groups, food co-ops, affordable Christmas markets, and informal, part-time employment programs.

Urban Alliance

Urban Alliance, a national youth development nonprofit, was founded in 1996 in Washington, DC., to provide students at risk of disconnection with the opportunity, support, and training to transition to higher education or employment after high school and, ultimately, to place them on the path to self-sustaining careers and lifelong economic self-sufficiency.

Urban Alliance's core program, the High School Internship Program, matches underserved high school seniors with paid, professional internships, job skills training, one-on-one mentoring, and ongoing post-program support. The program now serves over 500 interns annually and has expanded to new locations in Baltimore, Chicago, and Northern Virginia.

In 2017, the Urban Institute released the results of a six-year evaluation of the Urban Alliance High School Internship Program in Washington DC and Baltimore. The study revealed that the programs have a significant positive impact on their participants. All program alumni have graduate high school on time. Within one year of graduation, 80 percent of program alumni are connected through employment, college, a vocational training program, or the military. Participating in the program increased the likelihood that young men would attend college by 23 percentage points, and the likelihood that middle-tier students (those with a 2.0 to 3.0 high school GPA) would enroll in a four-year college by 18 percentage points. The study additionally concluded that participation in the program increased students' retention of critical professional skills.

Urban Institute

The Urban Institute, a Washington-based think tank, was established as an independent research organization in 1968 by the Johnson administration to study the problems in urban communities and to evaluate the impact of Great Society initiatives. Over the past fifty years, institute experts have immersed themselves in urban communities to collect data on the effectiveness of public and private efforts to strengthen families, cities, and neighborhoods and reduce poverty and societal deprivation. The institute has additionally expanded the scope of its research to include topics such as the challenges of short- and long-term unemployment, the effectiveness of crime prevention efforts, and the need for education reform. Since its inception, the organization's research into urban communities and its policy recommendations for tackling complex social and economic barriers to opportunity in such communities has been funded by a variety of entities including the federal government, state and local governments, private foundations, corporations, individuals, and international organizations.

William E. Simon Foundation

The William E. Simon Foundation is named after its principal benefactor, a former deputy secretary of the Treasury and catholic entrepreneur, who was committed to helping those in need experience the blessings of American opportunity and liberty by realizing the full promise of their own talent and drive.

In line with its founder's vision, the foundation's primary aim is to strengthen the free-enterprise system by helping inner-city youth and families gain access to education and community-based services that promote their character development and help them become independent, contributing members of society. The foundation works to achieve this goal by funding direct services in Jersey City and South Bronx and engaging in public policy research and advocacy. The foundation's direct service and policy research efforts focus largely on the themes of education, faith, and family. In the realm of education, the foundation supports research on school reform, accountability, and transparency and the promotion of ideas with the potential to improve school governance, teaching, and learning. The foundation funds private scholarship programs and supports the start-up and maintenance of public charter, independent, and parochial schools that feature academic rigor, respectful learning environments, attention to students as unique individuals, and an unwavering belief that their students can succeed. In the realm of faith, the foundation funds research on the positive impact of faith in the lives of young people and supports programs and churches that provide youth mentoring, after-school and summer enrichment, literacy and tutoring, sports and recreation, and community service. In the realm of family, the foundation supports research on the negative impact of increasing family fragmentation on the lives of children and their capacity for economic and educational success. The foundation additionally supports programs designed to strengthen the family, such as parenting courses and emergency support, as well as programs that provide mentoring, advocacy, and educational and career guidance for young people who lack a strong family support system.

Work Colleges

Work Colleges are accredited institutions of higher education that help low-income students—many of whom are first-generation college students—obtain a quality liberal arts college education and developing transferable real-world professional skills without being burdened by debt. Work Colleges award bachelor degrees based on a model that incorporates traditional learning with work responsibilities and service. Most students are required to work an average of ten to fifteen hours a week and participate in community service in a way that enhances their academic learning.

The work programs have a proven track record of enabling students of limited means to earn a college degree, while cultivating career-ready qualities and skills. Graduates also leave with considerably less debt than their peers at traditional colleges. There are currently eight geographically and academically diverse Work Colleges in the United States that run distinctive work programs designed to meet campus need and complement relevant coursework.

Alice Lloyd College, located in Pippa Passes, Kentucky, is the only liberal arts college in the nation to exclusively recruit its students from Appalachia. Full-time qualifying students from this region do not have to pay out-of-pocket tuition, which helps generate its *U.S. News and World Report* ranking as the Top College in America for graduating students with the least amount of debt. A large majority of the college's graduates return postgraduation to Appalachia to serve and work in their former communities.

Berea College, located in Berea, Kentucky, was named the top liberal arts college in the nation in 2011 by *Washington Monthly* based on the school's record of promoting social mobility, excellence in education, and community service. Founded in 1855, the college was the first interracial and coeducational college in the South. It recruits students who could not otherwise afford a high-quality liberal arts education and is the only top college in America that awards four-year full tuition scholarships to all of its students.

Blackburn College, located in Carlinville, Illinois, was established more than 175 years ago. In 2012 it was ranked as the #2 Best Value College in the Midwest by *U.S. News and World Report* and was ranked as a top performer on social mobility in 2024. Blackburn's ten campus buildings were constructed in part by students. Students are required to hold work positions that support campus operations in the bookstore, administration, academic tutoring, informational technology, and maintenance. The work program is run by student managers.

College of the Ozarks, located in Point Lookout, Missouri, is consistently ranked by a variety of national publications as "a best buy" and one of the best colleges in the nation. The college, also known as "Hard Work U," is a Christian school where students are able to cover their tuition through student work, grants, and scholarships offered by the college. Students are assigned to one of eighty diverse work assignments that are selected to complement their career path. Work performance grades are included along with academic grades on students' transcripts.

Ecclesia College, located in Springdale, Arkansas, has been awarded a place on the President's Higher Education Community Service Honor Role. The Christian college, which serves students regardless of their family resources, focuses on developing good work ethic and character among its students, while allowing them to offset educational expenses through work. Students also participate in a wide variety of community service projects in the local community and around the world.

Sterling College, located in Craftsbury Common, Vermont, is a small progressive liberal arts college with a focus on environmental protection and grassroots sustainability. Students can design their own environmentally focused major or choose from a variety of established majors, such as Conservation Ecology, Sustainable Agriculture, and Outdoor leadership. Students put their coursework to practice by monitoring campus energy use and food production, teaching classes on sustainability in the local public school system, participating in wildlife mapping projects, and engaging in environmental activism.

Warren Wilson College, located just outside of Asheville, North Carolina, is known for its international and environmental emphasis. It was named one of the "25 Best Buys" among private colleges and universities in the *Fiske Guide to Colleges* and was referred to as "one of the most earth-friendly colleges on the planet" by *Outside Magazine*. The college offers full tuition scholarships to every incoming student from North Carolina who qualifies for state or federal need-based aid. The school has also introduced twenty-five merit-based scholarships for middle-income or out-of-state students. The campus contains a working farm, gardens, and forests that are tilled and harvested by students.

Profiles

Jacob Riis (1849–1914)

Jacob Riis was a reporter and social reformer, who became one of the most influential photojournalists in American history. Born in Denmark, Riis immigrated to the United States at the age of twenty-one in 1870, a time when thousands of European immigrants were moving into New York's crowded apartment buildings called tenements. Working various jobs, Riis experienced first-hand homelessness and poverty before he eventually became a police reporter tasked with covering New York City's Lower East Side. This experience made him even more aware of the squalid, unsanitary, and violent conditions of New York's urban slums. Riis discovered that in some tenements the conditions were so abysmal that the infant death rate was one in ten. These experiences drove Riis to continue his efforts in investigative journalism.

In 1888, Riis took a job as a reporter for the *New York Evening Sun* and began conducting in-depth investigations of New York's slums using flashbulb photography to capture the deplorable living conditions. Two years later, Riis published the groundbreaking exposé *How the Other Half Lives: Studies among the Tenements of New York*. Riis's real-life photos of the deplorable conditions in New York City's slums shocked public opinion and brought attention to the plight of the urban poor. The book launched Riis's career as a social reformer, contributed to the passage of local laws regulating the quality of tenements, and motivated an extensive tenement study published by the Department of Labor in 1895. His work additionally inspired the housing and labor reforms later advocated by President Theodore Roosevelt, who had befriended Riis during his earlier stint as New York City police commissioner.

Jane Addams (1860–1935)

Jane Addams was a progressive social reformer and activist, who helped spur the settlement house movement in the late nineteenth and early twentieth centuries. Though her mother died in childbirth when Addams was only two years old, she lived a privileged childhood as the daughter of a politically connected businessman, who was one of Illinois's wealthiest citizens. In her early adulthood, Addams pursued an education, graduating at the top of her class from Rockford Female Seminary and enrolling at Philadelphia's Women's Medical College before dropping out for health reasons. She eventually stumbled upon what became her lifelong mission while on a trip to England with her friend Ellen Gates Starr. Impressed by Toynbee Hall, a settlement house that encouraged educated men to interact with and provide services to poor industrial workers on London's East End, Addams and Starr decided to introduce the settlement house model to the United States.

In 1889, Addams and Starr founded Hull House in a decaying mansion in one of Chicago's most destitute immigrant neighborhoods. Hull House's resident staffers and volunteers provided an array of social and educational opportunities and meals and daycare for poor children and working-class families. The Hull House complex was eventually expanded to thirteen buildings, which included libraries, museums, spaces for cultural events and trade union meetings, and a boarding house for single-working women. The Hull House model inspired the establishment of more than 400 other settlement houses throughout the country.

Eventually, Addams expanded her efforts as a progressive social reformer. She played an instrumental role in the development of a juvenile court system, the passage of protective labor laws and urban sanitation measures, and the launch of the School of Social Work at the University of Chicago. She became active in the women's suffrage movement, was among the founders of the National Association for the Advancement of Colored People (NAACP), and won a Nobel Peace Prize for her role in the formation and leadership of the Women's International League for Peace and Freedom.

Frances Perkins (1880–1965)

Frances Perkins was the first woman to serve as a presidential cabinet secretary and was one of the leading architects of President Roosevelt's New Deal. Perkins, who changed her legal name from Fanny to Frances in adulthood, was born in Boston to a family with historical prominence in the American Revolution and Civil War. After graduating from a classical college preparatory high school, Perkins attended Mount Holyoke College with a major in physics and a minor in chemistry and biology. During her final semester at Mount Holyoke, she took a course in American economic history and observed the mills along the Connecticut River as part of her course work. Horrified by the dangerous working conditions and lack of labor regulations, especially among women and children, Perkins was inspired to do what she could to help change those abuses. Following college, she worked in various teaching positions, spent her free time volunteering at settlement houses, and began studying sociology and economics at the University of Pennsylvania's Wharton School under the tutelage of progressive economist Simon N. Patten. In 1909, Perkins gave up teaching and began a fellowship with the New York School of Philanthropy investigating childhood malnutrition among school children in New York's Hell's Kitchen. That same year she enrolled at Columbia University to pursue a master's degree in economics and sociology.

In 1910, Perkins became the executive secretary of the New York City Consumers League. In this position, she effectively advocated for a variety of state labor and social reforms, including sanitary regulations for bakeries and legislation limited the working hours for women and children in factories. Following a catastrophic fire that killed nearly 150 workers at New York's Triangle Shirtwaist Factory, Perkins was hired as the executive secretary of the citizen's Committee on Safety. Under her leadership, a commission was formed to recommend practices to prevent similar tragedies in New York City's factories. The commission successfully lobbied for comprehensive state health and safety legislation that spurred reform nationwide. In 1928, after Perkins served a successful stint as labor advisor for New York Governor Al Smith, newly elected Governor Franklin D. Roosevelt invited her to oversee the state labor department as Industrial Commissioner. In this capacity, Perkins studied long-range programs to increase employment. Following his inauguration as president in 1933, Roosevelt appointed Perkins as Secretary of Labor. The following year, he invited her to head the Committee on Economic Security. In this capacity, Perkins helped construct a blueprint for legislation that was eventually passed as part of Roosevelt's New Deal, including social security, unemployment compensation, public works, and federal wage and labor regulations.

Cesar Chavez (1927–93)

Cesar Chavez was a labor union activist, inspired by Martin Luther King Jr. and Mahatma Gandhi's commitment to nonviolent change, who advocated for better wages, safer working conditions, and less exposure to pesticides for American farm workers. Chavez was born in 1927 to a Mexican immigrant farming family in Yuma, Arizona. When he was eleven years old, his family lost their farm at the height of the Great Depression and became migrant farmers. After completing eighth grade, Chavez worked in the fields full-time to help support his family. This experience gave him firsthand exposure to the hardships and injustices suffered by migrant farm workers. Following service in the Navy during the Second World War, Chavez returned to California where he helped organize striking agricultural workers and national boycotts to protest abusive labor conditions and the fact that the National Labor Relations Act of 1935 did not protect farm workers.

In 1962, Chavez moved with his wife and eight young children to Delano, a farm town in California's Central Valley, and formed the National Farm Workers

Association (NFWA). Under Chavez's leadership the NFWA, later renamed the United Farm Workers of America (UFW), became the first successful farm workers union in American history. With the help of the farm worker movement, Chavez established health clinics, daycare centers, job-training programs, affordable home-ownership communities, the first credit union for farm workers, and the Fred Ross Education Institution which trained negotiators, contract administrators, and union organizers. He simultaneously founded two educational-style Spanish language farm worker radio stations, which eventually grew into the thirteen-station Radio Campesina network. Chavez additionally became well-known for his successful hunger strikes and his role in convincing the California legislature and Governor Jerry Brown to pass the Agricultural Labor Relations Act of 1975, the nation's first law guaranteeing farm workers the right to organize, choose their own union representative, and negotiate with their employers. When Chavez passed away in 1993, more than 50,000 people attended his funeral services in Delano, California.

Elizabeth Warren (1949–)

Elizabeth Warren is a former law professor, a consumer advocate, and a United States Senator representing Massachusetts. Born to a lower-middle-class family in Oklahoma, Warren married at nineteen and began her career as an elementary school teacher before pursuing a law degree at Rutgers School of Law. After graduating from law school, Warren practiced law for a short time before becoming a law professor, teaching courses at several universities including the University of Pennsylvania and Harvard on commercial law, contracts, and bankruptcy. As part of her career in academia, Warren wrote 12 books and more than 100 articles on topics related to consumer protection and poverty in America.

Following the global financial crisis of 2007–8, Warren lobbied for the creation of the Consumer Financial Protection Bureau (CFPB), an executive branch agency with the stated goal of protecting consumers from predatory and corrupt practices by regulating financial products and services. She was also invited by Senator Majority Leader Harry Reid in 2008 to chair the Congressional Oversight Panel for the Troubled Asset Relief Program (TARP)—the oversight board created to oversee the Wall Street bailout.

Warren eventually became the first female senator to represent the state of Massachusetts when she was elected to the US Senate as a Democrat in 2012. As a senator, she focused primarily on consumer protection and expanding funding for childcare and the social safety net. In 2020, she placed third in the race to become the Democratic presidential nominee. After withdrawing from the presidential race, she continued her service in the Senate. Warren's most ambitious policy proposals include canceling student debt, promoting free college, renegotiating the North American Free Trade Agreement (NAFTA), funding universal childcare and medical care, and adopting a sizable wealth tax.

J.D. Vance (1984–)

J.D. Vance is an author, venture capitalist, a US senator representing Ohio, and the 2024 Republican Vice-Presidential candidate. Vance was born James Donald Bowman to Donald Bowman and Bev Vance in Middletown, a once-flourishing Rest Belt city in southwestern Ohio. Over time, the decline of manufacturing and the good jobs associated with it contributed to the decimation of the city's once-thriving middle class. Vance and his older half-sister Lindsey had a tumultuous upbringing. They were partially raised by their grandparents whom they called "Mamaw and Papaw," as their birth fathers abandoned them and their mother suffered from addiction. Eventually, J.D. adopted his grandparents' surname Vance and changed his middle name to David. Following high school, Vance enlisted in the US Marine Corp and served in Iraq before going on to attend Ohio State University. After graduating from college with a degree in political science and philosophy, Vance pursued a Juris Doctorate from Yale Law School. He subsequently worked for a multinational law firm and several investment firms.

In 2016, Vance published the best-selling autobiography *Hillbilly Elegy: A Memoir of a Family and Culture in Crisis*, which was eventually made into a major motion picture. In the memoir, Vance recounts his family's cultural roots in the poverty-stricken region of Appalachia and the violence and instability he experienced growing up in the white working class. Vance credits, in large part, the involvement and encouragement of his grandmother for his later-in-life achievements. The book was acclaimed by many for providing valuable insight into the lives of working-class Americans. Due to the book's success, Vance found himself in demand as a lecturer and political commentator. In 2022, he successfully won the US Senate race for Ohio running as a Republican, and in 2024 Donald Trump chose him as his vice-presidential running mate.

500+
NEW ARRIVALS!
SHOP
WHAT'S NEW
NOW

5

Data and Documents

Introduction

This chapter contains figures and primary resources for further research on the topic of poverty in America. The first section presents data on viewpoints regarding attainment of the American Dream; percentages of people living below the poverty line by demographic characteristics; share of aggregate household income held by lower-, middle-, and upper-income households; and labor force participation rates. The second section provides excerpts from a variety of government documents including speeches, laws, and testimonies that demonstrate changing ideological approaches toward poverty in America organized in chronological order.

Figure 5.1 Essential, Important, and Not Important Components of the American Dream

This figure presents Americans' views on what factors are essential, important, or not important to achieving the American Dream. Interestingly, very few people view "becoming wealthy" as essential to their vision of the American Dream.

A homeless man sits outside of a luxury shopping mall in San Francisco. Although individual vulnerabilities such as addiction, domestic violence, and tragedy may increase the risk, homelessness is exacerbated by the fact that there is not enough affordable housing. (Acelya Aksunkur/Dreamstime.com)

Do you think each is essential, important but not essential, or not important to your own view of the American Dream? (%)

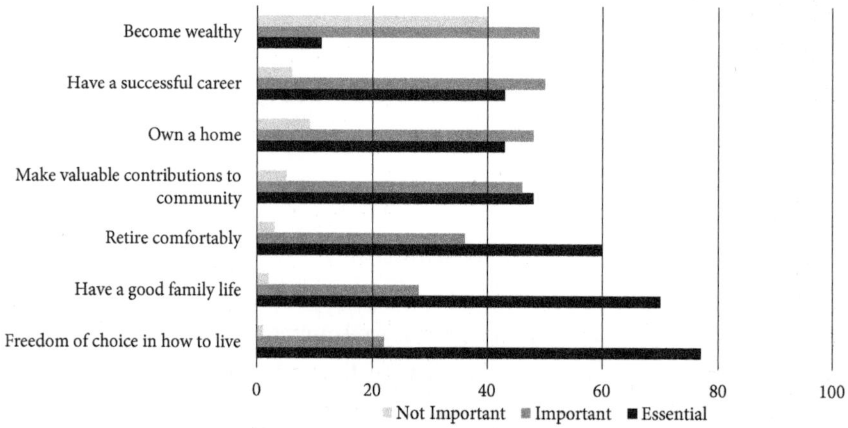

Source: Pew Research Center. 2017. "Few See 'Becoming Wealthy' as Essential to Their View of the American Dream." October 31. https://www.pewresearch.org/short-reads/2017/10/31/most-think-the-american-dream-is-within-reach-for-them/ft_17-10-31_americandream_definitions/

Table 5.1 Percentage of People in Poverty by Different Poverty Measures: 2022

Percentage of people living below the poverty line in 2022 by sex, age, type of family unit, and race based on the Official and Supplemental Poverty Measures.

Characteristic	Official Poverty Measure (%)	Supplemental Poverty Measure (%)
All People	11.5	12.4
Sex		
Male	10.5	11.9
Female	12.5	12.8
Age		
Under 18	14.9	12.4
18 to 64	10.6	11.9
65 years and Older	10.2	14.1
Type of Family Unit		
Married Couple	5.4	7.6
Cohabiting Partners	23.7	12.3
Single Female	22.5	22.6

Characteristic	Official Poverty Measure (%)	Supplemental Poverty Measure (%)
Single Male	10.0	14.7
Race		
White	10.5	11.4
Black	17.1	17.2
Asian	8.6	11.6
American Indian or Alaska Native	24.9	23.2
Two or More Races	12.2	11.4
Hispanic	16.9	19.3

Source: United States Census Bureau. 2023. "Poverty in the United States: 2022." September 12. https://www.census.gov/library/publications/2023/demo/p60-280.html

Figure 5.2 Share of US Aggregate Household Income

This figure shows the percentage of US aggregate household income held by lower-, middle-, and upper-income households in 1970 and 2020.

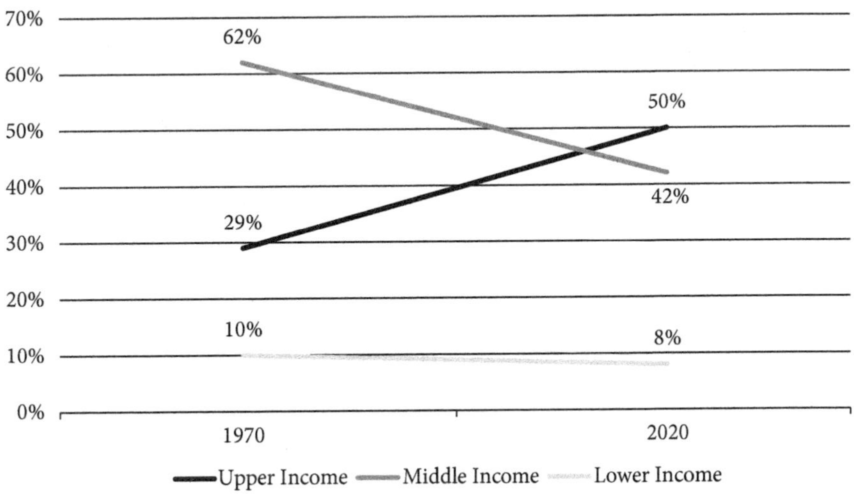

Source: Pew Research Center. 2022. "Share of Aggregate Income Held by U.S. Middle Class Has Plunged Since 1970." April 14. https://www.pewresearch.org/short-reads/2022/04/20/how-the-american-middle-class-has-changed-in-the-past-five-decades/ft_2022-04-20_middleclass_03/

Table 5.2 Annual Average Labor Force Participation Rates for 2000 and 2015

Average labor force participation rates in 2000 and 2015 of people ages twenty to twenty-four years not enrolled in school, by gender and educational attainment.

Characteristic	2000 (%)	2015 (%)	Change 2000–2015 (%)
Men			
Total, 20 to 24 years	91.2	86.1	–5.1
Less than a high school diploma	86.7	76.3	–10.4
High school graduates, no college	91.0	84.7	–6.3
Some college, no degree	92.8	87.1	–5.7
Associate's degree	97.4	92.2	–5.2
Bachelor's degree and higher	95.6	93.4	–2.2
Women			
Total, 20 to 24 years	77.4	77.3	–0.1
Less than a high school diploma	53.3	52.6	–0.7
High school graduates, no college	77.2	72.6	–4.6
Some college, no degree	84.1	80.0	–4.1
Associate's degree	88.0	84.9	–3.1
Bachelor's degree and higher	90.1	90.7	+0.6

Source: U.S. Bureau of Labor Statistics. 2016. "Labor Force Participation: What Has Happened Since the Peak?" September. https://www.bls.gov/opub/ted/2023/labor-force-participation-rate-for-people-ages-25-to-54-in-may-2023-highest-since-january-2007.htm#:~:text=The%20labor%20force%20participation%20rate,to%20its%20pre%2Dpandemic%20level

Documents

Thomas Jefferson's "Bill for the Support of the Poor" (1779)

In 1779, Thomas Jefferson proposed draft legislation in Virginia for the care of the poor, which was eventually adopted by the state legislature with some modifications and amendments. This draft demonstrates several features of the general approach to poverty and poor relief in early America: that government, in addition to private charities and churches, bears responsibility for the care of the poor; that poor relief ought to be implemented at the local level; and that the able-bodied should be required to work. Following are notable excerpts from Jefferson's draft.

Be it enacted by the General Assembly, that the Aldermen of every county wherein such provision, as is herein after required for setting the poor of the county to work, shall not have been made, shall, so soon as conveniently may be, purchase the inheritance, or procure a lease, of one hundred acres of land, or any less quantity that is sufficient for the purpose intended, in the county, and thereon cause a house to be built, if a proper one be not there already, and kept in repair, and shall cause all persons in their county, who are maintained thereby, or who seek relief therefrom, to be put into such house, to be there maintained and employed in such work as they shall be able to perform; and may also, by their warrant, apprehend and send to the same place all persons found wandering and begging alms, in the county … and shall put such beggar to work for any time not exceeding twenty days. And the said Aldermen shall hire some discreet man to oversee those who shall come or be put into such work-house, and shall, from time to time, ordain rules for his conduct, and for the government, employment, and correction of the persons subject to him, restraining him from correcting any of them with more stripes than ten, at one time, or for one offence. And in order to keep them at work shall provide wool, cotton, flax, hemp and other materials, with the tools and implements necessary for the manufacture thereof. And the said Aldermen shall meet together, at the court-house of their county, at some time between the second Tuesday in July and the first day of August in every year, and by taxation of the persons and property, in their county, according to the mode of assessment prescribed by the law which shall be then in force, for raising money for the public exigencies, shall raise competent sums of money for the necessary relief of such poor, lame, impotent, blind, and other inhabitants of the county as are not able to maintain themselves. And also for the putting out the poor children apprentices, as well as for defraying the expences of putting so much of this act in execution as relates to setting the poor to work and keeping them so employed; they shall collect appropriate taxes.

… All able bodied persons not having wherewithal to maintain themselves, who shall waste their time in idle and dissolute courses, or shall loiter or wander abroad, refusing to work for reasonable wages, or to betake themselves to some honest and lawful calling, or who shall desert wives or children, without so providing for them as that they shall not become chargeable to a county, shall be deemed vagabonds, and shall be sent, by order of an Alderman, to the poor house, there to be kept to labor during such time as shall be limited by the order, not exceeding thirty days; … unless, … the vagabond shall give surety for his good behavior, and that he shall betake himself to some honest and lawful calling for twelve months; from which order the party thereby condemned may appeal to the county court, who, if the order be affirmed, shall award him to pay the costs.

Source: Thomas Jefferson. "A Bill for Support of the Poor, June 18, 1779." *Founders Online.* National Archives. https://founders.archives.gov/documents/Jefferson/01-02-02-0132-0004-0032

James Madison on "Property" (1792)

Between 1791 and 1792, James Madison published a series of articles, referred to as his Party Press Essays, in the National Gazette. *In one of these essays, titled "Property," Madison outlines the idea of a comprehensive right to property, which includes all rights of personhood. The right to property, Madison contends, extends not only to external possessions but to the right to be safe from bodily injury, the rights of conscious and free exercise of religion, the right of freedom of speech, and the right to the free use of one's faculties (or physical and intellectual talents and abilities), and the right to choose one's employment. He then contends that government has a responsibility to secure individuals these rights, both by protecting them from injury by private persons and by refraining from the establishment of government monopolies or actions that arbitrarily infringe on the right to property or favor some individuals or types of enterprise more than others.*

This term in its particular application means "that dominion which one man claims and exercises over the external things of the world, in exclusion of every other individual."

In its larger and juster meaning, it embraces every thing to which a man may attach a value and have a right; and *which leaves to every one else the like advantage.*

In the former sense, a man's land, or merchandize, or money is called his property.

In the latter sense, a man has a property in his opinions and the free communication of them.

He has a property of peculiar value in his religious opinions, and in the profession and practice dictated by them.

He has a property very dear to him in the safety and liberty of his person.

He has an equal property in the free use of his faculties and free choice of the objects on which to employ them.

In a word, as a man is said to have a right to his property, he may be equally said to have a property in his rights.

Where an excess of power prevails, property of no sort is duly respected. No man is safe in his opinions, his person, his faculties, or his possessions.

Where there is an excess of liberty, the effect is the same, tho' from an opposite cause.

Government is instituted to protect property of every sort; as well that which lies in the various rights of individuals, as that which the term particularly expresses. This being the end of government, that alone is a *just* government, which *impartially* secures to every man, whatever is his *own*.

According to this standard of merit, the praise of affording a just securing to property, should be sparingly bestowed on a government which, however scrupulously guarding the possessions of individuals, does not protect them in the enjoyment and communication of their opinions, in which they have an equal, and in the estimation of some, a more valuable property.

More sparingly should this praise be allowed to a government, where a man's religious rights are violated by penalties, or fettered by tests, or taxed by a hierarchy. Conscience is the most sacred of all property; other property depending in part on positive law, the exercise of that, being a natural and unalienable right. To guard a man's house as his castle, to pay public and enforce private debts with the most exact faith, can give no title to invade a man's conscience which is more sacred than his castle, or to withhold from it that debt of protection, for which the public faith is pledged, by the very nature and original conditions of the social pact.

That is not a just government, nor is property secure under it, where the property which a man has in his personal safety and personal liberty, is violated by arbitrary seizures of one class of citizens for the service of the rest. A magistrate issuing his warrants to a press gang, would be in his proper functions in Turkey or Indostan, under appellations proverbial of the most compleat despotism.

That is not a just government, nor is property secure under it, where arbitrary restrictions, exemptions, and monopolies deny to part of its citizens that free use of their faculties, and free choice of their occupations, which not only constitute their property in the general sense of the word; but are the means of acquiring property strictly so called. What must be the spirit of legislation where a manufacturer of linen cloth is forbidden to bury his own child in a linen shroud, in order to favour his neighbour who manufactures woolen cloth; where the manufacturer and wearer of woolen cloth are again forbidden the oeconomical use of buttons of that material, in favor of the manufacturer of buttons of other materials!

A just security to property is not afforded by that government, under which unequal taxes oppress one species of property and reward another species: where arbitrary taxes invade the domestic sanctuaries of the rich, and excessive taxes grind the faces of the poor; where the keenness and competitions of want are deemed an insufficient spur to labor, and taxes are again applied, by an unfeeling policy, as another spur; in violation of that sacred property, which Heaven, in decreeing man to earn his bread by the sweat of his brow, kindly reserved to him, in the small repose that could be spared from the supply of his necessities.

If there be a government then which prides itself in maintaining the inviolability of property; which provides that none shall be taken *directly* even for public use without indemnification to the owner, and yet *directly* violates the property which individuals have in their opinions, their religion, their persons, and their faculties; nay more, which *indirectly* violates their property, in their actual possessions, in the labor that acquires their daily subsistence, and in the hallowed remnant of time which ought to relieve their fatigues and soothe their cares, the influence [inference?] will have been anticipated, that such a government is not a pattern for the United States.

If the United States mean to obtain or deserve the full praise due to wise and just governments, they will equally respect the rights of property, and the property in rights: they will rival the government that most sacredly guards the former; and by repelling its example in violating the latter, will make themselves a pattern to that and all other governments.

Source: James Madison. "Property," March 27, 1792 in Philip B. Kurland and Ralph Lerner, eds. *The Founders' Constitution* Vol.1. Chicago: University of Chicago Press, 1987: 598–9.

The Freedmen's Bureau Act (1865)

On December 6, 1865, in the aftermath of the Civil War, the necessary number of states ratified the Thirteenth Amendment to the US Constitution. This amendment declared: "Neither slavery nor involuntary servitude, except as a punishment for crime whereof the party shall have been duly convicted, shall exist within the United States, or any place subject to their jurisdiction." The task of assisting the four million newly freed people to adapt to the conditions of economic and political freedom, however, remained. This was a particularly daunting task as the Southern states sought to re-create a situation of de facto Black slave labor.

On March 3, 1865, just before the Civil War officially ended, Congress passed "An Act to Establish a Bureau for the Relief of Freedman and Refugees." The Bureau, which was to operate for the remainder of the war and for one year thereafter, was created to provide food, shelter, clothing, medical services, and land to freed slaves and destitute southerners who had been displaced during the war. Housed in the Department of War, the Bureau was additionally tasked with reuniting Black families, establishing schools for freed people, and supervising labor contracts between them and their employers.

In 1866, Congress overrode President Johnson's Veto and extended the life of the Bureau for two years. While the Bureau was short-lived, it marked a major transformation in terms of federal involvement in poverty relief. Perhaps its greatest legacy is the educational institutions for freed people it helped establish, many of which are still in operation today.

Be it enacted by the Senate and House of Representatives of the United States of America in Congress assembled, That there is hereby established in the War Department, to continue during the present war of rebellion, and for one year thereafter, a bureau of refugees, freedmen, and abandoned lands, to which shall be committed, as hereinafter provided, the supervision and management of all abandoned lands, and the control of all subjects relating to refugees and freedmen from rebel states, or from any district of country within the territory embraced in the operations of the army, under such rules and regulations as may be prescribed by the head of the bureau and approved by the President. The said bureau shall be under the management and control of a commissioner to be appointed by the President, by and with the advice and consent of the Senate, whose compensation shall be three thousand dollars per annum, and such number of clerks as may be assigned to him by the Secretary of War, not exceeding one chief clerk, two of the fourth class, two of the third class, and five of the first class. And the commissioner and all persons appointed under this act, shall, before entering upon their duties, take the oath of office prescribed in an act entitled "An act to prescribe an oath of office, and for other purposes," approved July second, eighteen hundred and sixty-two, and the commissioner and the chief clerk shall, before entering upon their duties, give bonds to the treasurer of the United States, the former in the sum of fifty thousand dollars, and the latter in the sum of ten thousand dollars, conditioned for the faithful discharge of their duties respectively, with securities to be approved as sufficient by the Attorney-General, which bonds shall be filed in the office of the first comptroller of the treasury, to be by him put in suit for the benefit of any injured party upon any breach of the conditions thereof.

SEC. 2. And be it further enacted, That the Secretary of War may direct such issues of provisions, clothing, and fuel, as he may deem needful for the immediate and temporary shelter and supply of destitute and suffering refugees and freedmen and their wives and children, under such rules and regulations as he may direct.

SEC. 3. And be it further enacted, That the President may, by and with the advice and consent of the Senate, appoint an assistant commissioner for each of the states declared to be in insurrection, not exceeding ten in number, who shall, under the direction of the commissioner, aid in the execution of the provisions of this act; and he shall give a bond to the Treasurer of the United States, in the sum of twenty thousand dollars, in the form and manner prescribed in the first section of this act. Each of said commissioners shall receive an annual salary of two thousand five hundred dollars in full compensation for all his services. And any military officer may be detailed and assigned to duty under this act without increase of pay or allowances. The commissioner shall, before the commencement of each regular session of congress, make full report of his proceedings with exhibits of the state of his accounts to the President, who shall communicate the same to congress, and shall also make special reports whenever required to do so by the President or either house of congress; and the assistant commissioners shall make quarterly reports of their proceedings to the commissioner, and also such other special reports as from time to time may be required.

SEC. 4. And be it further enacted, That the commissioner, under the direction of the President, shall have authority to set apart, for the use of loyal refugees and freedmen, such tracts of land within the insurrectionary states as shall have been abandoned, or to which the United States shall have acquired title by confiscation or sale, or otherwise, and to every male citizen, whether refugee or freedman, as aforesaid, there shall be assigned not more than forty acres of such land, and the person to whom it was so assigned shall be protected in the use and enjoyment of the land for the term of three years at an annual rent not exceeding six per centum upon the value of such land, as it was appraised by the state authorities in the year eighteen hundred and sixty, for the purpose of taxation, and in case no such appraisal can be found, then the rental shall be based upon the estimated value of the land in said year, to be ascertained in such manner as the commissioner may by regulation prescribe. At the end of said term, or at any time during said term, the occupants of any parcels so assigned may purchase the land and receive such title thereto as the United States can convey, upon paying therefor the value of the land, as ascertained and fixed for the purpose of determining the annual rent aforesaid.

SEC. 5. And be it further enacted, That all acts and parts of acts inconsistent with the provisions of this act are hereby repealed.

APPROVED, March 3, 1865.

Source: U.S., *Statutes at Large, Treaties, and Proclamations of the United States of America*, vol. 13. Boston, 1866: 507–9. https://freedmen.umd.edu//fbact.htm

Franklin D. Roosevelt, Commonwealth Club Address (September 23, 1932)

Like his progressive forebears, Roosevelt envisioned an unencumbered state and discretionary rule by public-spirited experts to bring about a new economic constitutional order. The progressive project, however, had been largely curtailed by the attachment that many Americans continued to have to the idea of natural rights, individual liberty, limited government, and local governance. Consequently, when he took office, the federal government still operated within a very limited range of authority. FDR's rhetorical innovations and skillful ability to calm reactionary elements, however, made him far more successful than previous progressives in spurring substantial and lasting institutional change.

One of the first and clearest examples of this rhetorical strategy is Roosevelt's 1932 campaign speech on progressive governance delivered to the Commonwealth Club in San Francisco, California. In the speech (excerpted below), Roosevelt cloaks his vision for the creation of a new economic order in the language of individualism. Given the current economic circumstances, the cause of individualism, he claims, demands the extension of the powers of government into new areas of life. Thus, he proposes a new social contract in which those who conduct government redefine individual rights to meet the demands necessary for economic security in a changing and growing social order.

... I want to speak not of politics but of Government. I want to speak not of parties, but of universal principles. They are not political, except in that larger sense in which a great American once expressed a definition of politics, that nothing in all of human life is foreign to the science of politics.

I want to invite you, therefore, to consider with me in the large, some of the relationships of Government and economic life that go deeply into our daily lives, our happiness, our future and our security.

The issue of Government has always been whether individual men and women will have to serve some system of Government or economics, or whether a system of Government and economics exists to serve individual men and women. This question has persistently dominated the discussion of Government for many generations. On questions relating to these things men have differed, and for time immemorial it is probable that honest men will continue to differ ...

The American colonies were born in this struggle. The American Revolution was a turning point in it. After the Revolution the struggle continued and shaped itself in the public life of the country. There were those who because they had seen the confusion which attended the years of war for American independence surrendered to the belief that popular Government was essentially dangerous and essentially unworkable. They were honest people, my friends, and we cannot deny that their experience had warranted some measure of fear. The most brilliant, honest and able exponent of this point of view was Hamilton. He was too impatient of slow-moving methods. Fundamentally he believed that the safety of the republic lay in the autocratic strength of its Government, that the destiny of individuals was to serve that Government, and that fundamentally a great and strong group of central institutions, guided by a small group of able and public spirited citizens, could best direct all Government.

But Mr. Jefferson, in the summer of 1776, after drafting the Declaration of Independence turned his mind to the same problem and took a different view. He did not deceive himself with outward forms. Government to him was a means to an end, not an end in itself; it might be either a refuge and a help or a threat and a danger, depending on the circumstances. We find him carefully analyzing the society for which he was to organize a Government. "We have no paupers. The great mass of our population is of laborers, our rich who cannot live without labor, either manual or professional, being few and of moderate wealth. Most of the laboring class possess property, cultivate their own lands, have families and from the demand for their labor, are enabled to exact from the rich and the competent such prices as enable them to feed abundantly, clothe above mere decency, to labor moderately and raise their families."

These people, he considered, had two sets of rights, those of "personal competency" and those involved in acquiring and possessing property. By "personal competency" he meant the right of free thinking, freedom of forming and expressing opinions, and freedom of personal living, each man according to his own lights. To insure the first set of rights, a Government must so order its functions as not to interfere with the individual. But even Jefferson realized that the exercise of the property rights might so interfere with the rights of the individual that the Government, without whose assistance the property rights could not exist, must intervene, not to destroy individualism, but to protect it …

So began, in American political life, the new day, the day of the individual against the system, the day in which individualism was made the great watchword of American life. The happiest of economic conditions made that day long and splendid. On the Western frontier, land was substantially free. No one, who did not shirk the task of earning a living, was entirely without opportunity to do so. Depressions could, and did, come and go; but they could not alter the fundamental fact that most of the people lived partly by selling their labor and partly by extracting their livelihood from the soil, so that starvation and dislocation were practically impossible …

It was in the middle of the nineteenth century that a new force was released and a new dream created. The force was what is called the industrial revolution, the advance of steam and machinery and the rise of the forerunners of the modern industrial plant. The dream was the dream of an economic machine, able to raise the standard of living for everyone; to bring luxury within the reach of the humblest; to annihilate distance by steam power and later by electricity, and to release everyone from the drudgery of the heaviest manual toil. It was to be expected that this would necessarily affect Government. Heretofore, Government had merely been called upon to produce conditions within which people could live happily, labor peacefully, and rest secure …

During this period of expansion, there was equal opportunity for all and the business of Government was not to interfere but to assist in the development of industry …

A glance at the situation today only too clearly indicates that equality of opportunity as we have known it no longer exists. Our industrial plant is built; the problem just now is whether under existing conditions it is not overbuilt. Our last frontier has long since been reached, and there is practically no more free land. More than half of our people do not live on the farms or on lands and cannot derive a living by cultivating their own property. There is no safety valve in the form of a Western prairie to which those thrown out of work by the Eastern economic machines can go for a new start. We are not able to invite the immigration from Europe to share our endless plenty. We are now providing a drab living for our own people …

As I see it, the task of Government in its relation to business is to assist the development of an economic declaration of rights, an economic constitutional order …

The Declaration of Independence discusses the problem of Government in terms of a contract. Government is a relation of give and take, a contract, perforce, if we would follow the thinking out of which it grew. Under such a contract rulers were accorded power, and the people consented to that power on consideration that they be accorded certain rights. The task of statesmanship has always been the re-definition of these rights in terms of a changing and growing social order. New conditions impose new requirements upon Government and those who conduct Government …

I feel that we are coming to a view through the drift of our legislation and our public thinking in the past quarter century that private economic power is, to enlarge an old phrase, a public trust as well. I hold that continued enjoyment of that power by any individual or group must depend upon the fulfillment of that trust. The men who have reached the summit of American business life know this best; happily, many of these urge the binding quality of this greater social contract.

The terms of that contract are as old as the Republic, and as new as the new economic order.

Every man has a right to life; and this means that he has also a right to make a comfortable living. He may by sloth or crime decline to exercise that right; but it may not be denied him. We have no actual famine or dearth; our industrial and agricultural mechanism can produce enough and to spare. Our Government formal and informal, political and economic, owes to everyone an avenue to possess himself of a portion of that plenty sufficient for his needs, through his own work.

Every man has a right to his own property; which means a right to be assured, to the fullest extent attainable, in the safety of his savings. By no other means can men carry the burdens of those parts of life which, in the nature of things, afford no chance of labor; childhood, sickness, old age. In all thought of property, this right is paramount; all other property rights must yield to it. If, in accord with this principle, we must restrict the operations of the speculator, the manipulator, even the financier, I believe we must accept the restriction as needful, not to hamper individualism but to protect it …

Faith in America, faith in our tradition of personal responsibility, faith in our institutions, faith in ourselves demand that we recognize the new terms of the old social contract. We shall fulfill them, as we fulfilled the obligation of the apparent Utopia which Jefferson imagined for us in 1776, and which Jefferson, Roosevelt and Wilson sought to bring to realization. We must do so, lest a rising tide of misery, engendered by our common failure, engulf us all. But failure is not an American habit; and in the strength of great hope we must all shoulder our common load.

Source: Franklin D. Roosevelt. "Campaign Address on Progressive Government at the Commonwealth Club in San Francisco, California," September 23, 1932. *The American Presidency Project*. https://www.presidency.ucsb.edu/node/289312

Lyndon B. Johnson's Great Society Speech (1964)

Though Lyndon B. Johnson began his presidency by declaring "an unconditional war on poverty," he soon made clear that his aspirations extended far beyond the mere elimination of poverty. For Johnson, ending poverty was just the first step toward the loftier goal of realizing what he termed the "Great Society." On May 22, 1964, in a commencement address at the University of Michigan, Johnson gave what became the signature speech of his presidency. At the outset of the address, Johnson states that the first century and a half of American history involved the struggle to create "an order of plenty for all of our people." Having accomplished this goal, the challenge now lies, Johnson asserts, in using that material security and prosperity as a foundation to "enrich and elevate our national life" and "to advance the quality of our American civilization."

I have come today from the turmoil of your Capital to the tranquility of your campus to speak about the future of your country.

The purpose of protecting the life of our Nation and preserving the liberty of our citizens is to pursue the happiness of our people. Our success in that pursuit is the test of our success as a Nation.

For a century we labored to settle and to subdue a continent. For half a century we called upon unbounded invention and untiring industry to create an order of plenty for all of our people.

The challenge of the next half century is whether we have the wisdom to use that wealth to enrich and elevate our national life, and to advance the quality of our American civilization.

Your imagination, your initiative, and your indignation will determine whether we build a society where progress is the servant of our needs, or a society where old values and new visions are buried under unbridled growth. For in your time we have the opportunity to move not only toward the rich society and the powerful society, but upward to the Great Society.

The Great Society rests on abundance and liberty for all. It demands an end to poverty and racial injustice, to which we are totally committed in our time. But that is just the beginning.

The Great Society is a place where every child can find knowledge to enrich his mind and to enlarge his talents. It is a place where leisure is a welcome chance to build and reflect, not a feared cause of boredom and restlessness. It is a place where the city of man serves not only the needs of the body and the demands of commerce but the desire for beauty and the hunger for community.

It is a place where man can renew contact with nature. It is a place which honors creation for its own sake and for what it adds to the understanding of the race. It is a place where men are more concerned with the quality of their goals than the quantity of their goods.

But most of all, the Great Society is not a safe harbor, a resting place, a final objective, a finished work. It is a challenge constantly renewed, beckoning us toward a destiny where the meaning of our lives matches the marvelous products of our labor.

So I want to talk to you today about three places where we begin to build the Great Society—in our cities, in our countryside, and in our classrooms.

Source: Lyndon B. Johnson. "Remarks at the University of Michigan," May 22, 1964. *The American Presidency Project.* https://www.presidency.ucsb.edu/documents/remarks-the-university-michigan

Ronald Reagan on Welfare Reform (1986)

In April 1982, President Ronald Reagan revived a practice first started by Franklin D. Roosevelt of delivering weekly radio addresses to the nation. Reagan typically used these talks to bring a policy issue to the nation's attention. In the address included here, Reagan denounces the nation's current welfare system claiming that it made the problem of poverty worse rather than better by keeping recipients in a state of perpetual dependency. Citing data on the decline of marriage and the increase of babies born out of wedlock to teenage mothers and absent fathers, Reagan contends that federal aid programs discourage family formation and marriage and were consequently leading to a permanent culture of poverty in America. Reagan concludes the address with a call for reshaping the system to encourage self-sufficiency and financial independence. This address marked the start of Reagan's campaign to further public support for welfare reform legislation.

My fellow Americans:

Today I'd like to speak to you about a gathering crisis in our society: It's a family crisis. To some it's hidden, concealed behind tenement walls or lost in the forgotten streets of our inner cities. But for millions of Americans, the crisis is ever present and growing, and it threatens to become a permanent scar on the American promise of hope and opportunity for all.

I'm talking about the crisis of family breakdowns, especially among the welfare poor, both black and white. In inner cities today, families, as we've always thought of them, are not even being formed. Since 1960 the percentage of babies born out of wedlock has more than doubled. And too often their mothers are only teenagers. They're children—many of them 15, 16, and 17 years old with all the responsibilities of grownups thrust upon them. The fathers of these children are often nowhere to be found. In some instances you have to go back three generations before you can find an intact family. It seems even the memory of families is in danger of becoming extinct. And what of the babies born out of wedlock, these children born to children. Statistically, we know that they're much more likely to have a low birth weight and, thus, serious health problems. We know that out-of-wedlock children often suffer abuse and neglect as well. And what sort of future can they look forward to?

The family is the most basic support system there is. For two centuries now, it's been families pulling together that has provided the courage, willpower, and sense of security that have enabled millions of Americans to escape poverty and grab hold of the rungs on the ladder of opportunity. How often have we heard about the immigrant father laboring long into the night to give his children the advantages he never had? How many self-made men and women in America of all ethnic backgrounds owe their success to the strength of character given them by hard-working, loving parents? But for the children of child mothers and absentee fathers, there is often only a deepening cycle of futility, hopelessness, and despair.

We're in danger of creating a permanent culture of poverty as inescapable as any chain or bond; a second and separate America, an America of lost dreams and stunted lives. The irony is that misguided welfare programs instituted in the name of compassion have actually helped turn a shrinking problem into a national tragedy. From the 1950s on, poverty in America was declining. American society, an opportunity society, was doing its wonders. Economic growth was providing a ladder for millions to climb up out of poverty and into prosperity. In 1964 the famous War on Poverty was declared and a funny thing happened. Poverty, as measured by dependency, stopped shrinking and then actually began to grow worse. I guess you could say, poverty won the war. Poverty won in part because instead of helping the poor, government programs ruptured the bonds holding poor families together.

Perhaps the most insidious effect of welfare is its usurpation of the role of provider. In States where payments are highest, for instance, public assistance for a single mother can amount to much more than the usable income of a minimum wage job. In other words, it can pay for her to quit work. Many families are eligible for substantially higher benefits when the father is not present. What must it do to a man to know that his own children will be better off if he is never legally recognized as their father? Under existing welfare rules, a teenage girl who becomes pregnant can make herself eligible for welfare benefits that will set her up in an apartment of her own, provide medical care, and feed and clothe her. She only has to fulfill one condition—not marry or identify the father.

Obviously something is desperately wrong with our welfare system. With only about half of what is now spent on welfare, we could give enough money to every impoverished man, woman, and child to lift them above the poverty line. Instead, we spend vast amounts on a system that perpetuates poverty. But the waste of money pales before the sinful waste of human potential-the squandering of so many millions of hopes and dreams.

In my State of the Union Address, I directed our administration to study the welfare system with a keen eye to making reforms. We already have in place a low-income assistance working group, which is hard at its task. In addition, I've instructed Attorney General Edwin Meese, as Chairman pro tem of our Domestic Policy Council, to convene a working group to evaluate the effect of a wide range of government programs on American families, especially poor families. These groups will report back to me by December 1st. The welfare tragedy has gone on too long. It's time to reshape our welfare system so that it can be judged by how many Americans it makes independent of welfare.

Until next week, thanks for listening. God bless you.

Source: Ronald Reagan. "Radio Address to the Nation on Welfare Reform," February 15, 1986. *The American Presidency Project*. https://www.presidency.ucsb.edu/documents/radio-address-the-nation-welfare-reform-0

Testimony of Anti-Poverty Activist Tianna Gaines-Turner (2013)

On July 31, 2013, in recognition of the forty-ninth anniversary of President Johnson's declaration of a war on poverty, the US House of Representatives' Budget Committee held a hearing focused on the progress or lack of progress in the war to alleviate poverty in America. The following includes an excerpt from the prepared statement of Tianna Gaines-Turner, a mother who had struggled with poverty and homelessness, and the Chair of Witness to Hunger, a research and advocacy group made up of members with lived experience with hunger and poverty. Gaines-Turner recounts the challenges her own family faces every day trying to get by on part-time, low-paying jobs, and government food assistance.

Chairman Paul Ryan and distinguished members of the Committee, thank you for requesting and considering this written testimony. My name is Tianna Gaines-Turner. I am married to the father of our 3 biological children. I have a son who is 9 years old and on the honor roll, going into 4th grade, and I have twins, age 5, who are starting kindergarten in September. I also have three teenage stepchildren, whom I love dearly. I have worked with the Witnesses to Hunger program, a growing group of parents who speak out as the true expert witnesses on hunger and poverty in America.

I work part time for a childcare provider at a recreation center making about $10 dollars an hour and my husband works behind the deli counter at a grocery store making $8 dollars an hour. We haven't been able to find full-time jobs. With the part-time jobs, our incomes go up and down. Not only do we have incomes that are inadequate, but they are also unstable and unpredictable. When programs like SNAP (food stamps) rely on stable income reports, it makes it harder to keep this nutrition support steady. So we may lose food stamps one month because we make too much, and then a few months later, when our companies choose to reduce our hours at their own convenience, we make less money and we need to turn to food stamps again to feed our kids healthy meals. But, then we might get an opportunity to work a few more hours, and then we lose the food stamps again—all in the space of six months, and never with the right timing. What happens, then, is we often run out of money for food. There is a research study I read that's called "Working for Peanuts" that shows when families have unpredictable hours at low paying jobs, that the families are more likely to be "food insecure." That's my family.

My three children have medical issues that concern me every day. All of my children suffer from epilepsy and have to take life-saving medication every day. All three of my children also have moderate to severe asthma. I worry about a day that might come where my children won't be able to see a specialist because I can't afford the co-pay. In addition, neither my husband nor I qualify for medical assistance because we make too much money in our part time jobs, but our jobs do not offer health insurance. I, too, suffer from asthma and epilepsy. I currently can't afford to get an inhaler. The thought that my own children may not be able to get the care they need worries me every day. Just like you want the best for your children, I want the best for my children.

This is very important for you to know. What I am going to show you is that issues of medical care, housing, and food all go hand in hand.

There have been times when my oldest son was sick or having seizures, and of course, as would you, I wanted to be at the hospital to care for him and help him get the care he needed, and to comfort him. But that meant my husband had to stay home to take care of the twins. And then we were both unable to work, so we lost money that month, and ultimately had to make a choice—do we pay the rent or do we pay the light bill? Not to mention, how do we buy food?

No family should have to choose between paying a bill or putting food on the table. In my work with Witnesses to Hunger, I read many research studies by Children's HealthWatch that showed that food, medical issues, paying for utilities and housing all go hand and hand.

Poverty is not just one issue that can be solved at one time. It's not just an issue of jobs, or food, or housing, or utility assistance, and safety. It's a people issue. And you can't slice people up into issues. We are whole human beings. Poverty has to do with a whole person who is in a family, in a neighborhood, in a community, and our country. The policies you work on in the House of Representatives affect me and my family in very deep and important ways. I am living out your policy-making and I see how your decisions affect both physical and mental health, especially the physical and mental health of my children and me.

Let's get something straight. We've heard some leaders say that people who are poor are lazy, or that they need to work harder. But that is a very wrong view. Most low-income families I know are working harder than many other people who make a lot more money, and they're working sometimes 2–3 jobs to make ends meet. We're playing by the rules, but we're not getting ahead.

Playing by the Rules—Working

I am not sure at what point the American Dream—of knowing that if you worked hard, you would survive—ended. But it has for my family, and for many in my communities. Working one or even multiple jobs is no longer enough. Wages are so low and expenses are so high that even if you are able to find work, it may not be enough to even pay for the expense of childcare. I have heard too often the story of people finally getting a job, just to have their childcare assistance taken away. They no longer qualify for the assistance at the exact moment they need it most. Just when someone is moving forward, the rug is ripped out from under "Every time my son got sick, their dad had to take off of work. That's money we're missing. That means: Do we pay the rent or do we pay the light bill?" them. This cycle pushes families deeper into poverty than they were before they took the job. This system needs to change in order for people like myself to forge a better future for myself and my children, one where I will never need to turn to public assistance again.

Good Nutrition

Relying on food stamps is not an easy process. When I hear the story about a person buying lobster using their SNAP benefits, I am frustrated because it is not the reality. People on SNAP count every penny they have and cut every corner they can to make sure their children do not starve. I know of many families through my work with Witnesses to Hunger who describe having to put their children to bed before dinner because there was nothing to feed the children, or others who look at food menus delivered to their door so that they can imagine ordering dinner and trick themselves into thinking they've eaten, when actually they have not eaten in days. The reality is that SNAP keeps us from starving. It is critical to the survival of the 50% of American children who will rely on the program at some point in their lives.

For me, feeding my family properly has become a strategic obsession. No matter how diligent I am to cut coupons or only buy things on sale, the benefits never last. Most nights my husband and I make our dinners on what is left over on our children's plates—we call it "kids plate surfing." We are able to get by thanks to SNAP, but we are not eating well.

I know that a proper diet is critical for the health and well-being of my children, that nutrients are key to their development. I also know that if my benefits are cut that means less meals and less nutritious food. Cutting a person's benefits by $10, $15, or $20 might not seem like a lot to legislators, but it would cut meals out completely for families like mine. Without SNAP, I would still feed my kids, but it would be cheap Oodles of Noodles with lots of sodium and a bunch of ingredients I can't recognize or pronounce. They would not get fresh vegetables and fruit.

Because I am active in addressing hunger, and work with researchers around the country, I've seen that this year, the Institute of Medicine proved that SNAP benefits do not last, because the monthly SNAP benefit is not enough for a healthy diet. My family, friends and community could have told you that years ago. But the thing is, people wouldn't believe us because they would somehow think it was our fault. The Institute of Medicine shows that it's not our fault. It is the system we have that needs improvement.

Safe and Affordable Housing

My family and I have been homeless twice in the last several years.

There was a house that we could afford to rent when the twins were newborns. The day we moved in, people in the neighborhood told us to stay inside because there was going to be a shoot out. There were children everywhere on this street. That's not a safe place to live, but it's all I could afford! And there was a terrible rodent problem on the block—mice and cockroaches. And, as you know, those are the things that make asthma worse—they are asthma triggers. So I was spending too much money on an exterminator to no avail, and spending too much time in the emergency room. We moved out because it was unsafe and unhealthy. We took our tiny savings to stay in a hotel until we could find a place that we could afford that was safe and wouldn't make us sick.

When we were homeless we would sleep on my mother-in-law's couch, and take the kids to the playground so they wouldn't have to think about their situation. At the playground, they could just be kids.

During this time, I was on the waiting list for Section 8. And it turns out my name in the system—after 10 years of waiting—was actually approved. They tried to send the forms to our old address, but they had the spelling of the street wrong, so it never reached us. We didn't know about this for months. And because we never responded, we were put back to the bottom of the waitlist. All of the housing forms are still paper based. It is a system that is still in the Stone Age.

It took a call from a legislator's office to get that situation fixed. Thanks to Section 8 finally working out, I now live in a slightly safer neighborhood. Yet there are still abandoned homes on our street, shootouts in the bar down the street, and several homeless people who stay under the bridge in the nearby subway.

Giving Back

Chairman Ryan recently said that people need to get involved in their communities and help each other out, because getting together to help each other out is much better than government benefits. But, if you actually came into our communities, actually invited us to talk with you about what it's like to be on government benefits, you would learn that government benefits are actually helping us stay healthy.

You would also see that helping each other out is exactly what we do, every day to survive.

The hardship of being homeless with children is what I would like people to see. When you look into my children's faces and in their eyes in that picture, they're only one and five years old, but you can see the stress and the loneliness. When you're homeless it seems like it's not just being homeless from having a home; it's being homeless from having selfrespect and self-worth, and just not being able to do what you want to do.

I used to take them to the playground when we were homeless so they wouldn't have to think about the situation they were in. They could just be kids. …

Source: U.S. House. Hearing before the Committee on the Budget. "Prepared Statement of Tianna Gaines-Turner." *The War on Poverty: A Progress Report.* 113th Cong. 1st Sess. (July 31, 2013). https://www.govinfo.gov/content/pkg/CHRG-113hhrg81981/pdf/CHRG-113hhrg81981.pdf

"Is the American Dream in Crisis?" (2019)

On July 17, 2019, the Senate Subcommittee on Economic Policy of the Committee on Banking, Housing, and Urban Affairs held a hearing on status and attainability of the American Dream and whether the nation is helping or harming individual Americans in their attainment of it. The following excerpts from that hearing include the opening remarks of Senator Tom Cotton (R-AR) and Senator Catherine Cortez Masto (D-NV).

Opening Statement of Senator Tom Cotton

... We are here to discuss economic mobility and the American Dream. When economists discuss these things, they often think in terms of GDP growth and consumer prices. To exaggerate just a little, they often seem to believe that so long as the economy grows 2 at 3 percent and Americans can afford more cheap plastic stuff from China, America must be doing great. But is that really true?

When I talk to Arkansans, I hear a different story. Most of them do not dream of extravagant wealth, much less abstract ideas like "'economic growth'" and "'consumer surplus.'" They know a life of getting and spending cannot hope to fulfill one's dreams.

Instead, they dream of a career that pays an honest wage so they can live in a decent neighborhood. They dream of getting married and starting a family. And, ultimately, they dream of passing on this standard of living to their children—plus a little bit more. That is the American Dream I hear, according to the Arkansans that I know.

The question for today is: Is our Nation helping Americans achieve this American Dream, or are we failing them?

I have to say, I think in some important ways our Nation is failing our fellow citizens. The labyrinth of subsidies, regulations, and misguided priorities constructed here in Washington often does little to help a large majority of Americans who do not graduate from college, the "'Silent Majority'" who work with their hands and on their feet.

Our government does not offer these Americans much beyond occasionally moralizing about their supposed shortcomings: "'go to college,'" "'abandon your hometown,'" "'learn to code.'"

What they really need are more viable career paths that do not require expensive educations. There are many good-paying, honorable jobs for people without college degrees in this country. But how do we create even more of them? How do we prepare workers so they are ready for those jobs?

There is another urgent context for today's hearing as well: our economic competition with China. For decades, Washington has pursued a policy of integration with China. The architects of this policy hoped naively that enriching the Chinese Communist Party would make it more pliable and less communist. Instead, it gave China the means to challenge America around the world—all while decimating the American heartland.

If we want to remain the world's strongest economy, we need to marshal every citizen, every skill, every talent at our disposal. We will need to recover the vitality, productive abilities, and indeed the patriotism that contributed to America's resounding triumphs in the past century.

If we build a more productive economy, it will serve not only our strategic interests as a Nation, but the interests of the American people, by helping them achieve the American Dream. I look forward to your thoughts and to my colleagues' questions.

Opening Statement of Senator Catherine Cortez Masto

... Thank you, Chairman Cotton, and welcome to all our witnesses today.

I appreciate the Chairman suggesting a hearing to explore barriers to economic mobility in the United States. The Senate Banking Committee has jurisdiction over many of the most pressing issues facing Americans today—from housing, to lending, to transportation, and today we discuss how Congress can improve economic outcomes for children and families and entrepreneurs.

We want our children to grow up and become financially self-reliant. We want the children of renters to be able to own their own homes if they wish. And we want children whose parents struggled to put food on the table to be able to afford a full pantry and even a few meals out every month.

We want children who survived homelessness to grow up with an income adequate to not just pay the rent but save for their children's college education and their own retirement. We want workers retiring from one career to be able to open a small store and have it thrive.

Yet those dreams—the American Dream—are unattainable for too many. Parents who lack affordable bank accounts end up with financial products that can lead to a debt trap. As they struggle with bank fees, they may see their car repossessed, resulting in getting fired from their job and getting evicted from their home.

The average college senior graduates with more than $30,000 in debt, and total student debt nationwide has topped $1.5 trillion. And some college graduates cannot find jobs that pay enough to manage their crushing student loan debt. They delay starting a family, buying a home, and saving for retirement for a decade or more because of this. An entrepreneur buys a franchise business but finds the business never earns as much as she was promised. As she struggles to keep her store in the black, she does it all on her own. She cannot afford to hire employees and pay them a living wage. That is wrong.

It is wrong that the ZIP Code where a child is born and grows up affects their future income and financial success more than the child's education, aptitude, or work ethic.

It is wrong that a lack of affordable financial products prevents families from building up savings to respond to a broken arm or a broken car without a major financial crisis.

It is wrong that corporations use noncompete clauses, union busting, and arbitration clauses to keep wages low and corporate profits high.

And it is wrong that high housing costs, lack of affordable childcare, and inadequate transit restrain economic mobility for struggling families and young adults.

It is wrong that entrepreneurs who purchased a franchise—many of them immigrants, retirees, and veterans—were misled by unfair contracts, deceptive financial information, and non-disparagement clauses.

We need solutions. And we know many of them are already out there.

In their written testimonies today, the witnesses have suggested significant investment in education, health, and other public services. They want to empower workers and franchise owners. They recommend tackling monopolies and corporate concentrations that drive out competition and result in lower wages for workers.

We have seen how Government can protect homeowners, small business owners, and entrepreneurs from predatory and abusive practices and financial products.

I thank all of the witnesses for being here today. I look forward to hearing the testimonies, working with all of you as we move forward. In fact, I hope that, as Mr. Cotton said, what we are focusing here on Congress is how we ensure that everybody has the opportunity to achieve that American Dream …

Source: U.S. Senate. Hearing before the Subcommittee on Economic Policy of the Committee on Banking, Housing, and Urban Affairs. "Opening Statements of Senator Tom Cotton and Senator Catherine Cortez Masto." *Exploring Barriers to Economic Mobility and Making the American Dream Attainable for All Americans.* 116th Cong. 1st Sess. (July 17, 2019). https://www.govinfo.gov/content/pkg/CHRG-116shrg39541/pdf/CHRG-116shrg39541.pdf

Margaret Eaddy Testifies on Housing Affordability (2022)

In the wake of the Covid-19 pandemic, the US House of Representatives' Committee on Financial Services held a hearing focusing on the nation's inadequate housing supply and corresponding crisis in housing affordability that was only exacerbated by the economic trends following the pandemic. In the testimony included here, housing activist Margaret Eaddy shares her family's struggle to obtain stable housing after being evicted due to financial hardship.

My name is Margaret Eaddy. I am from Hampton, Virginia.

I am grateful to the office of Representative Maxine Waters for providing me an opportunity to speak to you today.

The topic of this hearing—fair and affordable housing—is personal for me. And that's because I and my husband John currently live in our car.

There are so many other things about me I'd rather be sharing with you today.

I am a visual artist who paints beautiful abstract paintings. I am a former librarian. I'm an advocate for other parents, like me, who have been impacted by gun violence.

But being homeless steals your identity. People like my husband and I need stable housing before we can accomplish our full potential.

So today, I wanted briefly to share our housing story with you. Our experience has also brought us into contact with other families who are facing similar challenges, and I hope to speak up for them as well.

When the pandemic hit in 2020, my husband saw his hours cut in his job hauling trash to the landfill. We fell about $150 short on our rent. Instead of working with us, the landlord evicted us.

My husband and I decided to move into our vehicle while we searched for other places. But we soon found that the barriers to finding a home were very steep. Whenever my husband and I would speak with rental offices, I would give them my name. They would type my name into some sort of data system, and then tell me: "We see an eviction on your public record, and we cannot help you."

My husband and I were able briefly to find a place to live after our story received news coverage. We received support from kind individuals on GoFundMe. But this year, after that attention faded, our landlord chose to do what many landlords have done recently. They failed to renew our lease after it expired, and they increased our apartment's rent beyond what we could pay. So for the last four months, my husband and I have been living in our car again.

In the parking lots where we sleep and in the homeless agencies we visit, I have met many other homeless families. It hurts so bad to see moms and dads out there with their kids. The dads look like their pride was sold away from them. And when they tell you their stories, they will tell you that their world was turned upside down because their rent went up by even just fifty or sixty more dollars, and that they couldn't afford that.

Even if an apartment were to be offered to us, the deposit and income requirements are so high. A landlord typically asks for three times the rent upfront—$3,000, for example, for a place that rents for $1,000. We don't have that. Landlords also can require you to show that you make three times the monthly rent just to qualify. We can't show that.

All of this makes people in our situation more vulnerable to any landlord who will accept you, even if they overcharge you and provide unsafe conditions.

When people have stable housing, it allows them to do so much more in life.

I know that it is hard for a member of Congress to imagine yourself living in your car. It was hard for my husband and I to imagine ourselves in this situation. But I am asking you, today, to imagine yourself in our situation.

You don't know how good it is to have a knob to turn every evening—to enter a space where you're safe, and not in danger—until that's taken away from you.

There are a lot of people out here that if they had safe, affordable housing—and if they could stay in it until the day they died—that would be something they really do desire. Anything you can do to help make that a reality would mean a lot to many people.

Thank you.

Source: U.S. House. Hearing before the Financial Services Committee. "Testimony of Margaret Eaddy." *Boom and Bust: The Need for Bold Investments in Fair and Affordable Housing to Combat Inflation.* 117th Cong. 2nd Sess. (December 1, 2022). https://democrats-financialservices.house.gov/uploadedfiles/hhrg-117-ba00-bio-eaddym-20221201.pdf

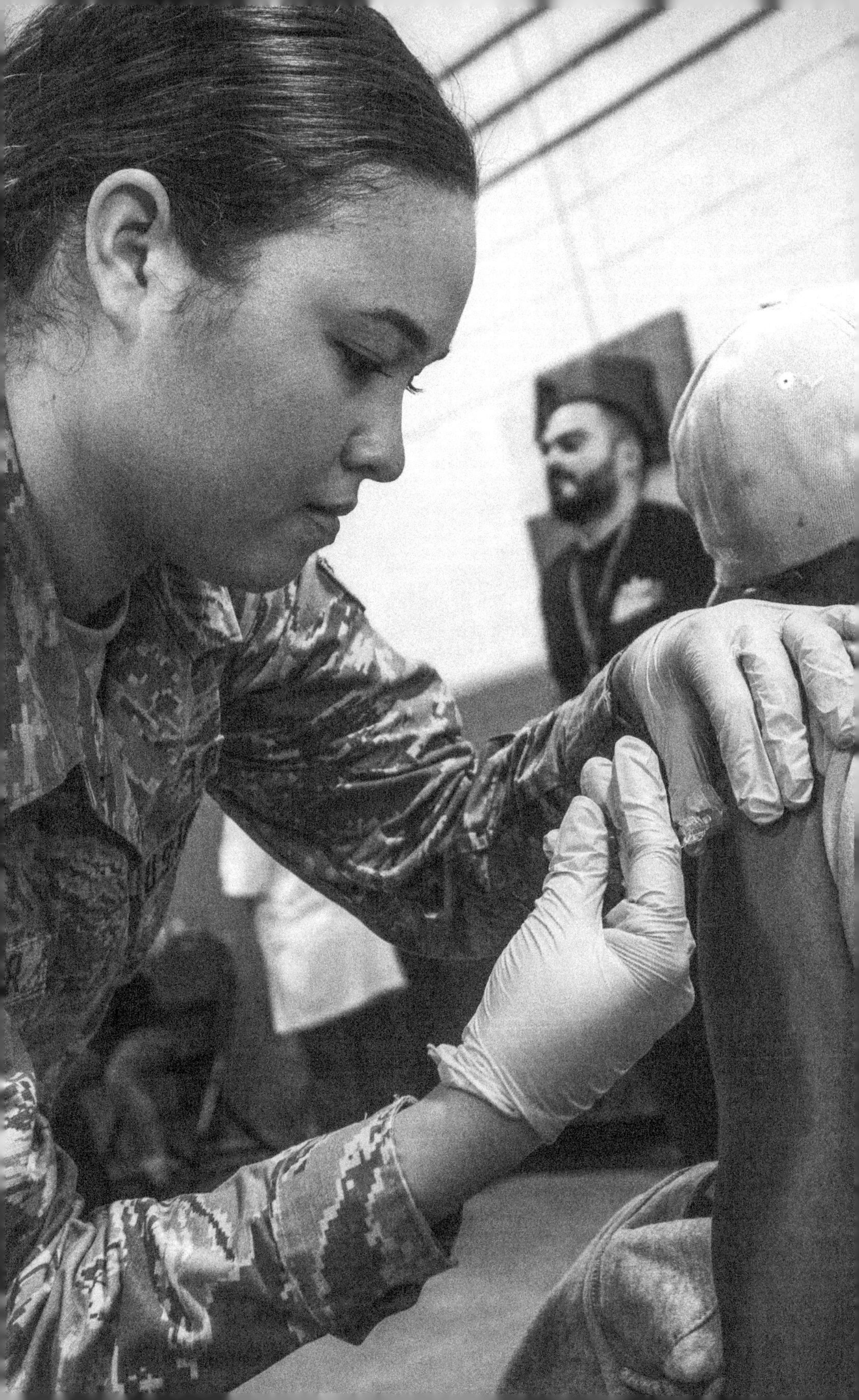

6

Resources

Introduction

This chapter provides an annotated list of selected books, articles, reports, and nonprint resources on a variety of topics related to poverty in America.

Books

Anderson, Elijah, ed. 2008. *Against the Wall: Poor, Young, Black, and Male.* Philadelphia: University of Pennsylvania Press.

This collection of sixteen original essays, edited with an introductory chapter by sociologist Elijah Anderson and a foreword by Cornel West, addresses the alienation and marginalization experienced by many urban, young Black males who are raised and socialized in concentrated poverty, segregation, failing schools, broken families, and communities that lack opportunity and upward mobility. Consequently, they are frequently trapped in a cycle of negative stereotypes, discrimination, unemployment, violence, crime, incarceration, and early death. Several essays focus specifically on the joblessness and economic plight of inner-city Black males and provide suggestions for how to re-engage urban youth through public policy, civic action, and programs such as youth entrepreneurship training.

A New Jersey National Guard Airman gives a homeless veteran a flu shot during a Stand Down event in Cherry Hill, New Jersey, in 2019. Stand Downs are grassroots, community-assisted programs organized to provide homeless veterans with healthcare, mental health screening, substance abuse counseling, social and legal services, food, clothing, and more, with the goal of helping them to re-enter mainstream society. (New Jersey National Guard photo by Mark C. Olsen)

Arnade, Chris. 2019. *Dignity: Seeking Respect in Back Row America*. New York: Penguin Random House.

In this up-close account of the class-divide plaguing modern-day America, Wall Street bond-trader-turned-photo-journalist Chris Arnade uses photography and real-life interactions to distinguish between what he calls "front-row America" and "back-row America." Front-row America includes the so-called meritocratic class, those who go to college and obtain advanced degrees, easily secure good employment, have access to useful social connections, and pass on their privilege to their children. Those in the back-row struggle to graduate high school, lack the credentials to secure gainful employment, and often find themselves left behind in dying communities, trapped in a generational cycle of violence, disaffection, and addiction.

After abandoning his career on Wall Street, Arnade began documenting poverty and addiction in the Bronx, where he spent hours in McDonald's and drug traps interviewing, photographing, and becoming friends with local homeless addicts. Eventually, he started driving across America spending time interacting with residents of similarly downtrodden communities. Arnade carefully recounts his conversations with individuals in these communities and describes how his experience gave him a new and deep respect for the dignity and resilience of back-row America.

While many in front-row America scorn and mock those who remain in dying towns, who cling to religion or tradition, or who find themselves caught in the grip of addiction, Arnade seeks to understand them. He demonstrates how the front row's narrow-minded focus on data-based economic growth and efficiency causes them to ignore the value of things that are harder to quantify like happiness, friendships, pride, and integration. He paints a vivid picture of the day-to-day life of back-row Americans, their desire to remain in the communities they call home, and how the policies of globalization have wreaked havoc in their lives, leaving them feeling excluded, rejected, and humiliated. This, he maintains, has left a vacuum easily filled by drugs, anger, and resentment. He ultimately concludes that improving the lives and communities for back-row Americans will require a reconsideration of the system in which economics is the central form of meaning, material goods are the primary form of valuation, and education and credentials are central to economic success.

Campbell, Andrea L. 2014. *Trapped in America's Safety Net: One Family's Struggle*. Chicago: The University of Chicago Press.

Andrea Campbell, professor of political science at the Massachusetts Institute of Technology, tells the story of her sister-in-law Marcella Wagner, who was left a quadriplegic after she was involved in a car accident with a hit-and-run driver on her way to nursing school. Campbell recounts how the accident not only caused physical and emotional devastation that ended Marcella's career plans but also plunged Marcella and her husband Dave into economic tragedy brought about by the means-tested social assistance programs that Marcella was forced to rely on as a severely disabled person.

Although Campbell had been teaching social policy for years, her firsthand experience helping her brother and sister-in-law's family opened her eyes to the fact that behind the statistics, government manuals, scholarly analyses, and ideological battles over policy design are real-life human beings whose lives are being molded, distorted, and stunted by the policies purported to help them. Using her family's experience as a case study, Campbell explores how social assistance programs affect the lives of the people who depend on them and their multiple failings and shortcomings. Campbell ultimately draws four conclusions about the nature of American social policy: first, that it is divided into different tiers that provide vastly different experiences for recipients; second, that many means-tested programs have designs that keep people trapped in poverty—they discourage work, savings, and marriage; third, that social protections for low-income people vary tremendously from state to state; and fourth, that American social policy provides insufficient protections from life's risks and cuts off socioeconomic mobility for recipients and their children. In closing, Campbell compares American social assistances programs to those in other developed countries that provide basic protections regardless of a citizen's employment status and that allow people to leave poverty with more training, better wages, and a more complete set of social benefits.

Carney, Timothy P. 2019. *Alienated America: Why Some Places Thrive While Others Collapse*. New York: HarperCollins.

For several years, columnist and American Enterprise Institute resident fellow Timothy Carney traveled Middle America, engaged in field work, and examined county-level maps, demographic data, electoral results, and social science findings. From this study, Carney ultimately concludes that the American Dream is no longer an achievable reality in many areas of the country. Unlike libertarians and Marxists, however, Carney maintains that the demise of the American Dream is a social phenomenon not an economic one.

To support this point, Tim Carney specifically examines how social isolation contributed to the success of Donald Trump in 2016 Republican primary election over more conventional GOP choices like Ted Cruz and Marco Rubio. Looking at the data from the 2016 primary election, Carney demonstrates how candidate Trump struggled in conservative areas with thriving religious, familial, and civic institutions that contribute to social capital and give people a sense of belonging. His earliest, strongest primary election supporters—those who said they'd never voted before but would drive long distances and wait hours to hear him speak at rallies—typically overwhelmingly lived in places defined by declining demographic conditions, even when they resided in slightly more affluent than average households. Candidate Trump's 2016 proclamation that the "American Dream Is Dead" and that he was the one to fix it resonated with these people who believed that their communities were falling apart and who saw their neighbors suffering from opioid overdoses and attempting suicide at record rates.

Carney uses this study of the 2016 primary as a segway to discuss the importance of location in analyzing current social pathologies, including rising rates of despair and social alienation, growing inequality, and declining levels of social and economic mobility, public health, and life expectancy. These maladies, Carney maintains, are not spread evenly throughout the country, but are concentrated in specific working-class towns and communities with failing social connections and support systems. Upper, middle, and working-class neighborhoods in which familial, civic, and religious ties and institutions are strong are far less likely to suffer from social alienation and physical and economic decline.

Carney attributes the erosion of civil society and alienation plaguing communities throughout the country to several factors that have left individuals and families disconnected from one another and isolated. These include the collapse of churches and other community organizations, a retreat from marriage, hyper-individualized capitalism, and the overcentralization of business, government, and culture. Ultimately, these trends have left many localities devoid of middling institutions that stand between the whole society and the individual and connect people to one another in supportive and productive relationships.

In his final chapter, Carney maintains that because the forces that have left so many Americans alienated are largely cultural, there are no big policy solutions. He does, however, suggest several smaller solutions to begin the process of rebuilding social connections and social capital at the local level. He also offers several suggestions for how to mitigate the abuses and exclusivity that sometimes accompany tight-knit religious and civic communities.

Case, Anne and Angus Deaton. 2021. *Deaths of Despair and the Future of Capitalism*. Princeton, NJ: Princeton University Press.

In this account of the plight of the American working class, economist Anne Case and Nobel Prize-winner Angus Deaton contend that despite the material progress and decline in poverty and deprivation that have occurred over the past two centuries thanks in large part to the twin forces of capitalism and globalization, all is not well. The authors document recent declines in overall physical and mental health and the dramatic rise in deaths of despair from suicide, drug overdose, and alcoholism among America's working class and examine the underlying economic and social roots of this crisis. They find that the increase in deaths of despair and declining quality of life has almost entirely occurred among those without a bachelor's degree and has been particularly acute among white working-class men.

The authors tie this crisis to several factors that have made the lives of the working class more difficult and have inhibited their ability to live dignified and meaningful lives. While they acknowledge the argument made by others concerning the effects of changing social norms, such as a decline in religiosity and community involvement and an increase in out-of-wedlock births, the authors of this work focus primarily on external economic factors that have contributed to social alienation and despair among Americans without a college degree. These factors include a long-term decline in median earnings and purchasing power, deterioration in job quality, reduced opportunity for promotion, an increased detachment from the labor force, and so on. In contrast to those who attribute globalization, technological change, and automation as the main causes of these maladies, the authors maintain that in America the rising economic and political power of corporations, the growth of high-tech firms that employ fewer workers, and the consolidation of industries (e.g., in hospitals and airlines) have contributed to the declining economic and political power of workers and ordinary working-class consumers. Added to this, the authors contend, is a pharmaceutical industry protected by government licensing that makes billions of dollars from sales of addictive opioids and a healthcare system that redistributes income upward to hospitals, physicians, device makers, and pharmaceutical companies while delivering poor health outcomes.

The authors conclude by recommending a series of policies to rein in and restrict rent-seeking, crony capitalism, lobbying, and the misuse of market power and to reform the American healthcare system.

Cass, Oren. 2018. *The Once and Future Worker: A Vision for the Renewal of Work in America*. New York: Encounter.

Over the past several decades, Americans have witnessed unprecedented growth in Gross Domestic Product (GDP). Despite this growth, workers' wages have stagnated, millions of people have dropped out of the labor force altogether, poverty rates have risen, drug addiction has surged, life expectancy and health have declined, and families and entire communities have collapsed. The characteristic response from opposite sides of the political aisle is either to trample the market with more regulations, mandates, and drastic increases in entitlements or to double down in support of an unhampered free market and maximum economic growth. Politicians incessantly speak about "good jobs," but the "jobs" programs and policies they embrace are typically focused on other priorities such as cutting taxes, shrinking government, expanding healthcare entitlements, and fighting climate change.

In this re-evaluation of society, economics, and policy, economist Oren Cass maintains that a thriving society and growing economy that benefits all classes is dependent not only on stable political institutions, but also on strong families and communities. These institutions in turn rely on a foundation of productive work through which people find purpose and satisfaction in providing for themselves and helping others. Thus, Cass's central claim, or what he refers to as his *Working Hypothesis*, is that a labor market in which workers can support strong families and communities is a necessary component of human flourishing and should be the primary focus of public policy. Cass further maintains in the first part of his book that creating the conditions that contribute to the productive employment of American workers will support not only a thriving, self-sufficient society but also economic dynamism and growth.

In Part II, Cass explores the policy areas that most influence the labor market and the availability of productive work. These include environmental regulations and their effect on what kind of labor our economy demands, education and the kind of labor workers can provide, trade and immigration policy and their effect on who produces and consumes in the market, organized labor and its effect on how agreements are made in the market, and taxes and subsidies and their effect on what jobs are created at what wages.

In Part III, Cass considers factors beyond the labor market that influence work. These include the challenge of constructing a safety net that protects those who cannot work while ensuring gainful employment of those capable of work and the influence that social norms and culture have on either devaluing work or reinforcing its importance.

Cass concludes by exploring how to refocus public policy on the renewal of work and family, sustained by a healthy labor market, which he argues will ultimately contribute to economic prosperity.

Colburn, Gregg and Clayton Page Aldern. 2022. *Homelessness Is a Housing Problem: How Structural Factors Explain U.S. Patterns*. Oakland, CA: University of California Press.

While homelessness has increased throughout the United States, the problem is more acute in some cities and metro regions than others. Using data on housing availability and homelessness, housing scholar Gregg Colburn and data scientist and policy analyst Clayton Aldern explore the substantial regional variation in rates on homelessness and the individual, structural, and political causes ascribed to such disparities. The authors contend that the policy conversation regarding homelessness tends to focus too narrowly on mental health and drugs as chief driving factors, masking the more important root cause: housing market conditions.

The authors determine that although individual vulnerabilities such as addiction, domestic violence, tragedy, and so on may increase the risk, homelessness is ultimately caused by the simple fact that there is not enough affordable housing. They reach this conclusion first by providing an overview of existing academic social science research on the topic. Next, the authors consider various potential explanations for the substantial variation in per capita homeless populations around the country including disproportionate levels of drug use, mental illness, or poverty and variations in weather, local politics, mobility, and welfare provisions. They find that these common explanations do not account for the regional variations in rates of homelessness. Instead, they maintain that regional differences in homelessness rates result from variations in absolute rent levels and rental market vacancy rates. These housing market conditions, they posit, explain why high-poverty cities like Detroit and Cleveland (with cheaper, more abundant housing) have lower rates of homelessness than cities (with high rents and low vacancy rates) like Boston, Seattle, Los Angeles, and Portland. The authors use the game of musical chairs to illustrate their findings. In the game, a contestant who has a disability or who lacks physical strength will be more likely to end up without a chair at the end of the game, but the real reason that the contestant is without a chair is that there aren't enough chairs to go around. The same logic, the authors argue, applies to homelessness. Whenever housing shortages exist, a certain number of people will inevitably become homeless.

The authors conclude by calling on policymakers first and foremost to increase the number of affordable housing units (both emergency and long term) and to provide subsidies and rental assistance to households to ensure they can access housing. This response to homelessness, they contend, will ultimately require a change in the public perception of homelessness, far greater levels of resources from all levels of government, and a broader systems approach to addressing homelessness.

Desmond, Matthew. 2023. *Poverty by America*. New York: Crown.

Sociologist and Pulitzer Prize-winning author Matthew Desmond contends that although the United States is the richest country on earth, it has higher levels of poverty than other advanced democracies. In the opening chapter, Desmond recounts personal encounters with individuals living in various forms of poverty to demonstrate that the problem of poverty is not limited to small incomes and material scarcity but extends to the relentless piling on of problems that accompany pain, trauma, instability, fear, addiction, incarceration, shame, and indignity.

In contrast to other books that document the conditions of poverty and seek to understand its nature, however, Desmond states that his primary purpose is to identify why American poverty exists by looking beyond the poor to those living lives of privilege and plenty—the secure, the insured, the housed, the college educated, the protected, the lucky. He ultimately determines that poverty persists in the America not because of scarcity but because affluent and middle-class Americans knowingly and unknowingly benefit from and perpetuate it. He derides banks and payday-loan stores that rely on exorbitant overdraft fees and extortionate rates as a stream of income, landlords who profit from raised rents, residents who support exclusionary zoning, and consumers who demand convenience and low prices with little concern for the exploitive practices that make them possible.

Desmond further maintains the persistence of poverty is not due to a lack of public benefits. America's welfare state (as a share of its Gross Domestic Product) is the second largest in the world, behind France. Yet, he contends that much of this assistance is given to those who need the help the least. A large percentage of government subsidies and benefits is spent on programs such as government-subsidized retirement benefits for state employees, student loans, tax-free college savings plans, child tax credits, and homeowner subsidies (such as the mortgage-interest tax deduction) that disproportionately benefit Americans who are living well above the poverty line. Furthermore, a sizable percentage of money earmarked for the poor is wasted due to bureaucratic overhead and poorly defined block grants to the states.

Desmond concludes by building an ambitious case for ending poverty. His solutions range from helping eligible people claim government aid to raising the minimum wage, supporting unions, regulating banks and lenders, creating more public housing, and increasing access to contraception and abortion. He ultimately calls on his fellow Americans to mobilize and become poverty abolitionists by refusing to support companies with exploitive labor policies.

Eberstadt, Nicholas. 2016. *America's Invisible Crisis: Men without Work*. West Conshohocken, PA: Templeton Press.

Nicholas Eberstadt, a political economist at the American Enterprise Institute, draws attention to a growing crisis lurking below the surface of the positive employment numbers following the recovery from Great Recession: the growing numbers of not working able-bodied men who are becoming incapable of providing for themselves and others. This crisis is largely obscured by unemployment figures because such numbers only account for those who are unemployed but seeking work. Those who are neither working nor seeking work are excluded from the official unemployment rate. Eberstadt points out that the workforce participation rate among men of prime working age (twenty-five to fifty-four) has been on a path of decline for the past half-century and has now exceeded Depression-era levels. One in six men of prime working age is without work and one in eight has stopped looking for work altogether. According to the data Eberstadt presents, men are more likely to be detached from the workforce if they lack a high school diploma or higher-ed degree, are not married or raising children, are not immigrants, and are Black.

This widespread detachment of men from the workforce, Eberstadt warns, will have significant, long-term negative economic, social, and political consequences. Whereas women who leave the workforce, either voluntarily or not, are likely to engage in other meaningful activities such as caring for children or family members, only a small percentage of jobless men are engaged in these pursuits. Rather, men who are disconnected from the labor force are increasingly living lives alienated from civil society, engaged in unproductive and harmful pursuits. Such men self-report spending most of their day pursuing immediate sources of gratification, such as attending gambling establishments, using tobacco or illegal drugs, and watching an average of nearly six hours of movies and television each day. These men are also less likely than females or their working-male counterparts to spend time in religious or volunteer activities, read the newspaper, or vote.

While the causes of this male flight from work are varied, Eberstadt speculates that primary factors include a shift in work due to innovation, automation, and globalization; the large-scale incarceration of men (especially Black men) and the corresponding growth of the felon population; and the rapid increase in disability and social welfare claims which disincentivize gainful employment. Eberstadt concludes the book with a couple of chapters summarizing and responding to critiques of his findings and analysis.

Eide, Stephen. 2022. *Homelessness in America: The History and Tragedy of an Intractable Social Problem*. Lanham, MD: Rowman & Littlefield.

Increase in homelessness has been one of urban America's most intractable social challenges in recent years. In this book on the tragedy of homelessness in America, political columnist Stephen Eide examines the history of homelessness, public and private responses to the problem, and prospective solutions. He opens by identifying the elusive nature of the terms "homeless" and "homelessness." These terms, he explains, were essentially coined by advocates in the early 1980s who sought to replace stigmatizing terms like "vagrant" and "bum" and to promote their preferred government response of more money for subsidized housing. Eide maintains that while the terms "homeless" and "homelessness" lessen stigma, they create other problems in debating the issue and proposing solutions. The terms group together individuals who are facing very disparate life situations and social problems, such as single mothers with children, who may be living in cars, motel rooms, or with family members, able-bodied men without work, and encampment dwellers suffering from untreated schizophrenia and/or opioid addiction. The universal use of these terms frustrates debate over solutions, causing policymakers to talk past one another and to neglect solutions other than subsidized housing.

After discussing current policies and semantics, Eide first offers a historical account of homelessness, an overview of complications and contradictions involved in the various campaigns to end it, and an explanation of why it persists. Tragically, Eide maintains, homelessness's current root causes relate to a range of policy improvements in other areas. These include urban renewal and better housing standards for the poor which led to a decrease in low-cost housing, increased respect for civil liberties, and higher expectations for the treatment of mental illness.

In proposing solutions, Eide emphasizes that the needs of the homeless population are diverse and that social policymakers should start by defining groups by their individual social and economic needs. Responding to homelessness in its modern variety, he contends, requires understanding four main problems: the problems of poor families, especially those headed by a single mother; untreated mental illness; public disorder; and inadequate low-rent housing in major cities. Eide concludes by exploring the intersection of homelessness with multiple other policy areas, including education, urban development, criminal justice reform, mental health, and he recommends reforms that reflect the underlying complexity of homelessness.

Freeman, John, ed. 2017. *Tales of Two Americas: Stories of Inequality in a Divided Nation*. New York: Penguin Books.

In his introduction to this edited anthology, literary critic and essayist John Freeman highlights the growing financial inequality in America which he argues has been produced by decades of injustice, structural inequality, and systemic oppression. He urges his readers to look beyond statistics and numbers and wage rates and to focus on what it feels like to try to get ahead in America today. The book contributes to this goal through a series of essays, short stories, and poems written by those who have experienced extreme economic struggle, inequality, prejudice, and oppression firsthand. Among the thirty-six separate accounts is an essay by Manuel Muñoz paying tribute to his dying father, who came from Central America to pick lettuce and cotton, a poem by Lawrence Joseph recounting the effect of global forces and the fleeing manufacturing industries on Detroit, Rebecca Solnit's account of how a police shooting in San Francisco came about as a direct result of the encroaching gentrification of the victim's neighborhood, and Karen Russell's piece detailing her relocation to Portland, Oregon, where she winds up renting an apartment directly above a homeless shelter. Other accounts likewise paint a picture of displacement, transience, violence, racism, estrangement, and stifling debt.

Kim, Anne. 2020. *Abandoned: America's Lost Youth and the Crisis of Disconnection*. New York: The New Press.

Today, a growing percentage of youth aged sixteen to twenty-four are entering adulthood disconnected from school, work, and family. Research shows that disconnected youth are far more likely to suffer from a range of pathologies, to participate in harmful, risky, or delinquent behaviors, to experience homelessness, and to generally disengage from their communities. In this exposé of America's crisis of disconnected youth, Anne Kim, contributing editor at *Washington Monthly*, explains that most young people enter adulthood cushioned by a web of connections to families, teachers, coaches, pastors, and other caring adults who help ease the transition. Such young people are equipped with the emotional, financial, and professional resources that enable them to navigate challenges and bounce back from mistakes. But many others—especially those who are from dying rural communities or lower-income backgrounds, who have spent time in foster care, or who have drug-involved or incarcerated parents—do not have the benefits of these extensive support networks. They experience the journey into independence of adulthood as an abrupt abandonment. Consequently, they are more likely to enter adulthood untethered to employment or education, which leaves them at a severe disadvantage for the rest of their lives.

Abandoned is broken into several parts. In the first part, Kim identifies how many young people are facing disconnection and surveys the increased recognition in neuroscience of emerging adulthood as a distinct developmental phase in need of specific supports. Next, Kim explains the various forces and factors that can push young people to become disconnected and how current public policy fails to meet the needs of disconnected youth, and in some cases leaves them worse off. Kim then highlights several extraordinary programs designed to provide young people in difficult circumstances with the positive supports they need to establish a lasting connection to work and school and to successfully achieve self-sufficiency. Finally, Kim concludes by laying out a blueprint for a youth policy agenda aimed at bipartisan appeal.

Kotkin, Joel. 2020. *The Coming of Neo-Feudalism: A Warning to the Global Middle Class*. New York: Encounter Books.

The mid-twentieth century was a time of robust and shared prosperity that witnessed a rapidly expanding middle class and an upwardly mobile working class in the United States and throughout much of the developed world. Beginning in the 1970s, however, this dispersion of wealth and opportunity began to stall and to decline—even during periods of economic growth—as the top income quintile acquired greater portions of overall growth. Professor, urbanist, and executive director of the Houston-based Urban Reform Institute, Joel Kotkin attempts to diagnose the trends that have led to a more stratified society.

Kotkin posits that feudalism—caused in large part by unfettered globalization, and marked by greater concentration of wealth and property, reduced upward mobility, demographic stagnation, and increased dogmatism—is on the rise. This emerging hierarchical society, Kotkin maintains, resembles the class divisions of medieval times. Corresponding to the medieval nobility and clergy—or the First Estate and Second Estate, as they came to be known in France—is today's clerical elite and clerisy. This class of feudal lords is made up of financial oligarchs and tech giants along with the educated professional class or cognitive elite (including academics, people in the arts and media, and bureaucrats) who benefit from their association with the wealthy and maintain inordinate influence over policy and culture. Beneath this group are the vastly larger group of "commoners" or what Kotkin refers to as today's yeomanry. This modern-day Third Estate has two parts. The first consists of small-business owners and lower-level professionals who can still achieve economic prosperity, but who are increasingly marginalized culturally and who see their economic prospects waning under the weight of oligarchy. The second consists of the working or low-skilled labor class who are becoming more like medieval serfs. They are experiencing deteriorating labor conditions, social disintegration, and alienation, and diminishing chances of owning significant assets or improving their lot except with government transfers.

Kotkin maintains that one of the consequences of an increasingly bifurcated society is growing despair and pessimism about the future throughout the high-income world which has contributed to declining birth rates and a lack of faith in capitalism and democratic liberalism. These trends, Kotkin argues, provide fertile ground for authoritarian leaders.

Kotkin concludes on a hopeful note with a manifesto for the Third Estate. Here he points out that reversing the slide into a neo-feudal order will first require an understanding of what is happening and a new political paradigm. The current "progressive" attachment to central government will only strengthen the clerisy by vesting more authority in the "expert" class. On the other hand, the refusal of conservative and libertarian devotees of market fundamentalism to acknowledge the dangers of oligarchic power and the harm being done to the middle and working classes will only further a political trajectory that threatens the viability of capitalism itself. A new perspective can emerge once the reality of neo-feudalism and its dangers are acknowledged. Ultimately, a class of younger workers and less affluent members of the clerisy have the numbers and capacity to develop a counterforce strong enough to stop and even reverse the disturbing rise of neo-feudalism.

Lind, Michael. 2023. *Hell to Pay: How the Suppression of Wages Is Destroying America*. New York: Penguin Random House.

The United States is currently plagued by a range of dystopian trends from declining fertility and family formation to loneliness, deaths of despair, bitter conflict over racial and gender identity, surging inflation, and extreme political division. Columnist and cofounder of New America, Michael Lind boils down these trends to four crises (a demographic crisis, a social crisis, an identity crisis, and a political crisis). These, he says, are ultimately worsened, if not caused, by a fifth underlying economic crisis: the existence of too many jobs with low wages, no benefits, and bad conditions in present-day America.

While many economists argue that low wages and the diminished bargaining power of workers are caused by market forces, Lind systematically recounts how corporate lobbies, aided by politicians and policymakers in both parties since the 1980s, have rigged the US labor market and welfare state to keep wages low and to reduce the bargaining power of American workers. Lind specifically derides bipartisan American elites who condescendingly tell laid-off and struggling American workers that instead of complaining about declining wages and that their jobs have been offshored to low-wage workers, they should "learn to code." He similarly calls out large firms in Silicon Valley and Wall Street who use displays of social progressivism to conceal their anti-worker efforts such as offshoring jobs in some sectors to poorly paid workers abroad; substituting unskilled immigrants willing to work for low wages in other sectors like meatpacking, construction, farm labor, and commercial and residential cleaning;

replacing full-time workers with part-time or gig-workers; and smashing private sector unions. Together politicians, corporations, and policymakers have created a multiracial underclass of "working poor" who can only survive with the help of the welfare state. Perversely, Lind contends, many welfare programs, such as the Earned Income Tax Credit (a wage subsidy for the working poor), create a vicious cycle by encouraging employers in sweatshop like sectors to continue paying low wages knowing that their employees won't starve thanks to government assistance. Furthermore, Lind maintains that degree inflation and occupational licensing have contributed to the crisis as American students spend more and more years and money on campus pursuing credentials in a destructive and wasteful competition for access to a limited number of good jobs. This competition of too many people for too few good jobs contributes to other social pathologies, including delayed and failed marriage, decline of civic associations, and the rise of identity politics and political polarization.

Lind concludes by outlining a series of trade, immigration, labor, and benefits policies that, he contends, will help transform the current low-wage/high-welfare model into a revitalized American economy in which all workers can share the gains from growth in the form of earned benefits and a living wage.

Mink, Gwendolyn and Alice O'Connor eds. 2004. *Poverty in the United States: An Encyclopedia of History, Politics, and Policy*. Vols. I and II. Santa Barbara, CA: ABC-CLIO.

This two-volume set explores how poverty and the shifting political and social responses to it have been central to the evolution of the United States. The first volume opens with a series of chronologically organized essays written by respected historians that explore the historical contexts of poverty in the United States and the changing approaches to it. These essays cover the colonial period, the nineteenth century, the Progressive Era and the 1920s, the Great Depression and the New Deal, and the 1940s to the early 2000s. The volume next turns to a series of topical, alphabetically organized entries that identify, describe, and interpret the core issues, events, debates, concepts, social and political movements, legislative developments, and social experiences that have shaped poverty and social welfare historically and that continue to influence policy debates in the twenty-first century. These topical entries are written by a variety of experts, including historians, political scientists, economists, legal scholars, and social welfare practitioners, and thereby provide a multi-faceted, interdisciplinary analysis. Interspersed with more than 300 topical entries, which continue into and are completed in the second volume, are various excerpts from key primary source documents, including speeches, congressional testimony, court decisions, and photographs that either influenced or illustrate the changing perceptions of and approaches to poverty in the United States.

Putnam, Robert D. 2015. *Our Kids: The American Dream in Crisis*. New York: Simon and Schuster.

Robert D. Putnam, a professor of public policy at Harvard, explores the disturbing trend of a growing class-based opportunity gap among America's youth. He provides evidence that youth born into poverty-stricken backgrounds today are far less likely than their counterparts in previous generations to experience upward mobility. In fact, Putnam demonstrates that although gender and racial bias are less of a barrier to upward mobility in modern America than they were in the 1950s, class origin has become a greater barrier.

Putnam weaves personal narratives with data throughout the book to demonstrate the contrasting daily realities of children from different socioeconomic backgrounds and to highlight distinct opportunities, resources, support systems, and social networks available to them. Putnam further explores how changes in neighborhoods, education, family structure, parenting styles, community, and religion have contributed to diminished opportunities for America's poverty-stricken youth.

Putnam concludes the book with a chapter on what individual communities and the country can do to reduce the opportunity gap between poor and rich children. He calls on civic leaders to reach across the boundaries of party and ideology in considering a range of potential solutions and to take advantage of the American federal system, which enables us to pursue innovative reforms and learn from the success and failures of others.

Articles and Reports

Cellini, Stephanie Riegg, Signe-Mary McKernan, and Caroline Ratcliffe. 2008. "The Dynamics of Poverty in the United States: A Review of Data, Methods, and Findings." *Journal of Policy Analysis and Management*. Vol. 27 (3): 577–605.

Since President Lyndon B. Johnson first declared a War on Poverty in the 1960s, a vast body of literature on poverty rates and the causes of poverty has been published. One strand of research examines static poverty measures or the changing proportion of Americans whose basic needs are not being met. Another strand examines the dynamics of poverty, providing information on how, why, and when families' incomes fall below or rise above the poverty threshold. The authors of this paper seek to review and synthesize the literature of poverty dynamics in the United States. Specifically, they describe and assess the most prevalent poverty measures, data, theories, and methods used to answer three questions: How likely are people to enter, exit, and reenter poverty? How long do people remain in poverty? And what events are associated with entering and exiting poverty? The authors then discuss the overarching patterns of poverty dynamics for the US population, differences among demographic groups, and how poverty probabilities, duration, and events have changed over time. The authors conclude with a discussion of the policy implications of their findings and avenues for future research. Specifically, they point out that it is not clear that poverty alone, no matter how it is measured, is the definitive benchmark for assessing well-being. Thus, they contend that studying the dynamics of other measures of economic or material well-being—such as food insecurity, difficulty paying bills, or unmet medical needs—would provide a broader and deeper understanding of the welfare of US families.

Chetty, Raj, David Grusky, Maximilian Hell, Nathaniel Hendren, Robert Manduca, Jimmy Narang. 2017. "The Fading American Dream: Trends in Absolute Income Mobility since 1940," *Science* 356 (6336): 398–406.

A defining feature of the "American Dream" is the idea that children will surpass their parents in income, wealth, and standard of living. Absolute mobility—the degree to which members of each class in a particular generation are better off and enjoy a higher standard of living, on average, than their counterparts in the previous generation—is also generally used by policymakers to determine the extent of economic opportunity in the country. The authors of this study, led by Harvard economist Raj Chetty, assess whether the United States is living up to the ideal of upward mobility by studying two questions: First, what fraction of children earn more than their parents today? And second, how have the rates of absolute mobility changed over time? Combining data from Census and Current Population Survey Income data with panel data from de-identified tax records for 1940–85 birth cohorts, the authors find that rates of absolute mobility have fallen from approximately 90 percent for children born in 1940 to 50 percent for children born in the 1980s.

To understand why upward mobility rates have fallen so sharply over the past half century, the authors examine two important macroeconomic trends that have affected the income of children born in the 1980s relative to those born in the 1940s: lower Gross Domestic Product (GDP) growth rates and greater inequality in the distribution of growth. The authors consider two counterfactual scenarios to assess the relative contribution of these factors. The first scenario considers what absolute mobility percentages would look like if growth rates were consistently as high over the years as those experienced by individuals born in 1940, but the distribution of that growth between income levels occurred at today's actual income distribution rates. The results demonstrated that higher GDP growth rates alone were insufficient to restore absolute mobility to the levels experienced by children in the 1940s and 1950s. Second, the authors examined a scenario using actual GDP growth rates but changed the distribution of total growth across income groups to the more equal distribution experienced by the 1940 birth cohort. Interestingly, changing the distribution of growth across income groups to the levels experienced by the 1940 birth cohort would reverse more than 70 percent of the decline in mobility. Thus, the decline in absolute mobility is more attributable to the unequal distribution of economic growth than it is to lower rates of growth in recent decades.

These results suggest that although economic growth is an important driver of absolute mobility, higher GDP rates alone will not restore absolute mobility to the levels experienced by children in the 1940s and 1950s. Rather, reviving the high rates of absolute mobility and thereby reinvigorating the ideal of the "American Dream" will require economic growth that is spread more broadly across the income distribution.

Chetty, Raj, Nathaniel Hendren, Patrick Kline, and Emmanuel Saez. 2014. "Where Is the Land of Opportunity? The Geography of Intergenerational Mobility in the United States," *Quarterly Journal of Economics* 129 (4): 1553–1623.

Using de-identified administrative records on the incomes of more than forty million children born between 1980 and 1982 and their parents, Harvard economist Raj Chetty and the other authors of this study examine three features of intergenerational mobility in the United States. First, the authors present statistics on intergenerational mobility in the United States as a whole, measuring the mean total family income of the children studied when they are approximately thirty years old in comparison to the mean total family income of their parents when the children were between the ages of fifteen and twenty. The authors find that a 10 percentile point increase in parent income is associated with a 3.41 percentile increase in a child's income rank on average, a 6.7 percentage point increase in college attendance rates, and a 3 percentage point reduction in teenage birth rates for women. Second, the authors characterize variation in intergenerational mobility across commuting zones (CZs), which are geographical aggregations of counties like metro areas but that cover the entire United States, including rural areas. The authors find that both relative and absolute intergenerational mobility vary substantially across geographical areas within the United States. Some CZs have relative mobility equivalent to the highest mobility countries in the world, while others have lower levels of mobility than the aggregate levels of any other developed country. For example, the probability that a child starting from a family in bottom quintile of the national income distribution will reach the top quintile is only 4.4 percent in Charlotte, North Carolina, but is 10.8 percent in Salt Lake City, Utah, and 12.9 percent in San Jose, California. Thus, the authors determine that rather than characterizing the entire country as the land of opportunity, the United States is better described as a collection of societies some of which are "lands of opportunity," while others offer little chance of escaping poverty. Finally, the authors explore factors correlated with upward mobility and discover that high mobility areas have less residential segregation, less income inequality, better primary schools, greater social capital, and greater family stability. The authors conclude that intergenerational mobility is a local problem that could potentially be improved using place-based policies. They express hope that the mobility statistics they have constructed might be used in the future to study the impacts of such local policy changes.

Dalaker, Joseph. 2017. "Introduction to Poverty Measurement." *Congressional Research Service* (March).

In 1964, President Lyndon B. Johnsson declared a War on Poverty, which generated public interest in developing a measure to determine the number of Americans living in poverty and how this number changed from year to year. A couple of years later, the Office of Management and Budget (OMB) issued a memorandum establishing the nation's official poverty measure and instructing the Census Bureau to publish annual poverty estimates.

This report prepared by the Congressional Research Service provides a synopsis of how poverty is defined and measured in the United States, focusing on the official measure of poverty, which is used to obtain official counts and percentages of the poor; the Supplemental Poverty Measure, put forth in 2009 by the OMB to consolidate the research and to ensure the refinement of methodology and data in the poverty measure's usage; and the Department of Health and Human Services (HHS) poverty guidelines, which are used in administering programs for low-income persons.

The author additionally summarizes several limitations of the official poverty measure and clarifies that the poverty measures discussed are financial measures that focus solely on economic privation in terms of income. As such, they do not directly capture the physical, mental, or social effects of being poor.

OECD. 2019. "Under Pressure: The Squeezed Middle Class." OECD Publishing.

The Organization for Economic Cooperation and Development (OECD), an international organization that works through member countries to promote policies that foster economic opportunity and prosperity, has been at the forefront of documenting the rising levels of income inequality and declining opportunities that many of its member countries have experienced over the past several decades. This OECD Report focuses specifically on the current global middle class as an economic and social group. It documents the extent to which members of the middle class have seen their standard of living stagnate or decline and their opportunities for upward mobility diminish, while higher-income groups have continued to accumulate income and wealth. This is particularly troublesome given the role that a strong and prosperous middle class plays in maintaining stable, cohesive, and economically thriving societies.

The report additionally examines the reasons behind the disappearance of middle-class jobs and the rising costs of the middle-class lifestyle, specifically focusing on trends such as occupation, consumption, wealth and debt, and perceptions and social attitudes. The report concludes by recommending a series of measures and initiatives to address the economic challenges faced by the global middle class and to protect middle-class living standards and financial security. These include improving fairness in the taxation system, addressing the increasing cost of living both on housing and education markets, building the skills of middle-class households, reducing risks of over-indebtedness, and improving access to business opportunities.

Isaacs, Julia B., Isabel V. Sawhill, and Ron Haskans. 2008. *Getting Ahead or Losing Ground Economic Mobility in America*. Washington D.C.: Brookings Institution (February 20). Accessed June 30, 2023. https://www.brookings.edu/wp-content/uploads/2016/06/02_economic_mobility_sawhill.pdf

This report, authored by a team of scholars at the Brookings Institutes in conjunction with the Pew Charitable Trusts' Economic Mobility Project, explores the question of whether America is still the land of opportunity and the degree to which upward mobility still exists. The authors aim specifically to spur and enlighten public dialogue on the issue of economic opportunity and mobility and to stimulate debate about which policies are likely to be most effective in ensuring that the American Dream endures for the next century. This is accomplished through a series of thematic essays focused on providing an objective and comprehensive look at the data. Essay topics include "Economic Mobility of Families across Generations," "Trends in Intergenerational Mobility," "International Comparisons of Economic Mobility," "Wealth and Economic Mobility," "Economic Mobility of Men and Women," "Economic Mobility of Black and White Families," "Immigration: Wages, Education, and Mobility," and "Education and Economic Mobility."

Sharkey, Patrick and Bryan Graham. 2013. "Mobility and the Metropolis: How Communities Factor into Economic Mobility." The PEW Charitable Trusts (December).

In a 2011, The PEW Charitable Trusts conducted a public opinion poll asking Americans what factors they thought were most important in determining whether people in the United States get ahead or fall behind economically. More than 80 percent of respondents identified hard work, ambition, and access to education as the most important factors in producing upward mobility. Few identified growing up in a good neighborhood as a key factor. Nevertheless, a growing body of evidence suggests that location contributes a great deal to Americans' prospects for upward mobility. For example, a 2009 study published by *PEW* found that a person who experienced high neighborhood poverty as a child had a much higher risk of downward economic mobility as an adult. Another 2012 *PEW* study on economic mobility at the state level found that several states, primarily in the Mideast and New England regions, had higher mobility than the national average, and other states, primarily in the South, had lower mobility.

In this study, sociology professor Patrick Sharkey and economics professor Bryan Graham examine the effect of neighborhood context across ninety-six US metropolitan areas on American families' prospects for upward or downward economic mobility. Using *PEW*-commissioned original research and datasets, they offer insight into why and how location matters, focusing specifically on neighborhood economic segregation, or the degree to which the poor and wealthy live apart from each other. They find that rates of economic segregation in many US metro areas have increased and that metro areas with distinct pockets of concentrated wealth and poverty have lower economic mobility than places in which the wealthy and poor are more integrated. The authors conclude with a call for further research that focuses on regional and local drivers of mobility and strategies and policies that reduce neighborhood economic segregation by expanding residential options for low-income families.

Siebens, Julie. 2013. "Extended Measures of Well-being: Living Conditions in the United States: 2011." *Household Economic Studies*. US Census Bureau.

While income level provides individuals with access to a variety of goods and services, measuring financial resources does not always provide a full picture of economic and social well-being. In 1992, to create a broader picture of well-being, the Census Bureau began using the Survey of Income and Program Participation (SIPP) to collect data on a variety of other measures. The SIIP asked householders questions from five broad "domains" of well-being: (1) appliances and electronic goods, such as possession of refrigerators, landline and cellular telephones, and computers; (2) housing conditions including the level of satisfaction with overall home repair, adequate living space, and sufficient privacy; (3) neighborhood conditions and community services, such as road conditions and the presence of abandoned buildings; satisfactory police, fire, and medical services; and attitudes toward local schools; (4) meeting basic needs, including the ability to pay bills in full to avoid eviction, and to have sufficient good; and (5) the expectation of help, should need arise, from friends, family, and the community. This report summarizes the data on each of these five domains of well-being focusing on the percentage of favorable conditions among all householders and the differences in levels of material well-being across groups based on age, sex, race, household income quintile, education level, householder disability, household family type, region, and renters versus homeowners. The report additionally summarizes changes in the achievement of favorable conditions by group across the five domains between 1992 and 2011.

Wang, Wendy and Brad Wilcox. 2022. "The Power of the Success Sequence for Disadvantaged Young Adults." *AEI and Institute for Family Studies.*

The Success Sequence refers to a series of life milestones that are associated with escaping poverty and achieving upward mobility in developed countries. This sequential formula includes completing high school, working a full-time job, and marrying before having children. In 2009, Brookings Institute scholars Ron Haskins and Isabel Sawhill generated widespread research interest in the sequence with the publication of their book *Creating an Opportunity Society.* Haskins and Sawhill overviewed the data demonstrating a correlation between the sequence and economic mobility and called for renewed norms and policies to encourage its achievement as an expected norm for young Americans. In a follow-up study published in 2017, researchers at the Institute for Family Studies Wendy Wang and Brad Wilcox found that among US Millennials who followed the sequence, 97 percent were not poor when they reached adulthood.

Critics of those who tout the success sequence as an effective means of escaping poverty have maintained that the formula ignores many of the obstacles and barriers that individual efforts cannot always overcome. In the study cited here, Wang and Wilcox respond to such critics by maintaining that though structural disadvantages undoubtedly make it more difficult to follow the three steps of the sequence, young adults in adverse circumstances who do follow the sequence—even in the face of significant disadvantages—are more likely to overcome challenges and achieve economic success. Wang and Wilcox cite research demonstrating that, though their percentages are slightly lower than those of whites, the vast majority of Black and Hispanic Millennials who follow this sequence are not poor in their mid-30s—upward of 80–86 percent are in the middle- or higher-income bracket. The authors found similar results among Millennials who grow up in lower income and non-intact families. Furthermore, even among Millennials who do not obtain a college degree, those who finish high school, work full-time, and marry before having children, 95 percent are not poor by their mid-30s.

Given the evidence linking the success sequence to better economic outcomes for young adults from disadvantaged backgrounds, the authors conclude by calling on policymakers, educators, and civic and business leaders to work to make each component of the success sequence more accessible to America's youth.

Winship, Scott, Christopher Pulliam, Ariel Gelrud Shiro, Richard V. Reeves, and Santiago Deambrosi. 2021. "Long Shadows: The Black-White Gap in Multi-generational Poverty." *AEI and Brookings Institute* (June).

Over the past several years, issues of racial injustice and inequality have taken center stage in American life and politics, especially regarding the status and treatment of Black Americans in terms of policing, criminal justice, labor market discrimination, educational opportunities, social capital inequalities, and the racial wealth gap. The authors of this report focus on long-term racial gaps in poverty and income mobility. Whereas previous studies have highlighted the disparities in poverty and mobility between Black and White Americans over two generations, this report addresses the gap in the literature by examining gaps across three or more generations.

Using the Panel Study of Income Dynamics (PSID), the longest running longitudinal household survey in the world, and the National Longitudinal Survey of Youth (NLSY), the authors find that Black Americans are over sixteen times more likely to be in the third generation of poverty than non-Hispanic White Americans are. More than 21 percent of Black adults between the ages of thirty and thirty-nine are in the bottom fifth of the income distribution for the third generation in a row, whereas the same is true for only 1.2 percent of White adults. Nonpoor Black Americans are also at greater risk of downward mobility into poverty. Based on this data, the authors conclude that a race-blind approach to increasing mobility and breaking cycles of poverty will not be sufficient if it does not account for the multigenerational experience of poverty.

Nonprint Sources

Flint Town. 2018. Directed by Zachary Canepari, Drea Cooper, and Jessica Dimmock. ZC/DC.

Flint Town, an eight-episode Netflix docuseries filmed between November 2015 and early 2017, captures the various plights of residents of Flint, Michigan, through the eyes of the dwindling, underfunded police force assigned to protect the city's urban areas, these officers' spouses, a local crime reporter, and the mothers in the community burdened by the lack of opportunity and safety they witness around them. Once a booming city, Flint is plagued by the decline of the auto industry, deindustrialization, depopulation, urban decay, drugs, poverty, crime, corruption, and public alienation and distrust. The city additionally experienced a widely publicized public health crisis, after a poorly managed resource decision poisoned the city's water supply. The series offers an opportunity to reflect on what it will take for Flint, and other cities like it, to be restored.

Growing Up Poor in America. 2020. Directed by Jezza Neumann. Frontline.

First aired on PBS, this documentary calls attention to the harsh realities of child poverty in America in the time of Covid-19 and increased racial tension told from the perspective of the children themselves. The film follows three children from different racial backgrounds and their families in battleground state of Ohio over the course of six months leading up to the 2020 election. As the pandemic and government shutdowns amplify their fears and their families' struggle to stay afloat, the children share their worries and hopes.

Inequality for All. 2013. Directed by Jacob Kornbluth. 72 Productions.

Inequality for All, which premiered at the Sundance Film Festival and won several awards, is a documentary film narrated by economist, former Secretary of Labor under Bill Clinton, and University of California, Berkley professor Robert Reich. The film is largely based on Reich's 2010 book *Aftershock: The Next Economy and America's Future*, which examines widening income equality in the United States. The film is organized around a series of lectures in Reich's wealth and poverty class at Berkeley, which are interspliced with news clips, interviews, graphics, and archive footage. Reich traces the growth of inequality back to the 1970s, when the middle class started shrinking and things started getting worse for most ordinary working people while top-income earners experienced increasing prosperity. He concludes that anti-union legislation, tax cuts, deregulation, and job outsourcing have each played a role among other contributing factors.

The film concludes with footage from the Occupy Wall Street and Tea Party protests, which Reich argues are both rooted in the angst people have that the game is stacked against them.

The Line: Poverty in America. 2012. Directed by Linda Midgett. Vision Video.

This short film highlights the plight of the millions of Americans living in poverty and struggles that have caused them to fall into poverty and that make it difficult for them to climb out of poverty. The documentary specifically chronicles the stories of individuals who live at or below the country's official poverty line. One man, a banker, struggles to get by and feed his three kids as substitute teacher after losing his high-paying job. Another woman, a single mom, battles the trauma of poverty and violence in Chicago's westside. A fisherman on the Gulf Coast of Louisiana sees his livelihood destroyed in the wake of Hurricanes Katrina and Rita, and a devastating offshore oil spill. Finally, a blue-collar man in North Carolina who lost his job after working most of his life becomes homeless and is forced to start over as a bus boy for the nonprofit restaurant The King's Kitchen.

Locked Out: A Mississippi Success Story. 2014. Directed by Sean W. Malone. Honest Enterprise.

This documentary film chronicles the struggles of Melony Armstrong, who fought to become the first professional African hair braider in Mississippi and to remove arbitrary regulations that stood in the way of other aspiring entrepreneurs seeking to enter the profession. After learning how to braid hair, Armstrong sought to start using her skills to earn a living, but when she tried to open the first professional hair-braiding salon in Mississippi, she was blocked by the Mississippi State Board of Cosmetology (MSBC). The MSBC demanded that Armstrong first obtain a cosmetology license costing nearly $10,000 and attend years of board-approved training, none of which had to do with hair-braiding. Although Armstrong did not have the means to meet these onerous requirements, she did not give up. Instead, she engaged in a legal battle against the state restrictions, which eventually sparked statewide reform and set a precedent for several other states to remove their hair-braiding licensing requirements. Armstrong not only offered new employment opportunities by establishing her own successful business, she also opened the door to hundreds of other aspiring entrepreneurs seeking to enter the hair-braiding business.

The Pruitt-Igoe Myth. 2012. Directed by Chad Freidrichs. Unicorn Stencil.

This documentary film details the history of Pruitt-Igoe, the 57-acre public high-rise housing complex in St. Louis that was eventually declared unfit for habitation and demolished in 1976. First completed in 1954, Pruitt-Igoe was championed as a solution to the overcrowding and deterioration that plagued inner city St. Louis. The project promised the replacement of rodent-infested slums in the city's downtown with "vertical neighborhoods for poor people." The buildings were designed with skip-stop elevators, which stopped only on certain floors, and long galleries and stairways to encourage residents to mingle with one another. The dream, however, was short-lived. By the late 1960s, the complex was plagued by vacancy, decay, vandalism, and violence.

The widely publicized images of vandalized hallways, broken windows, and the complex's eventual implosion helped perpetuate a narrative of failure that has been used to stigmatize modern architecture, public assistance, and government housing generally. *The Pruitt-Igoe Myth* seeks to counter these stereotypes by telling the stories of those who resided in Pruitt-Igoe and by recounting how the post–Second World War suburbanization, de-industrialization, and general urban decline of St. Louis made the Pruitt-Igoe project particularly vulnerable.

7

Chronology

Below is a chronological list of some of the defining moments and major events impacting poverty in America.

1600s Many localities throughout the American colonies begin to codify the English Poor Law, allowing tax assessments for the provision of the poor and the appointment of town leaders to oversee the administration of such aid.

1776 On July 2 the Continental Congress passes the Lee Resolution formally declaring the thirteen British American colonies free from allegiance to Great Britain. On July 4, the Continental Congress endorses the Declaration of Independence, which outlines a justification for the establishment of a new people and governing system rooted in what the Declaration refers to as self-evident truths (truths that are discoverable through reason and a common-sense observation of humankind). The central and most fundamental of these is the claim of natural human equality. This proposition is based on the logic that although human beings are unequal in many specific characteristics and circumstances; none of these inequalities establishes select human beings as the rightful and natural rulers over others. Human beings are not divided by nature into castes of rulers and ruled.

1785 The Congress of the Confederation passed the Land Ordinance. This act establishes a system in which settlers can purchase title to low-cost, subdividable lots of farmlands in the undeveloped western territories.

Surging inflation in recent years has increased the financial stress on most Americans, putting more people at risk of dropping below the poverty line. (Arne9001/Dreamstime.com)

1787 The US Constitution is written. It is ratified the following year and goes into effect on March 9, 1789. The Constitution allocates specific, enumerated powers to the federal government such as the power to provide for the nation's security and the power to regulate commerce. The Tenth Amendment, however, specifies that the exercise of all powers not granted to the federal government, nor forbidden to the states, is reserved to the states or to the people

1818 Congress enacts the Revolutionary War Pension Act—the Nation's first military pension program, designed to aid impoverished Revolutionary War veterans and then veterans of subsequent wars. Throughout most of the nineteenth century, military pensions were the sole form of federal assistance for poverty. These pensions, however, were considered an entitlement for service rather than charity or welfare.

1824 The New York legislature enacts the County Poorhouse Act. This law required that each county in the state establish one or more poorhouses for the care of all recipients of public assistance and created county boards to manage these almshouses. The measure initiated two trends in nineteenth-century America welfare policy: a transfer of responsibility for public assistance from the town to the county level and a shift in emphasis toward "indoor relief" or the use of institutional care through poor houses.

1862 Congress passes the Homestead Act encouraging widespread land ownership through the sale of public lands.

1863 On January 1, Abraham Lincoln issues the Emancipation Proclamation declaring that "all persons held as slaves," within the rebellious confederate states, "are, and henceforward shall be free."

1865 On March 3, just before the official conclusion of the Civil War, Congress passes "An Act to establish a Bureau for the Relief of Freedman and Refugees." The Bureau, which was to operate for the remainder of thc war and for one year thereafter, is tasked with providing food, shelter, clothing, medical services, and land to destitute freed slaves and southerners who had been displaced during the war. The Bureau is additionally given the responsibility of reuniting black families, establishing schools for freed people, and supervising labor contracts between them and their employers.

Following the assassination of President Abraham Lincoln on April 14, Vice President Andrew Johnson ascends to the presidency. In response to Johnson's leniency toward the Southern states and their readmission to the union and in anticipation of the ratification of the Thirteenth Amendment to the Constitution, numerous southern state legislatures begin to enact a series of Black Codes. These codes impose significant barriers to the protection of political rights and effectively re-enslave freed persons by severely restricting their movement, the free use of their labor, and their right to acquire and possess property.

On December 6, in the aftermath of the Civil War, the Thirteenth Amendment to the US Constitution is ratified. This amendment declares that "Neither slavery nor involuntary servitude, except as a punishment for crime whereof the party shall have been duly convicted, shall exist within the United States, or any place subject to their jurisdiction." Widespread disagreement, however, continued to exist over how to secure abolition and integrate back into the United States both the conquered Southern confederate states and the four million newly freed people.

1890 Journalist Jacob Riis publishes the widely read *How the Other Half Lives: Studies among the Tenements of New York.* Using the new technology of flash photography, Riis exposes New York's upper and middle classes to the squalid, unsanitary, and violent conditions of urban slums.

1909 President Theodore Roosevelt calls the first White Conference on the Care of Dependent Children in response to concerns about the institutional placement of children. The conferees recommend that measures be taken to prevent the removal of children from their homes and to place those that do have to be removed due to exceptional circumstances with families instead of institutions.

1912 On April 9, President William Howard Taft signs the law establishing the Children's Bureau in response to recommendations of the White House Conference of 1909. The Children's Bureau, the first federal government department devoted to the welfare of children, is given the responsibility to investigate and report on all matters pertaining to infant mortality, the birth rate, orphanages, juvenile courts, dangerous occupations, accidents and diseases of children, and employment. Originally part of the Department of Labor, the Children's Bureau is eventually moved to the Department of Health and Human Services' Administration on Youth and Families. The Children's Bureau remains the agency primarily responsible for implementing federal child welfare initiatives.

1913 The Sixteenth Amendment is ratified by the states on February 3, establishing Congress's right to adopt a federal income tax. The unhampered ability to tax incomes drastically increased the federal government's ability to produce revenue, paving the way for the expansion of its powers into the economic life of the nation.

1929 On October 29 a sharp decline in US stock values leads to a market crash. The crash is considered the official start of the crisis that led to the Great Depression.

1933 Congress passes and President Franklin D. Roosevelt (FDR) signs into law several of the centerpiece programs of his New Deal. These laws include, among others, the Emergency Banking Act; the National Industrial Recovery Act, which authorizes the creation of the National Recovery Agency and the Public Works Administration; The Reforestation Relief Act, which creates the Civilian Conservation Corps (CCC); the Federal Emergency Relief Act, which funds grants to the states for emergency unemployment relief; and the Agricultural Adjustment Act, which authorizes the creation of the Agricultural Adjustment Administration to administer rules and regulations governing subsidies, production, and supply restrictions on certain commodities.

1935 FDR signs the National Labor Relations Act, also known as the Wagner Act, into law on July 5. The law grants private sector employees the right to organize into trade unions, engage in collective bargaining, and participate in concerted action such as strikes. The act also creates the National Labor Relations Board (NLRB) to arbitrate disputes, oversee union elections, and penalize unfair labor practices.

FDR signs the Economic Security Act of 1935 (also known as the Social Security Act) on August 14. The landmark law establishes programs including Old Age Assistance (OAA) and Aid to Dependent Children (eventually renamed Aid to Families with Dependent Children, AFDC) to help fund state welfare programs for mothers and children, the destitute elderly, the crippled, and the blind; creates a federal-state unemployment and disability insurance program; and launches a compulsory old-age retirement system (now known as Social Security). Amendments to the act, passed in 1939, add benefit payments to a spouse and minor children of a retired worker and survivor benefits to the families of prematurely deceased workers.

1937 FDR signs the Wagner-Steagall Housing Act on September 1. The law creates the United States Housing Authority (USHA) to facilitate rent supplements for low-income tenants and construction of low-rent housing projects.

1938 FDR signs Fair Labor Standards Act establishing a federal minimum wage, a forty-hour work week, and mandatory overtime pay for all businesses engaged in interstate commerce.

1944 Congress unanimously passes and FDR signs the Servicemen's Readjustment Act, also known as the GI Bill, which provides Second World War veterans with funds for college education, unemployment insurance, and housing and access to low-interest mortgage and business loans. It also authorizes the establishment of veterans' hospitals. The act is later amended to include all those who have served in the Armed Forces.

1949 Under the provisions of the Agriculture Act, the Secretary of Agriculture is directed to distribute surplus food commodities acquired through federal price support to low-income families. The types and quantities of items provided depended entirely on the availability of surplus goods rather than on the nutritional needs of those participating in the program.

1950 Congress amends the Social Security Act to provide "caretaker" grants to mothers of dependent children and to add a new category of public assistance Aid to the Permanently and Totally Disabled (APTD).

1959 Congress authorizes the United States Department of Agriculture to issue food stamps.

1961 President Kennedy issues an executive order calling for the Secretary of Agriculture to work with the states to provide agricultural goods to impoverished populations. The US Department of Agriculture develops a pilot food stamp program in response. Under this voluntary program, several states allowed the needy to purchase food stamps that were worth more than the cash exchanged for them. These stamps could then be used like cash at grocery stores.

Congress creates the AFDC-Unemployed Parent program, which extends eligibility for AFDC benefits to two-parent families whose heads of households were still unemployed after exhausting their unemployment benefits in effort to discourage desertion by unemployed fathers.

1962 Under President Kennedy's urging, Congress passes the Public Welfare Amendments to the Social Security Act (often referred to as the Social Service Amendments) greatly increasing federal support to local welfare departments for the costs of providing casework, job training, job placement, and other services to recipients of public assistance. The amendments additionally allow states to require beneficiaries to engage in community work or attend job training programs.

The Manpower and Development and Training Act (MDTA) is enacted on March 15 to provide training or retraining for workers displaced by automation or technological change.

1964 President Johnson declares an "unconditional war on poverty" in his annual message to Congress on the State of the Union and lays out an ambitious legislative agenda which aimed "not only to relieve the symptom of poverty, but to cure it."

At the urging of President Johnson, Congress passes the Civil Rights Act of 1964 into law on July 2. The law prohibits discrimination based on race, color, religion, sex, or national origin in hiring, promoting, and firing. It further forbids discrimination and segregation in public accommodations, federally funded programs, and schools. The law additionally creates the Equal Employment Opportunity Commission to administer and enforce civil rights laws against workplace discrimination.

On August 20, President Johnson signs the first major initiative of his war on poverty, the Economic Opportunity Act (also known as the Poverty Bill). This act establishes several new programs including Job Corps, a nationwide job-training program; Neighborhood Youth Corps, which funds part-time jobs for underprivileged high schoolers and college students; Volunteers in Service to America (VISTA), the domestic version of the Peace Corps; the Community Action Program (CAP), which provided funds to local agencies and community organizations to develop activities aimed at empowering the poor; and founded Head Start, a preschool program for low-income children.

At President Johnson's request, Congress passes the Food Stamp Act in August creating a permanent food stamp program. The act required the states to develop eligibility standards and to operate the program.

1965 President Johnson signs the Elementary and Secondary Education Act (ESEA into law) on April 9 as a cornerstone of his War on Poverty legislation. The act authorizes the federal government to equalize educational opportunities by directing educational grant funding to the states. The act has is reauthorized many times to provide further funding and eligibility requirements for aid. Two of the most well-known re-authorizations and expansions include the No Child Left Behind Act of 2001 and the Every Student Succeeds Act of 2015.

In May, the Office of Economic Opportunity adopts a working definition of poverty and an official measure, known as the poverty line, based on methodology proposed by Social Security Administration analyst Mollie Orshansky. The measure compares household income and size against a set of thresholds defined by the cost of minimum necessities such as food, clothing, and housing. Two years later, the Office of Management and Budget codifies this measure for statistical purposes and charges the Census Bureau with providing annual poverty estimates based on the measurement.

President Lyndon Johnson signs the Housing and Urban Development Act on September 9. The act elevates the Housing and Home Finance Agency, which administered public housing and urban renewal programs, to a cabinet level department which is named the Department of Housing and Urban Development (HUD).

President Johnson signs the Social Security Amendments creating Medicare and Medicaid to provide federally subsidized health insurance to for the elderly and poor.

Motivated by the belief that higher education would provide an effective means of lifting people out of poverty, President Johnson signs the Higher Education Act into law on November 8. The act increases federal grants to universities and for scholarships, provides for low-interest loans to students, and establishes a National Teachers Corps.

1971 Congress amends the Food Stamp Act, setting national standards of eligibility, increasing funding for the program, and lowering the cost to make it easier for the poor to afford to purchase stamps. The legislation also allowed those with no income or little income to acquire them at no cost.

1973 The Agriculture and Consumer Protection Act requires all states to participate in the food stamp program.

1975 The Earned Income Tax Credit designed to refund low-income families through the tax scheme is implemented.

1988 President Reagan signs the Hunger Prevention Act of 1988, which increases the value of food stamps and changes the income requirement to all more people to qualify for food stamps.

The federal government begins to pilot programs to determine whether food stamps could be replaced with electronic benefits transfers (EBT), such as a debit card that could be electronically loaded every two weeks with money to buy food. States began to move to the EBT system in the 1990s and by 2002 the debit card system became a federal requirement.

1996 President Bill Clinton signs the Personal Responsibility and Work Opportunity Reconciliation Act (PRWORA) into law. The legislation replaces the Aid to Families with Dependent Children (AFDC) welfare entitlement program with the Temporary Assistance to Needy Families (TANF) program. Unlike AFDC, TANF places time constraints on the receipt of federal welfare benefits, limiting most recipients to a five-year lifetime limit on aid. PRWORA also imposes significantly stricter work requirements as a condition for receiving aid.

2007 The Great Recession begins in December following the subprime mortgage crisis and the collapse of the US housing market.

2008 Falling housing-related assets contribute to a global financial crisis and the failure or collapse of many of the United States's largest financial institutions, as well as a bankruptcy crisis in the automobile industry. Congress approves an unprecedented $700 billion bank bailout and a nearly $800 billion economic stimulus package that incorporates a combination of government spending and tax cuts. The nation enters into a prolonged economic downturn.

On May 22, 2008, Congress overrides a presidential veto and passes the Food, Conservation, and Energy Act of 2008. The act drastically increases funding for federal food assistance and changes the name of the federal food stamp program to the Supplemental Nutrition Assistance Program or SNAP. The federal government forbids states from disallowing purchases of unhealthy snack goods and carbonated beverages but funds a Food Stamp Nutrition Education Program. Over the years several reauthorizations have extended benefit levels and reduced eligibility requirements to enable more people to participate in the program.

2009 The Great Recession officially ends in June, but the economy continues to struggle as the country undergoes further job losses and anemic growth.

2011 Recovery from the Great Recession officially begins.

Economists at the Bureau of Labor Statistics and the Census Bureau introduce a new Supplemental Poverty Measure, which accounts for geographical variation and family resources (such as cash and noncash benefits) and expenses (such as taxes and medical costs) that are not included in the Official Poverty Measurement. The Census Bureau begins publishing two sets of yearly poverty estimates—one using the official method and the other using the Supplemental Poverty Measure.

2017 The US economy completes its eighth year of expansion following the Great Recession. The unemployment rate hits a seventeen-year low.

2020 Several governors begin issuing statewide school closure orders in response to the growing number of confirmed Covid-19 cases in the United States in early March.

President Donald Trump issues the Proclamation on Declaring a National Emergency Concerning the Novel Corona Virus Disease (Covid-19) Outbreak.

On March 18, California Governor Gavin Newsom issues the country's first state-wide stay at home order, prompting a wave of school closures, stay-at-home orders, and government-mandated closures of businesses based on policy distinctions between "essential" and "non-essential" operations. Unemployment skyrockets and hundreds of thousands of businesses permanently shut down. The federal and state governments respond with a multitude of financial relief efforts, including economic impact and stimulus checks, extended unemployment benefits, and so on.

2021 The passage of the American Rescue Plan's Child Tax Credit expansion and stimulus payments, in conjunction with other temporary relief measures, spurs the largest one-year drop in child poverty on record. As soon as temporary benefits are phased out, however, lower-income families experience a drastic drop in their calculated income. The child poverty rate more than doubles from a record low of 5.2 percent in 2021 (when families are still receiving temporary benefits) to 12.4 percent in 2022.

2023 The Census Bureau announces on September 12 that real median household income in 2022 fell in comparison to 2021 and that the Supplemental Poverty Measure (SPM) rate in 2022 had increased by 4.6 percentage points from 2021, marking the first increase in the overall SPM rate since 2010.

2024 US Representative Bonnie Watson Coleman (D-NJ) introduces a resolution to the House of Representatives commemorating the sixtieth anniversary of the War on Poverty and acknowledging its shortcomings.

Glossary

Absolute Mobility: A measure of whether the overall standard of living in a society has increased. Occurs when the members of each class in a particular generation are better off and enjoy a higher standard of living, on average, than their counterparts in the previous generation. Absolute mobility generally results from overall economic growth.

Absolute Poverty: The inability to access a minimal standard of life-sustaining essentials, such as food, clean water, clothing, shelter, sanitation, healthcare, and education.

Almshouses: A house supported by a church or private charity to house and support aged, infirmed, and/or extremely poor individuals.

Apprenticeship: A method of preparing workers to master occupational skills by allowing them to receive paid training through supervised work-based learning and instruction.

Assets: Resources with economic value owned or controlled by an individual, corporation, or other entity. Examples include land, houses or other buildings, stocks and other financial investments, equipment, inventory, and cash.

Child Abuse: Occurs when a parent or caregiver, whether through intentional action or failing to act, causes injury, death, emotional harm, or risk of serious harm to a child. The various forms of abuse include neglect, physical abuse, sexual abuse, exploitation, and emotional abuse.

Collective Bargaining: The process through which employees as a group negotiate contracts with their employer to determine the terms of their employment including pay, benefits, hours, leave, and son. Employees are typically represented by a labor union during collective bargaining.

English Poor Law: The body of laws first developed in sixteenth-century England that governed the provision of relief for the poor.

Faith-Based Organization (FBO): A nonprofit organization or service provider affiliated with or inspired by a certain religion or religious beliefs.

Gainful Employment: An employment situation in which an individual is steadily employed and receives consistent payment for work.

Gentrification: The process by which more affluent people move into, renovate, and attract new business to a poor area resulting in an increase in property values and the displacement of current inhabitants in the process.

Gross Domestic Product (GDP): The total market value of the final goods and services produced within the United States in a year. The per capita GDP refers to the value of the country's economic output divided by its population.

Intergenerational Mobility: The degree to which children move up or down the income spectrum or change social status relative to their parents' generation.

Joblessness: Refers to anyone who is not working. It is not the same as unemployment, which only includes those who are not working but who are actively looking for work.

Labor Force Participation Rate (LFPR): The percentage of those in the civilian noninstitutional population who are working or actively looking for work relative to the population from which they are drawn.

Labor Union: An organization of workers in a trade or profession formed to protect workers rights and represent them in negotiations with employers over issues of pay, benefits, and working conditions.

Laissez-Faire: A philosophy or practice of opposing governmental interference in economic affairs beyond what is necessary for the maintenance of peach and the protection of property rights.

Lower Class: Typically refers to those who are high school dropouts and whose family income is below the twentieth-income percentile.

Macroeconomic: The branch of economics that studies the behavior and performance of the economy as a whole. It is concerned with large-scale or general economic factors such as unemployment, inflation, economic growth, Gross Domestic Product, and so on.

Mal-Employment Rate: A measure of the number of workers who are underemployed or who are working in jobs below their skill capacity or level of training and education.

Means-Tested Welfare: Government benefit programs that limit eligibility to individuals and families whose income and or assets fall below a certain threshold.

Microeconomic: The branch of economics concerned with the economic behavior, incentives, decisions, and resource allocation of individuals, households, and firms.

Minimum Wage: The minimum amount of compensation an employer is required by law to pay each employee for a defined time period.

Monopoly: An enterprise that is the only sell of a good or service. Monopolies can lead to unfair consumer practices, such as limiting alternative products or creating barriers for competitors to enter the marketplace.

NEETs (Neither Employed nor in Education or Training): Individuals who are neither working nor in school.

Neglect: A form of child abuse in which a parent or caregiver fails to provide needed food, shelter, clothing, medical care, or supervision to the degree that a child's health, safety, and well-being are threatened with imminent risk or serious harm.

Neoliberalism: An economic philosophy associated with economic liberalization, deregulation, globalization, and free trade.

Nongovernmental Organization (NGO): Legally recognized, independent not-for-profit organizations that operate independently from government entities.

They include charities, nonprofits, voluntary groups, trade unions, professional associations, and human rights advocacy groups.

Nonprofit: Legally recognized, independent not for profit organizations that operate independently from government entities. They include charities, nonprofits, voluntary groups, trade unions, professional associations, and human rights advocacy groups.

Occupational Licensing: The process by which governments establish qualifications to practice a trade or profession, so that only those who have met the qualifications are legally permitted to receive pay or wages for engaging in work related to the trade or profession.

Opioids: A class of drugs naturally found in the opium poppy plant that work in the brain to produce a variety of effects, including the relief of pain. Opioids include the illegal drug heroin, synthetic opioids such as fentanyl, and pain relievers available legally by prescription, such as oxycodone, hydrocodone, codeine, morphine, and others.

Prime Working Age: The age of adults considered to be in their prime working years (ages twenty-five to fifty-four).

Recession: A period of at least six months of negative economic growth as measured by a country's Gross Domestic Product.

Relative Mobility: Refers to a dynamic in which individuals move up or down the social hierarchy in comparison to the socioeconomic position of their parents.

Relative Poverty: Refers to the disparities of wealth or inequality between groups in a particular social context rather than material deprivation.

Settlement Houses: Inner-city, reform-oriented community centers that provide educational, recreational, and other social services.

Social Capital: An individual's network of relationships and level of social connectedness—includes informal ties to relatives, friends, and neighbors as well as formal ties to civic associations, volunteer or professional organizations, and religious and educational institutions. These connections and relationship networks can help individuals successfully navigate society and its institutions.

Social Welfare: Private and public services for segments of society considered to be disadvantaged due to poverty, unemployment, low educational attainment, race, and so on.

Spatial Mismatch: A phenomenon that occurs when potential employees live in areas that are geographically isolated from job opportunities.

Substance Abuse: A pattern of harmful use or dependence on an addictive substance, especially alcohol or drugs.

Tribe, Tribal: An American Indian or Alaska Native Tribal entity that is federally recognized as having a government-to-government relationship with the United States, with the responsibilities, powers, limitations, and obligations attached to that designation.

Undereducated/Underskilled Workers: Workers who do not have sufficient education or skills for the jobs available on the labor market.

Underemployed: Those who are employed part-time, but desire and are able to work full-time.

Unemployed: Refers to individuals who are not employed, but who are actively seeking employment by sending out resumes, filling out applications, interviewing for positions, or otherwise engaging in job search activities.

Unemployment Rate: The share of those currently in the labor force who are without employment.

Upper Class: Refers to individuals who occupy the highest status of society based on wealth, education, and social rank.

Usury: The practice of lending money based on exploitive interest rates or terms.

Wealth: The accumulation at a given point in time of cash and other valuable economic resources. Net worth, which subtracts any debts owed from the total market value of all assets owned, is the most common measure of wealth.

Working Class: Typically refers to those whose family incomes is between the twentieth- and fiftieth-income percentiles and who have a high school degree, and possibly some post-high-school education, but have not completed a bachelor's degree.

Index

About the Author

Christina Villegas, PhD, is a Professor of Political Science at California State University, San Bernardino, where she teaches courses in American political thought, institutions, and public policy. She has co-authored and authored several books, including *Hard Drive: A Family's Fight against Three Countries*, *Democracy in California: Politics and Government in the Golden State*, and *Documents Decoded: Alexander Hamilton.* She is also the author of several other books in the Contemporary World Issues series on youth unemployment, the American foster care system, and modern slavery. She has also written extensively on the American founding, the US Constitution, and public policy.